THE ART OF MAKING SENSE

THE ART OF Making Sense

A GUIDE TO LOGICAL THINKING

SECOND EDITION

By LIONEL RUBY

J. B. LIPPINCOTT COMPANY

PHILADELPHIA AND NEW YORK

LIBRARY OF CONGRESS CATALOG CARD NUMBER 68-15730
PRINTED IN THE UNITED STATES OF AMERICA

To Norman

PREFACE

"THE NEW AND TRUE theory of the Preface," says Brander Matthews in his *Pen and Ink*, "is this: If you want to have your book criticized favorably, give yourself a good notice in the Preface." A Preface, he says, "should be appetizing, alluring, enticing." And so, in his Preface to the aforementioned work, he announced that book as "the most interesting, the most entertaining, and the most instructive book of the decade"—1880-1890. Few authors, however, have sufficient immodesty to make such remarks about their books, though they must surely believe such remarks to be absolutely true.

But a Preface ought to say something about what is to follow. And what is not to follow. There are some things this book does not attempt to do. It does not have the purpose of teaching anyone how to think, for everyone already knows how to think. Not only can all of us think, but all of us can think logically. Some years ago Mr. Mortimer Adler wrote *How to Read a Book*. If you didn't already know how to read a book, you couldn't have read Mr. Adler's book. What Mr. Adler had in mind, of course, was teaching people to read *better*. So here. We can all of us learn to think better, and "all of us," means *everybody*, without exception.

Nor does this book aim to impart new mental powers to the reader. It will not give you a photographic memory, or a powerful imagination. It will not give you the power to think at lightning speed. In other words, familiarity with "the art of making sense" will not give you a new mind. But you don't need a new mind; your old one is quite good enough if you will only make the most of it.

This book has a fundamentally practical aim. It is concerned with the principles of intelligent thinking. When we understand these prinicples we shall be more reasonable in our thinking and better able to evaluate what we read and hear. We shall carry on our discussions, and even arguments, in a more civilized manner. We shall learn how to distinguish between a good argument and a bad man, or between a good man and a bad argument. We shall see how our emotions interfere with our thinking. And perhaps the reader will become a bit more impatient with the sensationalism, intemperance, vituperation, and caterwauling that is all too often substituted for an appeal to reason in public debates.

Thomas Jefferson, in a somewhat cynical mood, once said that newspapers ought to divide their news columns into four departments: Truths, Probabilities, Guesses, and Lies. Unfortunately, newspapers cannot always do this even though they may have the best intentions, for they themselves do not always know which is which. A familiarity with the principles of semantics, logic, and scientific methods of thinking will help the reader to make these distinctions for himself. These principles will be examined as we go along.

Have you ever experienced a sense of being baffled and frustrated when someone accused you of being "illogical"? Do you know how to defend yourself against such a charge? The charge is unjustified as often as it is justified, so that even a slight acquaintance with logical principles will enable you to defend yourself against unjustified charges of this kind. The art of self-defense (not always the same thing as the art of making sense) gives one a sense of security, and this leads to more self-confidence. But, of course, it may have been the case that you *were* illogical. This might be because you committed a simple error you could easily have avoided if it had previously been pointed out to you. (Preferably in the quiet of your study rather than in the heat of controversy.) Logic, one of the essential elements in the activity of making sense, gives you a tool for checking your own thinking, as well as one for checking the thinking of others.

The art of making sense will be fostered by a familiarity with some of the principles of semantics, logic, and scientific methods of thinking. The study of these principles, incidentally, may also give you a new point of view toward the world, and even a new philosophy of life. If we can learn the difference between what it is reasonable to believe and what it is unreasonable to believe, then we may also become aware of what it is reasonable to fear and what it is unreasonable to fear. This may result, among other things, in our finding ourselves better adjusted to the world in which we live. And, being better adjusted, we shall be less anxious. The life of reason and serenity of spirit are closely related.

This book grew out of a series of ten radio talks called "How To Think Logically." This series was presented on FM station WBIK, Chicago, in the spring of 1952 and many of the talks were subsequently presented on television, over stations WBKB and WNBQ in Chicago. The substance of the original talks, plus much new material, makes up the present book.

The author's debts are many and varied. Acknowledgments and thanks are in order. An author who writes in a field so rich in literature as is the art of making sense must necessarily owe much to other writers. There are many books from which the author has learned much and borrowed freely. A list of these would be tedious but mention cannot be omitted of Cohen and Nagel's classic work *An Introduction to Logic and Scientific Method*.

Grateful acknowledgments are due to those who read the manuscript and proofs: to George Stevens, for excellent editorial criticism; to Wayne A. R. Leys for criticism of the last chapter; to Warner A. Wick for many valuable comments on the manuscript; to Elsie T. Micholson for reading the galleys and for many helpful suggestions; and, above all, to my wife, Louise Ramis Ruby, for her devoted and critical reading of this book.

PREFACE TO THE SECOND EDITION

IT IS NOW fifteen years since this book was first published. Some of its topical illustrations had become out-dated: what were contemporary events have now become part of history, even though it be recent history; one or two items became "quaint," such as man's inability to see the other side of the moon. An "up-dating" of illustrations seemed called for. Further reflection also resulted in some changes in emphasis concerning the elusive nature of language, and some material was re-arranged and rewritten to achieve greater accuracy and clarity. The most important change, however, will be found in the expansion of the discussion of formal logic, both in its traditional and modern forms.

Lionel Ruby

CONTENTS

I.

ON BEING LOGICAL

WE ARE SOMETIMES surprised to learn of our own powers. This is what happened to Monsieur Jourdain, the rich but uneducated hero of Molière's *The Bourgeois Gentleman.* Jourdain, in his eager quest for culture, has hired several teachers to instruct him in the arts and graces of polite society. In the following scene Jourdain is receiving his first lesson from his teacher of philosophy, but interrupts the lesson with a special request:

JOURDAIN: I'm going to tell you something highly confidential. I'm in love with a lady of high social standing, and I want you to help me write her a love note.

TEACHER: Very well.

JOURDAIN: It must be something quite gallant.

TEACHER: Unquestionably. You'd want it, of course, in verse?

JOURDAIN: No, no. Not in verse.

TEACHER: Nothing but prose, then?

JOURDAIN: No, I wish it written neither in prose nor verse.

TEACHER: But, Monsieur, it must certainly be in one or the other.

JOURDAIN: What do you mean by that?

TEACHER: Because, Monsieur, everything that is not prose is verse, and all that is not verse is prose.

JOURDAIN: And when one speaks, what is that?

TEACHER: That is prose, Monsieur.

JOURDAIN: What! When I say, "Nicole, bring me my slippers, and give me my nightcap"; is that prose?

TEACHER: Yes, Monsieur.

JOURDAIN: Well, well, well! To think that for more than forty years I have been speaking prose, and didn't know a thing about it. I am very much obliged to you for having taught me this.

In a perhaps similar fashion, the reader might be surprised to learn that all human discourse can be divided into the two categories of the logical and the non-logical, and that when he says, "I'm putting on weight; I must eat less," he is using a well-known form of argument called a "syllogism," though in a concealed form. (Perhaps the reader's attention should be called to the fact that "non-logical," in the last sentence, does not mean *il*logical. Illogicality means a violation of the rules of sound reasoning; "non-logical" refers to discourse which is non-argumentative, e.g., "I like to travel.")

Whether we know it or not, then, we are all of us logical creatures. Logical thinking comes as naturally to us as does breathing. To say that we use logic means that we reason, and there is no human being who is not capable of reasoning. Aristotle *defined* "human being" as "the reasoning animal." But this does not mean that we are always reasonable or that our reasoning is always correct. Improvement is possible; we can learn how to avoid certain obvious errors, we can learn to tackle our problems more methodically, and we can learn to check our thinking by critical standards and rules. If we make the right use of our powers, we shall do much better.

René Descartes, the great French mathematician and philosopher, sought for a method whereby we might guide our thinking more successfully. In the year 1637 he published his *Discourse on Method*, which opens with a somewhat surprising thought:

> Good sense is, of all things, the most equally distributed among men; for everyone thinks himself so abundantly provided with it, that those even who are the most difficult to

> please in all other matters do not commonly desire more of this quality than they already possess.

Our first response to this passage is apt to be one of amusement. Descartes seems to be poking fun, in a gently ironic manner, at those masters of the art of self-deception: human beings. But Descartes was not joking. He seriously meant what he wrote.

Our response when we learn that he was being serious is likely to be one of incredulity. "What!" we ask, "does a person's satisfaction with his good sense prove that he *has* good sense? May he not be mistaken? May he not be smugly complacent?" Now, first of all, let us be clear as to what Descartes means by "good sense." By this term he means the fundamental element in our power to reason: the ability to distinguish truth from error. Descartes admits that we may be mistaken when we think we have a sufficiency of this power and ability, but he is quite serious when he says that our self-confidence in our good sense is a fairly reliable index of human equality in this respect. Not complete equality of course, but only that we come closer to equality here than in any other respect. But let us follow him further, even though you may have some lingering doubts as to whether he himself is exercising his good sense.

"If I am right," Descartes now asks, "how shall we explain the great differences in the opinions of men?" That there are enormous differences in belief is an obvious fact. We differ about everything under the sun, particularly in politics and religion. The explanation of these differences, Descartes says, is not that some human beings are endowed with more reason or native good sense than others, but that some of us "conduct our thoughts along different paths, and do not fix our attention on the same objects." And why is it that some men's opinions are certainly more sensible and reasonable than those of others? His answer here is: "to be possessed of a vigorous mind is not enough; the important thing is rightly to apply our mind to what we are doing."

Descartes then goes on to say that "the greatest minds, though they are capable of the highest excellences," are likewise subject to the greatest errors, and "those who travel very slowly may yet make far greater progress, provided they keep always to the straight road, than those who, while they run, forsake it." For himself, he adds (despite his magnificent achievements in founding analytical geometry), he "never fancied his mind to be in any respect more perfect than that of the average man." On the contrary, he had often wished that he was "equal to some others in promptitude of thought, or in clearness and distinctness of imagination, or in fulness and readiness of memory." And these, he thought, are the only qualities that contribute to the perfection of the mind. But good sense, or reason, is the same in all of us.

To what, then, did Descartes owe his great success as a thinker? He tells us: "It has been my singular good fortune to have very early in life found a methodical way of thinking. In this way I have gradually augmented my knowledge, and raised it little by little to the highest point which the mediocrity of my talents and the brief duration of my life will permit me to reach." The method he found so useful, he tells us, involves four simple precepts:

1. Never to accept anything as true which you do not clearly know to be such; that is, to avoid hasty judgments and prejudice.
2. To divide each difficulty under examination into as many parts as possible, or into as many as necessary for the solution of the problem.
3. To begin with the things that are simplest and easiest to understand, and then to ascend to knowledge of the more complex.
4. To make enumerations so complete, and reviews so comprehensive, that you may be assured that nothing is omitted.

Let us briefly sum up what Descartes is telling us in the remarks we have quoted from his *Discourse on Method.* By and large, he says, all men[1] have reason (good sense) in equal degree. And so, though a man may admit that another is cleverer than he, or more learned, or possessed of wider knowledge, he will not admit that the other has more *capacity for distinguishing truth*

[1] The term "men," used in this very general way, is of course synonymous with "human being." Or, as someone once put it, we shall understand the term "man" as "embracing woman."

from error (when the facts are clearly known). And, by and large, he is right in this. There are of course enormous differences between one human being and another in quickness of apprehension, power of imagination, and in the fullness and readiness of memory. But the chief difference between one person's understanding and another's is due to the fact that some people use the proper methods of thinking, whereas others do not.

Now, whatever we may think of the usefulness of Descartes' own simple precepts for attacking a problem (and the full significance of these precepts in his philosophy is by no means simple), his general conclusions do point to an encouraging thesis: We are all capable of understanding, and we may improve our understanding by using the right methods of thinking. The right methods will help us to solve our problems more efficiently. Our problems may be "scientific" ones, in the narrow sense of that term, but they may also arise in business and social relations, in salesmanship (or anti-salesmanship, that is, sales-resistance when we play the role of consumer) and in politics or love.

But the reader may have been thinking of some further objections to Descartes' assumptions. One may question his assumption that all men are rational. Modern psychologists do not accept this assumption, the reader may say, and certainly it does not jibe with our own experiences with our fellow men. We all know people who do not seem to be reasoning creatures, and, if they are satisfied with their good sense, why, so much the worse for them. And, the reader may go on: Don't most people seem to be controlled by their emotions? Are people really interested in the truth? Don't people always believe only what they want to believe?

Let us examine the objection that man is essentially an irrational rather than a rational animal. Is this really the teaching of modern psychology? Now, it is true that many contemporary psychologists have tended to emphasize the unconscious rather than the conscious aspects of the human mind. Psychologists have made us familiar with the mental process called "rationalization"—a term which does *not* mean "being rational." Rationalization refers to an unconscious process of self-justification.

We seek to justify our beliefs or attitudes or conduct by "high-minded" motives. We may think that our refusal to speak out against injustice is based on the principle that "protests do more harm than good." The real reason for our refusal may be cowardice. We "rationalize" this discreditable motive by inventing a creditable reason. In uncovering these unconscious motives and in describing irrational forms of behavior, psychology is like medicine, which emphasizes the study of pathological rather than healthy states. Medicine, of course, studies diseases in order to eliminate them. And psychology emphasizes the importance of the irrational elements in our lives so that we may learn how to discount and control them, and so reach a more rational attitude.

It is unfortunately true that all too often we do believe in what we want to believe, regardless of the facts, because of some unconscious interest such as pride or vanity. It is sometimes impossible to argue with a man, as when he has prejudices so deeply rooted that he is beyond the reach of rational argument. Let us remember this possibility and we will not overestimate the power of logic and reason. And no one is wholly immune from these irrational influences, though hardly anyone is irrational in general and about everything. But, though we are not completely rational, we still assume that the normal state is one of rationality. And even those who doubt whether rationality is the norm usually take the position that it is the *other fellow* who is thinking with his glands instead of his mind. I say that it is impossible to reason with *him*, when it may be equally impossible to reason with me.

The anthropologist Franz Boas, in his *Mind of Primitive Man*, tells us that primitive man has the same kind of mind that we have, except that he is more entangled in emotion. Civilization, Boas says, does not improve the mind, but it decreases emotional association with ideas and thus helps us to think more clearly. If we wish to make sense we must try to eliminate emotion when emotion is irrelevant. Emotion is out of place in considering information contained in the multiplication table, and it is equally irrelevant in assessing a problem of legal evidence. Was Alger

Hiss guilty of perjury? If we say, "No, because I like the guy," or "Yes, I hate his guts," we are evading the fundamental duty of a rational person, which is to look into the evidence. If we have been in the habit of dealing with problems of guilt and innocence in this emotional manner, then it is time to correct this fault.

We must try to eliminate the personal equation from our thinking, when our thinking should be concerned with the facts. The worth of an idea has nothing to do with the personality of the speaker. Problems can be discussed without reference to persons. "We Germans dislike the French," a character in *Faust* says, "but we love their wines." This point has wider implications, as seen in this item from a statement by the American Library Association and the Book Publishers' Council:

> A book should be judged as a book. No art or literature can flourish if it is to be measured by the political views or private lives of its creators. No society of free men can flourish which draws up lists of writers to whom it will not listen, whatever they may have to say.

Admittedly, we often think irrationally, or fail to think at all, but we are *capable* of being reasonable. Not only are we capable of being reasonable and logical, but we ought to exercise these capacities when reason and logic are appropriate. Logic is appropriate when we deal with matters of proof or disproof, claims and counterclaims. There is apparently a good deal of misunderstanding of this point. The Chinese philosopher Lin Yutang, for example, admires "reasonableness" but disparages "logic." In *The Importance of Living* we find the following:

> Humanized thinking is just reasonable thinking. The logical man is always self-righteous and therefore inhuman and therefore wrong, while the reasonable man suspects that perhaps he is wrong and is therefore always right.

This quotation indicates the ambiguous place logic holds in human esteem. On the one hand, it is considered a mark of high praise when we say of a speaker's argument, "Now, that's good logic." (What we too often mean, unfortunately, is merely that the speaker agrees with us.) On the other hand, we are suspicious of logic. We say, "You can prove anything by logic, but that doesn't make it true." Mr. Lin even uses the word as one of dispraise, as if it were a pejorative term. Now, with respect to Mr. Lin's remarks, I think that practically everyone objects to those self-righteous individuals who regard themselves as infallible, who *know* that they know, who say: "Reason is always right, and *I* am the voice of reason." But this is not a picture of the logical man. Few persons are so vividly aware as the logical man is of the difficulties in demonstrating that *any* assertion is true. The logical man never forgets that perhaps he is wrong and the other fellow right. And even logicians like to think of themselves as human and reasonable. One further comment on Mr. Lin. It is perhaps right to suspect that you are wrong, but this does not mean that your *opinions* are thereby guaranteed to be true. Only by the use of logic can we tell whether they are.

And here is still another kind of objection to logic. The next quotation is from a speech by Austen Chamberlain, British foreign secretary following the first World War:

> "I profoundly distrust logic when applied to politics. . . . Instinct and experience alike teach us that human nature is not logical, that it is unwise to treat political institutions as instruments of logic, and that it is in wisely refraining from pressing conclusions to their logical end that the path of peaceful development and reform is really found."[1]

Chamberlain's remarks reveal a fear of logic, a disease to which we shall give the name "logophobia." The fear, that is, that logical thinking requires us stupidly to apply rigid principles to situations in which such principles are inapplicable. But such thinking is not logical; it is simply foolish. Political institutions, for example, are not instruments of logic. They are things that logicians, like others, try to understand. The world is made up of "stubborn, irreducible facts," such as political realities. A logical person will try to see all the complexities in whatever he studies,

[1] Quoted in L. Susan Stebbing, *Thinking to Some Purpose.*

and if anyone treats human beings as if they were nothing but abstract symbols, or confuses politics with mathematics, he follows no logical law in doing so. And it is just as unreasonable to condemn logic for bad thinking as it is to condemn the science of arithmetic because bookkeepers sometimes make errors in addition.

Our point, of course, is that Chamberlain's remarks indicate a misunderstanding of what logic is. Logic is the science of proof. What the logical man insists on is simply this: that if you claim that you have proved a point–about anything at all–then your proof should be scrutinized in terms of the adequacy of your evidence. Logic shows us how to make this scrutiny.

Though we are all capable of being logical, and are so for the most part, we develop bad habits of thinking in certain areas. It is difficult to think well in fields which involve our emotions and self-interest. We often simply forget that we ought to exercise our critical powers. We become dogmatic, and make positive and arrogant assertions without proof. We may become blind fanatics, and stop thinking altogether. We become blind followers of authorities, without ever inquiring as to whether their pronouncements can be justified by the evidence. A useful corrective here is Bertrand Russell's somewhat remarkable understatement concerning the role of expert opinion: "When the experts are agreed," he writes, "the opposite opinion cannot be held to be certain; when the experts are not agreed, then no opinion can be held to be certain." Let us respect the experts, in other words, but let us not follow them blindly. And above all, let us avoid that provincialism or narrow-mindedness which regards any ideas other than our own as outlandish, or perverse, or dangerous, or subversive.

Logic helps us to confound these irrational attitudes by showing us that there is much more room for doubt than is dreamed of by dogmatic prophets and proclaimers. Thus logic encourages a bit of skepticism, and, in this, logic is in accord with common sense. The skepticism of common sense is found in many of our popular though inelegant passwords, ranging from the "man from Missouri" who says, "Show me," to the watchword of the 'thirties: "Vass you dere, Sharlie?" to the utterly simple "Oh yeah?"

Skepticism and tolerance go together, as Mr. Lin suggested. The skeptical and tolerant man is no fanatic. Unlike the fanatic of Santayana's epigram, he does not "redouble his effort after he has forgotten his aim." But skepticism and indifferent tolerance are not enough. Nothing is more ineffectual than a wholesale skepticism, for life is intolerable without a belief in something positive, and those who have no positive beliefs whatsoever are usually easy prey for the first dogmatist who comes along. Instead of doubting everything, we should be ready to believe when there is sufficient evidence, and we should suspend judgment when evidence is lacking. In other words, we should be "critical-minded" rather than "negative-minded." Let us admit that 2 plus 2 is 4, and that the Russians were the first to put a satellite into orbit. The most reasonable attitude is that of the true scientist, who says: Let us test our beliefs by the evidence, showing a willingness to revise these beliefs as the evidence changes, never claiming finality for our beliefs, but recognizing that the probabilities are sometimes so overwhelming that we can really count on some important truths.

Logic, in other words, is not trying to put anything over on anyone. Logic is simply the study of the methods the human race has devised for acquiring reliable knowledge. This study helps us to clarify our beliefs, so that we shall think straight, not crookedly. And it appeals for its ultimate support to our own common sense. But, like everything else, it is appropriate only in its proper place. Its proper place is in determining whether a claim to truth deserves your assent.

A few words now as to what you are going to find in this book. The art of making sense involves an understanding of semantics and scientific methods of thinking, in addition to the analysis of reasoning, or logic. The "good thinker," in other words, must make a threefold analysis of a discussion. He will interest himself in the meanings of the words, he will look for the "argument" in what he reads or hears, and he will ask himself whether what he hears is true or false. Each of these interests represents a question to be asked, a problem to be solved. To illustrate the manner in which these questions arise, let us examine an "argument," by which we shall mean a unit of discourse that purports to prove something:

> Since a democratic nation is one in which the fundamental laws are approved of by the majority of the people, India must be a democratic nation even though they deny social equality to the untouchables, for the majority of the Indian people approve of the "outcast" system.

Let us put this argument to the test of our three questions:

(1) The semantical question: What do the words mean? (The crucial words, that is.) For example: What do you understand by "social equality"? What is "democracy"? A definition of "democracy" is presented. Do you agree with the definition? The principles which will help us to clarify questions of this kind are discussed in Chapters II through V.

(2) Let us consider the argument as a whole. What is the author trying to prove? What reasons does he give to justify what he is trying to prove? Do you think his argument is logical, i.e., does his conclusion follow from his facts and assumptions? Does your agreement or disagreement with his facts and assumptions have anything to do with the "logic" of the argument? A discussion of questions of this kind will be found in Chapters VI through XII.

(3) Finally, another type of question: Is it *true* that India denies social equality to the untouchables? Is it true that the majority of the Indians approve of the "outcast" system? If you have beliefs on these matters, and your beliefs are challenged, do you know how to support your position on matter-of-fact questions? The last part of the book is concerned with the problem of truth and probabilities, falsehoods and improbabilities.

One thing at a time, however. Let us now examine some aspects of the communication process, for "making sense" needs material to work on, and this material is words.

II.

WORDS, WORDS, WORDS

"WHAT DO YOU READ, my lord?" Polonius asks, and Hamlet answers: "Words, words, words." Unfortunately, there are times when this is all our reading and conversation give us: just words. Words are of little importance on their own account, or for their own sake. Their importance derives from their meanings. The function of words is to act as signs or symbols of something outside themselves. Words may be likened to checks drawn on a bank, worth nothing as paper, but valuable insofar as they represent cash in the bank. Words are "cashed" when we are directed to the things and events they stand for. Thus the admonition of Justice Oliver Wendell Holmes: "Let us think things, not words."

"Semantics" is a new word which has come to designate the study of words (and symbols generally) in relation to their meanings. Words are signs or symbols, that is, things that usually stand for something other than themselves. Another way of describing semantics is to say that it is the study of "the meaning of meaning." This is a rather curious expression, when we stop to think about it, for when we ask what "meaning" means, we assume that we know what "means" means, for otherwise we could not ask what meaning "means." The meaning of meaning, in other words, depends on the meaning of meaning. The simpler definition, however, is quite adequate for our purposes, and we shall define "semantics" as the study of symbols, such as words, and their meanings.

In recent years the study of semantics has received a great deal of attention from philosophers, logicians, and scientists, as recognition has grown of the importance of a proper understanding of language for clear thinking. The subject is not a new one, however. It is as old as philosophy itself, going back to Socrates in ancient Greece. For Socrates thought of philosophy as the "pursuit of meanings." He sought adequate definitions of words like "justice," "good," "right," and "wrong." He realized that unless there is agreement on the meaning of the words we use, communication between man and man is impossible.

Since the time of Socrates a concern with meaning and language has been a constant preoccupation of philosophers and logicians, from Aristotle to John Dewey. But it was not until the last fifty years or so that semantics has emerged as a full-fledged discipline. Today semantics covers a vast and complex field of investigation, with widely diverse branches of study. There are anthropological investigations into the origin and growth of language in human societies, linguistic studies of etymologies and changes in the meaning of words, psychological studies of the relation of language to human attitudes and behavior, logical analyses of symbolic structures, propaganda analysis, and many other investigations, all of which are concerned with semantical problems.

We shall not be concerned with a systematic investigation of semantics. Nor do we share the hopes of some semanticists that this subject offers a panacea for all of the world's ills. We are interested in some practical applications of the subject: to show how an understanding of semantical principles concerning the uses and functions of words may aid us in thinking more clearly, and thus in making sense. We are interested also in semantics insofar as it may improve the process of communication between man and man, and thus facilitate understanding. Many human problems have as their basis nothing but a failure to understand what the other fellow really wants. The importance of this truth should of course not be overestimated, for not all disagreements and disputes are the result of failures of communication. We may understand with perfect clarity that an aggressor nation wishes to control the world. Nevertheless, all too often, unnecessary and avoidable misunderstandings do arise. It would be well to avoid these, and semantics may help us to achieve this goal. A sound understanding of language, the instrument of communication, is a means to this end.

Before we discuss some of these practical applications, however, let us note the close relationship of language and thinking. No one really knows how much thinking human beings could do without language, but it is undeniable that our thinking would be very limited. Human intelligence is based on our ability to think and talk about things that are not in our actual surroundings. We use words to "point to" these things. Though animals can think, they have no words, and so their intelligence is limited. We can think and talk about Mary even though we don't see her. But suppose we mention the name "Mary" to a dog, and Mary is his mistress. The dog will react to the familiar sound, and will wag his tail in eager anticipation of seeing Mary. The dog reacts to the name much as he does to Mary. But human beings can think and talk about Mary, knowing that she is absent. In fact, knowing that Mary is absent makes it a good deal easier to talk about her. A girl can pick at a daisy and say, "He loves me, he loves me not," but no animal can do that.

Language is thus indispensable to human thinking, but this does not mean that mental ability is the same thing as having a large vocabulary. A limited vocabulary, it is true, restricts the range of our thinking. And this may lead us, mistakenly, to think of people as being unintelligent merely because certain words are unfamiliar to them. The children in an underprivileged neighborhood, for example, did very poorly in an intelligence test which contained questions such as this: "A hand is to an arm as a foot is to a ——." Only a few children filled the blank with "leg" and most of them were scored low in intelligence. But later it was learned that the expression "is to" was unfamiliar to these children. They would have said "goes with," that is, a hand "goes with" an arm, and when "goes with" was substituted for "is to" in the same test, they did very well, and scored high in "intelligence."

Language also influences the *content* of our thoughts. The phrasing of a question will influence our thinking about the subject matter. It is well to remember this point when we evaluate the results of public opinion polls. It makes a difference whether one is asked: "Do you favor continuation of the Foreign Aid program?" or "Are you opposed to sending more American dollars to support foreigners?" The phrasing of a question may convey an emotional tone, and most of us are suggestible, so that we have a tendency to agree with what the questioner seems to expect of us. Consider how we are apt to respond to the question: "How do you account for the great unpopularity of the foreign aid program with the great majority of the American people?" We may fail to stop short at this point to ask the question: "Is it really true that the majority of the people *are* opposed to foreign aid?"

A rather outrageous travesty, which satirized the suggestibility of the opinion-poll subject, occurred on one of the popular "Candid Camera" programs. The interviewer pretended that he was taking polls for a TV program called "Your Honest Opinion." He "rehearsed" one of the subjects, an elderly gentleman, before "going on the air." One of his questions was: "What do you think of women's clothes today?" The man answered, "I like them fine." "No, no," said the producer, "that isn't the answer we want. This is the 'Your Honest Opinion' program, and you wouldn't be expected to say you like them fine. People would expect your honest opinion to be 'I like the old-fashioned clothes better.' So that's what you have to say." The elderly gentleman dutifully complied.

Semantics, then, is concerned with language insofar as language is relevant to problems of thinking and communication. We shall now examine certain misunderstandings concerning words, and some of the fallacies and myths that cluster around the relationship words have to the things they stand for.

Words, the smallest units of speech, are not mysterious things. They are events in space and time, that is, they have a physical dimension, and they have meanings. As physical things, words are spoken or written. The spoken word comes before the written word, for men spoke before they wrote. What, now, is a spoken word as a physical thing? It is, first of all, a sound or noise, made by vibrating the muscles of your throat. The movement of these muscles causes a vibration of the air inside your mouth, and these motions cause a vibration of the air surrounding you, passing through the area where you speak, and these vibrations in the surrounding air hit the eardrums of the person you are talking to, causing movements in his nervous system and brain, and he then hears your words.[1]

But, more important than this physical dimension of the word, is its meaning. When we say that words have meanings, we say that human beings agree that a certain word, like "nylon," for example, shall refer to a certain kind of material. This material could have been called by any other name, but the Du Pont Company christened it "nylon." So now, when I think of this material, and say "nylon," the sound comes to your brain, and your mind is referred to the material I am thinking of, namely, the fabric used in women's hosiery, etc.

Now, this relationship of the word to the thing is an "arbitrary" relationship, in the sense that the word could have been any other word. There may be aesthetic or other reasons for choosing an "appropriate" name, but these considerations are never compelling. This principle, that the relationship of words to things is an arbitrary one, may seem absurdly simple to you, but it is a basic principle of semantics, and, though simple, it is unknown to some, and forgotten by others. Children, for example, are apt to be unfamiliar with the principle. When a

[1] There appears to be no scientific basis whatsoever for a story concerning the physical adventures of words as told by that unregenerate old liar, the celebrated Baron von Münchhausen. The story concerns a man who shouted a greeting to a friend on the other side of the Volga River, on a bitterly cold winter day. It was so cold, the Baron relates, that before the words crossed to the other side of the river they froze solid, and were not heard on the other side until the spring, when the thaw released them.

French semanticist asked a child whether the moon could have been called "the sun" and the sun "moon," the child said, "No, because the sun makes it warm and the moon gives light." Another little boy once asked his mother: "Mother, when I was born, how did you know that I was really Charlie, and not some other little boy?" Children often believe that a word is *necessarily connected* with a thing, so that it would be impossible to call the thing by any name other than the one by which it is known. Now, of course, after words come to be associated with specific things, a connection *is established*, and we would create confusion if we did not use these words in their customary meanings. But the point is that words, when they first come into being, can be anything at all.

And here is another amusing example of the same type of error. When the planet Pluto was discovered in 1930, the story goes, a young lady was reported to have asked an astronomer: "Professor, when you astronomers discovered the new planet, how did you know that this planet was *really* Pluto, and not some other planet?" Now this new planet, of course, could have been called by any other name, even Mickey Mouse, though in some ways that name would not have been so appropriate, for it is customary to name the planets after ancient Roman gods.

The kind of error we have just noted was the subject of an amusing bit of spoofing by Mark Twain. Somewhere in his writings he discusses chapter 2, verses 19 and 20 of the Book of Genesis, which deal with a semantical matter: "And out of the ground the Lord God formed every beast of the field, and every fowl of the air. And brought them unto Adam to see what he would call them, and whatsoever Adam called every living creature, that was the name thereof. And Adam gave names to all the cattle and to the fowl of the air, and to every beast of the field." The semantics of this account is unexceptionable, but Mark Twain, in his little jest, imagines that these animals pass in review before Adam. He gets along fine, until he is finally baffled by one animal. He can't think of a name for it. In desperation (like a man) he turns to his wife for help. "Eve," he asks, "what name shall I give this animal?" Without a moment's hesitation, Eve answers,

"Call it a horse." "But why a horse?" Adam asks her. "Well," says Eve, "it looks like a horse, doesn't it?"

We have been dealing with rather obvious examples. But the same kind of error also occurs on subtler levels than those just considered. For example, the system of government in the United States is commonly referred to as a democracy. There are some people, however, who argue that it is wholly improper to call our system of government a democracy. Some have gone so far as to demand that a law be passed forbidding the use of the word in this sense. These people argue that we are a *republic*, that we have a republican rather than a democratic form of government. The dictionary defines a republic as a system in which sovereignty resides in the people and in which legislative and administrative functions are carried on by elected representatives of the people. "Democracy," the argument goes, "means the rule of the people directly, and not through representatives," as in a small town where every voter has his say in a town meeting.

Now, there is no question that we are a republic, but we may *also* be a democracy *as that word is now used*. If the people of the United States, England, and France wish to refer to their systems as democracies, and define a democracy as "a system of representative government based on the principles of freedom, and legal and political equality," there is no one who can or should prevent the people from doing so. In other words, the word "democracy" has been broadened in its meaning by usage, and today it usually refers to a system of government in which the people elect representatives in regularly scheduled free elections, and in which there is a basic devotion to freedom and political equality. This at least is one meaning that democracy has acquired, and to argue that it is *wrong* to use the word in this manner represents a failure to acknowledge the arbitrary relationship of words and things.[1] Language is like a living thing in its growth and development, but its life depends on human decisions.

The uses and alleged misuses of the word "democracy" may

[1] But see Chapter IV for some apparent exceptions to this point.

appear to involve only a theoretical problem of semantics. The heat engendered by this apparently trivial matter, however, indicates that other issues may be involved. These other issues are not far to seek. The issue is the age-old one of conservatism vs. liberalism. To call the United States a democracy is to emphasize our ideals of freedom and equality, in addition to our representative system. Conservatives, who believe that an emphasis on equality will work against the public good, prefer the word "republic," which does not suggest equality. Many liberals, who want more equality, prefer "democracy."

Words, then, can have as many uses as people give them. As language grows and develops, it becomes permissible to use new names for things, or to use old names in new ways. Thus, the word "surgeon," from Greek roots meaning "one who works with his hands," once meant a laborer; today it means one who operates on a living organism. The word "doctor" today means a practitioner of medicine and surgery, among other things; but originally it meant a teacher, especially one of great learning. These are examples of old words that have acquired new senses. It would sound rather odd if we said that medical men were not really doctors, on the ground that "doctor" *really means* a teacher of great learning.

New names are invented not only for new things, like new drugs and synthetics (streptomycin, orlon) but we also give old things new names. Wigs are called "transformations," and corsets "foundations." Inflammable materials are now called "flammable," and a question concerning the meaning of a word is now called a "semantical question."

The principle that words are arbitrarily associated with things should of course not be abused. If we desire successful communication we should not capriciously assign new meanings to old words. The use of words in their customary senses also enables readers or hearers to devote more attention to the thought and less to the vocabulary. That famous character known as Humpty-Dumpty, however, was unconcerned with whether anyone understood him or not, and accordingly he was free to abuse the principle, as evidenced by the following colloquy:

> Humpty Dumpty said . . . : "There's glory for you."
> "I don't know what you mean by glory," Alice said.
> Humpty Dumpty smiled contemptuously. "Of course you don't—till I tell you. I meant, 'There's a nice knock-down argument for you.' "
> "But 'glory' doesn't mean a 'nice knock-down argument,' " Alice objected.
> "When *I* use a word," Humpty Dumpty said in rather a scornful tone, "it means just what I choose it to mean—neither more nor less." (Lewis Carroll, *Through the Looking Glass.*)

We have been discussing the failure to take note of the arbitrary relationship between words and things. We shall now examine a second type of error which arises from the failure to recognize the fact that words are merely symbolic sounds. This error is the belief in the magical power of words. It is the practice of certain primitive tribesmen to change their names after being cursed, so that they may escape the evil which has become attached to their names, and thus to themselves. Another example is the case of the benighted primitive who, when cursed by a fellow tribesman, dropped flat on the ground so that the words would fly harmlessly over his head. And do you remember the story in the *Arabian Nights,* about Ali Baba and the Forty Thieves? Ali said, "Open, Sesame," and lo! the cave door opened. These examples indicate the nature of the belief in the magical power of words: words have potencies to do things all by themselves; a name can become infected with evil; it can harm a man if it actually strikes him, and it can open cave doors.

Are these superstitious beliefs in the magic of words confined to primitive man? I am sure that you are not guilty of similar superstitions, but how about your friends? And, candidly, aren't we all, just a little bit? Don't we all know people who say, "Speak of the devil and he's sure to appear," and who really believe that there *may* be something in that expression? Don't we go to the race track and find a horse whose name has struck our fancy, and bet on that horse regardless of the form charts? And if this has happened to you, and your horse won, weren't you just a little bit persuaded that there really is some kind of magic in a name? And why do we say, "Knock on wood," when we express a thought concerning our good fortune? Well, obviously, because we assume that there are forces in the universe which don't like to hear people talk about their good luck. Again, the belief in the magic of words.

Have you ever watched a group of men engaged in a form of wagering known as "shooting craps"? It is a highly instructive area of investigation for the student of language. One of the players is hoping that he will throw a 7 or 11. He talks pleadingly to the dice, and informs them that his very young infant is in need of protective covering for its little feet. Or the player may commune mysteriously with "Little Joe" and "Big Dick." But alas! the dice roll regardless of his words. For words have no magical powers.

Or consider the radio broadcasting (or the telecasting) of baseball games. Many of the listeners (and televiewers) believe that words have magical powers. If the home team's pitcher is pitching a no-hit game, these believers in magic regard it as a terrible crime for the announcer to mention this fact, for if he does, then the spell will be broken, and the next batter will be sure to make a hit. Because of this superstition, which many announcers are afraid to challenge, millions of listeners are cheated, for they are denied knowledge of the dramatic intensity on the baseball field.

A third error is the assumption that words give us guarantees concerning things. This error usually occurs in this way: we assume that a fine-sounding name proves the fine quality of the thing referred to. This is a frequent source of deception. A Communist-front organization may call itself "The People's Committee for Peace," or some such name, because the words "people's" and "peace" sound trustworthy and good. In the same way, a group seeking to foster race prejudice may use words like "Christian" or "Fellowship" in its name in order to convey the impression that it upholds the principles of religion and love for one's fellow beings. We all know of the many fancy names which used to be common in the fur business, such as Hudson Seal for muskrat fur. The Federal Trade Commission may be going too far, however, in forbidding the expression "imitation fur" for materials that are not made of fur, on the ground that the word "fur" cannot be used for materials not made of fur! This reminds one of a famous cartoon showing a policeman beating a harmless-looking individual at a Communist demonstration. The man: "But, officer, I'm an anti-Communist." The policeman: "I don't care what kind of Communist you are!", and continued to whack.

One must guard against these sources of deception, but there are also many harmless forms of this sort of thing which involve willing self-deception. Thus on transatlantic liners, many years ago, "third class" was changed to "tourist class" because third class sounded too inferior. In the Soviet Union, we may note, the name Third Class was changed to "Third Category," for there can be no class distinctions in a communist society! The accommodations are the same, objectively, but the change of name may have a pleasing psychological effect, for it seems to eliminate a stigma.

We also often assume that evil-sounding names imply that the thing is evil. The implication does not follow. But again, we must emphasize the fact that "brutal" and ugly names may have undesirable psychological consequences, and this is particularly unfortunate when such names are not strictly accurate in their descriptive aspects. For example, the expression "Home for Incurables." This name was based on the assumption that certain diseases are actually incurable, but this is a big assumption, and the present tendency is to change this name to "Institution for Chronic Diseases." Not only is such a name truer to the facts, but it also gives the patients more hope, and hope may have beneficial psychosomatic consequences. Furthermore, who knows but that science may some day find cures for such diseases? In other words, let us not call a spade a spade even when it isn't one.

Names, then, guarantee nothing in themselves. As Shakespeare's Juliet remarked:

> "What's in a name? That which we call a rose
> By any other name would smell as sweet."

Shakespeare's semantical point here was neatly distilled in the lines of a nameless poet:

> Shakespeare was right.
> Names never quite
> Turn white to black
> Or wrong to right.

So much for three semantical errors. One of the basic points of this chapter is that the meanings of words are based on arbitrary human choices. An understanding of this point will also help to clarify the semantic relevance of the etymologies of words. The word "etymology" refers to the study of the history of words, to their derivations from their roots, with all their changes of form, spelling, and meaning. Etymology describes the manner in which words came to acquire their present meanings. For example, the word "philosophy" is based on two Greek roots, *philein* and *sophia. Philein* means "the love of," and *sophia* means "knowledge" or "wisdom," so that the etymological derivation of the word "philosophy" indicates that it means the "love of wisdom." "Philanthropist" is based on *philein* and *anthropos,* meaning "man," so that a philanthropist means a "lover of mankind." "Sophomore" comes from *sophos* and *moros,* the latter root meaning "fool." A sophomore is a wise fool.

Other examples could be multiplied endlessly. The word "assassin" is based on the Arabic word *hashashin,* which is derived from "hashish," an intoxicating drug found in the Middle East. The first assassins were hashish-addictive eleventh-century Syrians and Persians who were members of secret societies which murdered their political enemies. "Planet" comes from a Greek word meaning "wanderer," for planets change their positions among the fixed stars.

But the important point for semantics is this: etymologies enlighten us concerning meanings, and sometimes give precision to words whose meanings are somewhat vague to us. The etymology of "definition," for example. This word comes from the Latin roots *de* (off) and *finis* (end, limit, boundary). A definition, then, *delimits* the meaning of a word. The study of etymologies will help us in using the right word to express a precise shade of meaning. But etymologies do not control the use of language. No matter how a word may have originated, it means today what people use it for. Custom is king in matters of language, and if human beings customarily use words in new senses, it cannot be said that they are wrong in doing so, for words are noises arbitrarily associated with things. An assassin today means one who commits murder because of fanaticism or for a reward, not a person who smokes hashish. And etymologies may also be misleading. The word "etymology" itself, for example. The word is based on *etymon*, meaning "the true sense," plus *logos*, or "word," but there are no "true" or "false" senses of words. There are only customary or uncustomary senses. And so, though etymologies illuminate the meaning of many words—like "philanthropist," and "planet"—they do not establish the "real" meaning of the word. Words mean what people intend that they shall mean. We are the masters of the words, not the words of us.

Words are wonderful engines of communication, but we must know what they mean, and how to handle them. And we must guard against being "taken in" by them. As that wise old English philosopher Thomas Hobbes wrote: "Words are wise men's counters—they do but reckon with them, but they are the money of fools."

III.

SPEAKING AT CROSS-PURPOSES

"CASSIUS CLAY IS a great fighter," says Fred. "You are wrong, Fred," says Phil, who is slightly deaf, "Henry Clay was a great statesman, not a greater writer." A clear misunderstanding. But even those among us who hear perfectly sometimes misunderstand each other as badly as Phil misunderstood Fred. We shall now examine one of the major causes of failures of communication: the fact that words have more than one meaning. This characteristic of words, called "ambiguity," is responsible for many unnecessary disagreements.

Let us imagine that we are listening to a conversation between two men, Bill and Jim, at one of those informal debating societies known as "cocktail parties." They are arguing a frequently debated topic, the principle expressed in our Declaration of Independence, that all men are created equal. Bill has the floor:

"Jim, I tell you that men aren't equal. Don't let anyone tell you they are. They don't know what they are talking about. Use your own eyes! Do you *see* the equality of mankind? Do you find in your own experience that people have equal abilities, or equal characters? Do you find that they are equal in any respect whatsoever? Everyone is different from everyone else. In my opinion Thomas Jefferson uttered preposterous nonsense when he said, and I quote, 'We hold these truths to be self-evident, that all men are created equal.' This so-called truth is not self-evident to me, so it can't be self-evident. In my opinion this so-called truth is actually a falsehood."

Let us now hear from Jim: "Just a minute, Bill. You are the one who doesn't know what he is talking about. Men *are* equal, and I agree completely with Jefferson. The equality of mankind is the foundation of our democracy. No man has the right to think of himself as better than any other, or as entitled to special privileges which others aren't entitled to. Every person is entitled to equal opportunities, and no one should suffer discrimination because of his race, color, or creed. This is the basis of our legal system, which tells us that all men are equal before the law. A legal decision should not depend on the color of a man's skin. Do you deny that? Are you in favor of racial and religious discrimination?"

Bill now takes the firing line: "No, Jim, I don't believe in racial and religious persecution or discrimination. But I repeat once more: men aren't equal. Why, most people don't even have the intelligence to vote properly; that's why we have so much corruption and inefficiency in the government. Your equality is a myth."

And so on. Let us be merciful, and tune out Bill and Jim at this point, though they are probably still arguing, unless they have already reached the point of mutual exhaustion. Now, the argument we have just overheard can never have an ending, because it was really not an argument at all, but just two fellows talking at cross-purposes. In order to have a genuine argument there must first of all be an agreement or meeting of minds about the issue in dispute; that is, there must be a common understanding of the question to be answered. But there was no such agreement between Bill and Jim. They were talking about different things, and so their minds never really met. They were engaged in what we shall call a "verbal dispute."

A verbal dispute is one in which the two speakers engage in what merely looks like an argument, but really is not, because the speakers do not understand each other. The reason why they do not understand each other is that they are using a *key word* in two different senses. The key word in this case was "equal." In other words, there can be no argument concerning whether or not men are equal, if Bill means one thing by "equal" and Jim means something else. Let us recall what they were saying.

Bill said that men were not equal. By "equal" he meant having the same size, shape, mental and physical powers, talents, and so on. Jim said that men were equal. By "equal" he meant that all men should be given the same opportunities, and that they should have the same chance of getting justice in a court of law. Bill's mind and Jim's mind did not meet, for they were thinking about different things. Though each used the same word, "equal," they meant quite different things by the word, and so were engaged in a verbal dispute, rather than in a genuine discussion or argument.

As you listened to Bill and Jim, you perhaps felt yourself agreeing with each in turn, for obviously each was right in the sense in which he defined the word "equal." Bill was right in saying that there are physical and other differences in human beings. Jim, thinking of the word's moral connotations, was right in saying that men should have the same opportunities.

Now, it is of course easy for us to see the mistakes Bill and Jim were making. It is easier for the outsider than for a participant to recognize verbal disputes, just as it is easier to think of witty repartee after the party than during it. Even though we may recognize the foolishness of carrying on a verbal dispute, this is no guarantee that we will not fall into the same trap ourselves. But being forewarned, is, to a degree, being forearmed. Let us try, henceforth, to catch ourselves before wasting too much time in such disputes. In any case, verbal disputes are fruitless, and we can all improve our conversational habits by watching out for, and thus avoiding them.

The basic foolishness of the verbal dispute lies in the fact that we argue when there is in fact no real difference of opinion. A real argument involves a genuine disagreement, in which one person contradicts or denies what the other is saying. (This should be done politely, of course.) But when Bill said that human beings are physically different, he was not denying that all men should have the same opportunities, and when Jim insisted that men are entitled to justice, he was not denying that there are physical differences. Their only disagreement, if any, was over what Jefferson meant by "equal." But they were not aware of the fact that this was the only difference between them. Both Bill and Jim appeared to be in agreement that in one interpretation of Jefferson's meaning, Jefferson would be wrong; in the other sense, right. Parenthetically here, let us recall exactly what Jefferson did say. He said: "We hold these truths to be self-evident, that all men are created equal; that they are endowed by their Creator with certain unalienable rights; that among these are life, liberty, and the pursuit of happiness." This fuller statement indicates that by "equal" Jefferson meant an equality of rights. But, though Bill may have misunderstood the sense in which Jefferson used "equality," Bill used the term "equal" in one of its standard meanings. Well, then, *are* all men equal? Our answer should be "Yes and No"; Yes, in Jim's sense; No, in Bill's.

But the chief point is that we should not disagree with anyone until we first find out what he means by his words. To understand before we disagree is not only a rule of courtesy but also good sense.

The basis for the troubles we have just described is the fact that words are ambiguous. The key words in many disputes have more than one meaning, or more than one sense and this leads to misunderstandings.

Words stand for things, but we don't have just one word for each thing, like a buttonhole for each button. More than one word may stand for the same thing: such words are synonyms. One word, on the other hand, may stand for several different things. When there is uncertainty as to the meaning which the speaker or writer intends, there is ambiguity. For example, the word "secretary" usually means "a person who attends to correspondence." But a big-game hunter may tell you that on his last trip to Africa he captured two secretaries. If you look the word up in the dictionary you will find that "secretary" also means "a South African bird with very long legs." Or, a business acquaintance may tell you that he recently moved his blonde secretary into his home. He is referring to a writing desk made of light-colored wood. The ambiguity of words may create embarrassing misunderstandings! The word "equal," similarly, may be understood in different senses, and this opens the door to misunderstandings of the kind we have just described. Words are not ambiguous by themselves but only in a context which makes their meaning uncertain. There is no ambiguity, of course, in "I wish to dictate a letter to my secretary."

When words are spoken, rather than read, their phonetic sounds may be ambiguous. The sound "*teers*," for example, in "The audience sat in *teers*." Tears or tiers? The next example also involves phonetic ambiguity: "Some people pray on their knees on Sundays and on their neighbors the rest of the week."

Let us now look at another example of a discussion in which a key word is used in different senses. Let us suppose that there is a disagreement over the number of unemployed in the United States at the present time, and that two collectors of statistics have reached different results in counting the unemployed. The difference between the statisticians may be due to biased figures, or unrepresentative samples. But the difference may be a semantical one–the statisticians may have *defined* the word "unemployed" in different ways. There are some industries which employ seasonal workers, such as the canning industry. Is a seasonal worker unemployed during the winter months, when he is regularly laid off? One statistician may consider him unemployed; the other may say he is employed, for he expects to return to his job in the spring. Or the statisticians may differ with respect to the classification of workers who are ill, or on strike. These matters should be settled by definitions, otherwise a verbal dispute may occur because of the different meanings given to the word "unemployed." If we are not agreed on what we mean by a word, we shall talk at cross-purposes.

A verbal dispute frequently engaged in by college students arises over the old chestnut: When a tree falls in an uninhabited forest, does the crash make a sound? The argument goes on and on. One side argues that there is no sound because there is no one present to hear it; the other that longitudinal air waves, known as "sound waves," will occur in the air whether or not anyone is present to hear them, so sound is present. Now, the sciences of physics and psychology tell us that "sound" occurs when waves in the air hit our eardrums and cause motions in our nervous systems, finally reaching the brain. When the motion finally reaches the auditory nerve, we experience what is called "sound." This analysis reveals the presence of two elements: (a) a certain kind of mental experience and (b) a physical cause of that experience. In the dispute we just noted, "sound" was used in both of these senses: (a) for the experience itself and (b) for the physical cause, the sound waves that cause the mental experience. In sense (a) the crash does not make a sound in the uninhabited forest; in sense (b) it does.

Is rhumba music being played in your home *now?* This question is exactly like the one just considered. It is almost certain that there are radio waves in your home that could be transformed into rhumba music if you would tune them in, but you do not hear the music if your radio is silent. So there is rhumba music in your home in one sense, but not in another.

Verbal disputes indicate the manner in which the ambiguity of a word may result in our talking at cross-purposes. Precisely the same sort of thing happens in *verbal agreements*, as distinguished from disputes. Verbal agreements are "merely apparent" agreements. We may find ourselves in apparent agreement with another person only because of ambiguity and speaking at cross-purposes. Just as a verbal dispute conceals a possible real agreement, so a verbal agreement may mask a real dispute. The latter is obviously the more dangerous, for we have more to fear from false friends than from merely supposed enemies. As an example of a verbal agreement, consider the agreements reached at the World War II Yalta Conference in February, 1945. In these agreements between Stalin, on the one hand, and Roosevelt and Churchill, on the other, Stalin agreed that he would permit free and democratic elections in Poland after the war. All he wanted, he said, was a friendly Polish government. Roosevelt and Churchill had one sort of thing in mind by the words "free," "democratic," and "friendly"; Stalin had something quite different in mind. To Stalin, a friendly government meant one that was completely controlled by the Communist Party. So, though there was *agreement in words* at Yalta, the ambiguity of the words "friendly" and "democratic" resulted in a failure in the meeting of minds. Once again, talking at cross-purposes.

So much for verbal disputes and verbal agreements. The problem of ambiguity has much wider ramifications, some of which we shall now explore. Ambiguity is an ever-present aspect of language, for most words have many meanings. This leads to difficulties in communication, as noted, but it also vastly enriches language. A word like "fast," for example, which refers to abstention from food, to a quality of colors, to certain kinds of characters, and so on, is the equivalent of many words. But we are primarily interested in ambiguity insofar as it is an obstacle to communication. There are four types of ambiguity that cause trouble of this kind, and we shall briefly survey each type. The four types: the ambiguity of single words, of sentences, of emphasis and of significance.

Thus far, all of our examples were of the first type, the ambiguity of single words, words like "equal," "sound," "unemployed," "friendly," and so on. Verbal disputes usually involve the ambiguity of a single word or expression. One of the ways in which we can detect the presence of this kind of ambiguity is to ask a question containing the suspected word, and phrase the question so that it can be answered by Yes or No. If a Yes or No answer requires a specification of the sense, then the question is ambiguous. "Are all men equal?" Whether we answer by Yes or No, we must *specify* the sense of "equal." The best answer: "Yes *and* No, depending on the sense of 'equal.' "

Similarly, the question; "Do you believe in God?" requires clarification of the sense of the ambiguous term "God." Now, there are many people who object to this kind of analysis, and who say that they want no quibbling; they want a simple Yes or No answer. But philosophers have defined the word "God" in different ways. When the American philosopher Arthur O.

Lovejoy applied for his first teaching position, the application asked the question "Do you believe in God?" Lovejoy appended a list of more than 30 philosophical definitions of God and asked, "In which of these senses is the question to be answered?" (He got the job). Or consider the conception of God held by the philosopher Spinoza, who was a pantheist. The pantheistic conception of God holds that God is the system of Nature as a whole, in all its existential and dynamic aspects. For Spinoza, everything in the world is part of God, and God is everything. Spinoza regarded himself as a profoundly religious man; for him, God is the only Being who can be loved by man without fear of man's ever being disappointed, for God is eternal, infinite, and perfect. But most people think of God as a personal Being, as the creator of the Universe, and pantheism denies that God is a Person. The Catholic Church has condemned pantheism as a form of atheism. It is thus apparent that one may believe in God, in one sense of that term, and yet be considered not to believe in God, in a different sense. To the question, "Do you believe in God?" Spinoza would have answered, "Yes, in one sense; No, in another."

Unless we are alert to the possibility of ambiguity we may find no sense where sense is present, as in this sentence from Paul's First Epistle to the Corinthians: "And though I bestow all my goods to feed the poor . . . and have not charity, it profiteth me nothing." This is an apparent contradiction, for 'charity' *means* almsgiving. But in an older sense, charity means love (from the Latin *caritas*), and certainly charity in the modern sense is possible without love.

Ambiguity may also result in fallacious reasoning, as in this example of a bad argument:

> Science has discovered many laws of nature. This is proof that there is a God, for a law implies the existence of a lawgiver, and God is the great Lawgiver of the universe.

This argument is vitiated by the ambiguity of the word "law." In "laws of nature," law is used in its scientific sense. It means "a description of the uniform behavior of natural events." In another sense, i.e., in the sense of "legal law," law does imply the existence of a lawgiver, for law in this sense means "regulations emanating from legislatures and courts, rules enforcible by the State, etc." A simple way of differentiating the two is to say that a natural law is a *description;* a civil law is a *prescription.* We need a lawgiver to prescribe, or issue a command, but scientists use the term "law of nature" to mean that they have found some kind of invariant behavior in nature. Their description of this behavior has nothing to do with commands. To use an ambiguous term in two different senses, as this argument does, and to draw a conclusion based on this confusion of two senses, is to be guilty of the fallacy of "equivocation."

The first type of ambiguity, the ambiguity of single words, is also a prolific source of humor: "If I had a mind to," Wordsworth said, "I could write like Shakespeare." In the following example, the humor was unintentional: It was reported that at Oxford and Cambridge, "Half of the school population are poor students on scholarships." "Poor": in money or studies? Good, bad, and indifferent puns are based on the same kind of ambiguity. Sydney Smith, the wittiest of English divines, once described how two women used to lean out of their windows, on opposite sides of the street, and argue with each other. "They will never agree," he said, "for they are arguing from different premises." Benjamin Franklin coined a famous pun when he warned his fellow colonists that they had better work in co-operation against England. "We must indeed all hang together," he said, "or, most assuredly, we shall all hang separately." And here is another, a delightful example, which parodies the syllogistic form of reasoning: "Some dogs have shaggy ears. My dog has shaggy ears. Therefore, my dog is *SOME* dog!"

So much for our discussion of the ambiguity of single words. Let us now look at the second type of ambiguity, the ambiguity of sentences, as distinguished from the ambiguity of single words or expressions. Ambiguous sentences are statements whose grammatical construction may lead to possible misinterpretation. Such sentences are called "amphibolous." This is the kind of ambiguity involved in the "Help Wanted" sign at the factory entrance: Wanted: Young Girls to sew Lace Trimmings on the 4th Floor. This "grammatical ambiguity" is the kind employed in the messages which diplomats like to send to each other. The ambiguous language permits the writer to claim that he did not mean what the reader thought he meant. Literally and strictly interpreted, his language may commit him to nothing. For example, a diplomatic editor wrote a short note to a would-be author: "I shall lose no time in reading your manuscript."

This type of ambiguity was used by the famous oracle at Delphi in ancient Greece. The oracle made predictions of things to come, and the predictions always came true, because of the form in which they were cast. For example: If the oracle were questioned concerning the outcome of a battle between the Greeks and the Persians, the oracle would deliberately cast its prediction in amphibolous language, something like this: "The God Apollo says that the Greeks the Persians shall subdue."

Our third type of ambiguity we call the "ambiguity of emphasis." It occurs when we are uncertain as to the emphasis which words require. This is one of the reasons why it is so much more interesting to hear a play performed by competent actors than to read the play, for the actors give the words their proper emphasis. An example of this type of ambiguity is found in "Nothing is too good for her." Consider how the meaning will vary with the emphasis!

Errors in emphasis occur when we stress the wrong words in a sentence and thus distort the meaning of the writer. Consider the Ninth Commandment: "Thou shalt not bear false witness against thy neighbor." Now, if one reads this commandment with the accent on *neighbor*, this suggests that it is permissible to bear false witness against those who are not our neighbors, a meaning obviously not intended.

Improper emphasis is sometimes the result of making biased selections, as in quotations which misrepresent the speaker's meaning. Such improper emphases, however, are usually due either to carelessness or to deliberate design, rather than to actual ambiguity. For example, a professor made the following comments on a student's thesis: "Your thesis is both good and original. Unfortunately, the good things in it are not original and the original things are not good." The student, an expert excerpt-lifter, quoted his professor's remark: "Your thesis is both good and original."

Our fourth and final type of ambiguity is called the "ambiguity of significance"; ambiguity, that is, concerning the significance of what is being said. This often occurs with respect to what is "left unsaid," as when Zaharias, a wrestling promoter, quoted Zbysko, the famous old-time wrestler. "Wrestling is faked, today," said Zbysko, "and I could have licked any of the young guys today." "That last remark is untrue," said Zaharias. Does saying that "the last remark is untrue" imply that the first is true? But more typically, this type of ambiguity occurs when a perfectly true statement has misleading connotations, as if one were to say, "John didn't beat his wife last week." (Was this his usual practice?) Or this one: "British statesmen always put the interests of Britain first." True, but what is its significance? It insinuates that British statesmen are more selfish than others. But every statesman puts the interests of his country first. It is not the statesman's job to sacrifice his country's interest to the interests of other countries. And when a characteristic is true of everyone, as this one is, specific individuals or nations deserve neither credit nor discredit for sharing it with everyone else.

An old story about a sea captain and his first mate will serve as a final illustration. The captain and his mate alternated in writing the happenings of each day in the ship's log. One day the mate drank too much, and the next day he found the entry, "The mate was drunk today." Very much annoyed, the mate asked the captain why he had made that entry. "It's true, isn't it?" the captain asked. The mate admitted it was. "Well, then," said the captain, "if it's true then it is properly entered in the log." The next day the captain (who was a sober man) opened the log and found the mate's revenge in the notation, "The captain was not drunk today."

So much, then, for the subject of ambiguity and its four forms, ambiguity of single words, of sentences, of emphasis, and of significance. Is there anything we can do to avoid these fertile sources of misunderstanding and thus improve the process of communication? There is. Whenever we find ourselves in a dispute we can ask whether a key word is being used in different senses. Whenever we read editorials or other discourse containing opinions and arguments, we can check to determine whether any of the four forms of ambiguity are present, and if so, whether our first interpretation of the meaning is the only possible one that makes sense in the given context.

The cure for the troublesome aspects of ambiguity lies in making our ideas clear. And this means that we must define our terms. The general problem of definition will be discussed in the next chapter.

IV.

DEFINE YOUR TERMS!

THE GREAT PRACTICAL PROBLEM of semantics is communication. We have seen how ambiguity is responsible for failures in communication, as in verbal disputes. But communication fails for other reasons, too, such as sheer lack of understanding. We don't know what the other fellow's words mean; he doesn't understand what we mean, and we may not even understand what we ourselves are saying. This state of affairs is amusingly presented in a bit of doggerel:

> See them underneath the tree
> Gather round the goose-girl's knee
> While she reads them by the hour
> From the works of Schopenhauer.
> But do they really comprehend
> What Schopenhauer's driving at?
> Oh! Not at all! But what of that?
> Neither do I, neither does she,
> And, for that matter, neither does he.

The point is that we ought to know what we are talking about. When we use high-level abstractions, words like "democracy," "freedom," "capitalism," or "communism," we should make our meanings clear. We should never forget that a word is like a check drawn against the world of experience, and that it has no meaning for us unless we can "cash it in" by "pointing" eventually, to that to which it refers. When we speak, let us beware of "glittering generalities" which we do not understand, and let us not speak unless we know what we are saying. It is this necessity for making our meanings clear that was in the mind of the French philosopher Voltaire when he said, "Before I will discuss anything with you, you must define your terms."

The habit of using words which have no meaning, however, is unfortunately widespread, and meaningless terms may even pass for profundity. We may cite Reginald Bunthorne, the "fleshly poet" of *Patience:* Bunthorne gives us a recipe for acquiring a reputation as a "man of culture rare." "Speak in transcendental terms," he advises:

> "The meaning doesn't matter if it's only idle chatter of a transcendental kind.
> And everyone will say,
> As you walk your mystic way,
> 'If this young man expresses himself in terms too deep for *me*,
> Why, what a very singularly deep young man this deep young man must be!' "

The late George Orwell, critic and author of *Animal Farm* and *1984*, once remarked that art critics often seem to use words that have no meaning. "In art criticism," he wrote, "words like 'romantic,' 'plastic,' 'values,' 'human,' 'dead,' 'sentiment,' 'natural,' 'vitality' are strictly meaningless, in the sense that they not only do not point to any discoverable object but are hardly expected to do so by the reader." Orwell may have been unduly pessimistic concerning the language of art critics, but it will be instructive to ask ourselves just what these words do mean, the next time we encounter them in criticism.

A common misinterpretation of the warning against the use of "meaningless terms" should be noted here. Mr. Stuart Chase, in his *Tyranny of Words*, had great fun with a definition of fascism by Harold Laski, which went like this: "I suggest the conclusion that fascism is nothing but monopoly capitalism imposing its will on the masses which it has deliberately transformed into slaves." Mr. Chase tells us that he "never saw an 'ism imposing its will," and he derides Laski for talking about such "timeless, spaceless, descriptionless entities" as "fascism" and "capitalism." These words, says Mr. Chase, are meaningless abstractions, standing for nothing at all.

Now, it is possible that Laski was using words which had no meaning even for him, in the sense that he could not translate these words into events in experience. Big abstractions charged with emotional content are an invitation to stop thinking. But Mr. Chase's razor cuts too sharply when he says that he never saw an 'ism imposing its will. This is quibbling, for when Laski says that fascism is "imposing slavery on mankind," he may simply mean that certain men, with certain ideas, are making slaves of other men. And we should also remember that no word is meaningless in itself. Laski *may* have had something definite in his mind when he spoke of "monopoly capitalism," doubtful as this may seem. And even the art critic's words may conceal real insights, though his words are often used carelessly. The wise man knows that there are cheats in the world, but that does not make him condemn or distrust everyone.

Communication often fails, then, because words are ambiguous, or vague, or because they are used loosely, or carelessly, or without meaning. Ambiguity is not quite the same thing as vagueness. An ambiguous word is one capable of being understood in more than one sense in a given context. We are not sure which sense is intended. By a vague word, we mean one whose meaning may be fairly well understood, but whose limitations are unclear. Thus, the term "obscene" is vague, for we don't know where to "draw the line." A statute which forbids vehicles in a public park obviously applies to motorcycles. Bicycles also? Tricycles? Roller skates?

The use of most of the words in ordinary language becomes vague when we are confronted with "fringe" applications, but each word also refers to clear-cut examples, called "paradigm" cases, to which the word typically refers. There is no question that automobiles, airplanes, and railroad trains are vehicles, as are boats.

In mathematics and the sciences, and also in law, terms are precisely defined, but such words are taken out of everyday circulation. Words in ordinary speech cannot be defined with such exactness.

Vagueness can sometimes be eliminated by "drawing a line." The expression "the West" as used in American history, is a vague term. Bernard DeVoto gave this term a specific meaning when he said that "the West begins where the average rainfall drops below twenty inches. When you reach the line which marks that drop—for convenience, the one hundredth meridian—you have reached the West."

There are some important words which are both ambiguous and vague, i.e., they have several unclear meanings. This is a kind of "double-barrelled" ambiguity. The words "freedom" and "liberty" fall into this category. Consider the famous "Declaration of the Four Freedoms" which mentions Freedom of Speech, Freedom of Religion, Freedom from Hunger, and Freedom from Fear. Note that the first two of these Freedoms have a "negative" connotation, referring to the limitation of the power of the State with respect to the rights of the individual. The third and fourth Freedoms, on the other hand, imply that the State must take positive action to provide the people with food and security. Or consider words such as "liberal," or "conservative." There are no universally accepted definitions of these terms; dictionaries can merely list their various uses.

In serious discussions, when key words are subject to varying interpretations, i.e., when words like "liberal" or "conservative" are used, the speaker or writer who wishes to make his meaning clear should stipulate definitions of his terms. By "stipulation" we mean "specifying or particularizing": The speaker announces the precise sense in which he will use the word. He should begin by saying, "In this discussion the word X will mean . . ." This is now the meaning the word will have whenever he uses it. Three possibilities are open to the stipulator: (1) He may find one of the several customary meanings of a word adequate,

(2) he may choose to stipulate a modified version of a customary meaning, or (3) stipulate a brand-new meaning.

Stipulations would be unnecessary if words had one and only one meaning. But since this is not the case, stipulations of definitions are often an indispensable element in making our meanings clear. The stipulator has a great deal of freedom, but great caution should be used in stipulating new meanings. Readers and audiences find it difficult to follow a speaker who uses words in unfamiliar ways, and the speaker's freedom is limited by his desire to hold his audience. Confusion is likely to result when new meanings are used, for old habits are hard to get rid of and we usually persist in giving familiar words their customary meanings. And worse: The stipulation of new meanings may involve dangerous traps for the innocent. There ought to be a code of linguistic ethics for all speakers: when they stipulate new meanings they should warn the reader that they are doing just that. The danger is that the stipulator may give us a new meaning as if he were merely giving us one of the customary meanings that all of us accept, and thereby get us to believe things we otherwise would not.

As an example of the stipulation of a new meaning without prior notification that this is being done, let us examine a passage in the book *Soviet Communism: A New Civilization?* (1936), by Beatrice and Sidney Webb. The Webbs, who were prolific writers in the fields of economics and sociology, and who founded the British Labour Party, were not Communists, but they admired the socialistic aspects of the Soviet Union and sought to win friends for Russia. They were apparently not above using semantical tricks to gain their end. Here is a passage from the book, page 479:

> Our own conclusion is that, if by autocracy is meant government without prior discussion and debate, either by public opinion or in private session, the government of the USSR is, in that sense, actually less of an autocracy than many a parliamentary cabinet.

The net effect of this passage is to make the reader think that the Soviet Union in 1936 was not as autocratic, or, to use the word more common today, not so much of a "dictatorship" as was commonly supposed. Why not? Because of the very novel definition of dictatorship invented by the Webbs. To them dictatorship means government "without prior discussion and debate, either in public opinion *or* in private session." The crucial word is the "or." The Webbs were really saying that if Stalin and the Politburo decided to send political dissenters to slave labor camps, but talked the matter over in private, among themselves, before acting, then their conversations removed the stigma of dictatorship from their government. But dictatorships, as usually understood, are governments which do not permit *public opinion* to decide issues. To give force to public opinion requires freedom for opposition parties, so that the people may change the government when they so desire. The Webbs, one may say, attempted to "put one over" on their readers. A new meaning has been insinuated in order to give a bad thing a good odor.

There is another type of trick that may be used in the stipulation of a definition. The stipulator may take familiar words having favorable connotations–like "democracy," or "freedom"–and redefine them with a quite different content than is customary. The unwary may fall into the trap of carrying the favorable connotations of the old word to the new content, thinking that the new must be as good as the old because it is called by the same name. This, of course, is the fallacy of thinking that words are guarantees of things.

For example, we sometimes hear people say, "The Russians have democracy, just as we have democracy, except in a different way. They have democracy as *they* define the word, namely, as a system in which 'the people,' rather than private capitalists, own the industrial plant." Now, of course, the Russians may call their system a "people's democracy," and they have "democracy" in accordance with their stipulated meaning. There is no international law which forbids this kind of linguistic behavior. But they mean something quite different from what we mean, and they adopted this term "democracy" for very special purposes. Having their own aims in view, and knowing that the slogan of "democracy" has great appeal to people because of the libertarian and egalitarian ideals it usually stands for, they adopted this word, but gave it a new meaning. The fact that the same word is used makes people feel that the thing is the same. And since we regard democracy as good, and they use the same word, the innocent may conclude that their system must be as good as ours, though in a different way.

This is the sort of thing Mr. Sidney Hook had in mind when he said of the Communists: "They talk of 'peace' without meaning peace, and of 'democracy' without meaning democracy. They take over the slogans of democracy and fill them with opposite content. Debasing the coinage of the mind is worse than debasing the currency."

When confusions of this kind occur in a discussion it is better to discard the word "democracy" altogether, and thus avoid the possibility of these confusions. The important thing is to compare the actual practices of the rival systems, regardless of what they are called.

A similar confusion occurs in the following: Jack and John are arguing over the question: "Does Russia have freedom?" Jack says they have no freedom, for in Russia there are no opposition parties, or secret ballots, or uncontrolled newspapers. The Russian workers lack the right to strike, and the people lack the right to leave the country. John, on the other hand, says the Russians do have freedom, not *our kind*, it is true, but a special kind called "economic freedom." The Russians have economic freedom, John says, because the government guarantees work for everyone, thus eliminating the possibility of unemployment. According to John, the workers under capitalism lack this freedom, for they face the possibility of being unemployed.

The expression "economic freedom" employs the term "freedom" in a highly unusual way. If we do not notice the novelty of this usage, we may accept the conclusion that the Russians have a free society, on the ground that a guarantee of employment is really a form of "freedom" (in our sense). And since we love freedom (in our sense) we are expected to conclude that the Russians really enjoy this great blessing.

The unusual sense in which "freedom" is employed here, however, becomes evident when we consider its implications. If a guarantee of employment gives us freedom, then the strange result follows that there is a select and privileged class of people in the United States who enjoy this kind of freedom. This class live in institutions called penitentiaries, where everyone is guaranteed employment, or, as it is called in these institutions, "labor." The labor that is guaranteed may be very hard–it may consist in breaking rocks–but it gives the inhabitants economic freedom. It should be obvious that people don't really want economic freedom (in the sense of guaranteed employment) above all else. Slaves have that kind of "freedom." What people want is the elimination of unemployment while they continue to enjoy their *ordinary* freedoms, in the usual sense of that word. For labor union members, for example, the right to strike is an essential condition of freedom.

We have been discussing some problems with respect to the stipulation of meanings. It is desirable for speakers to tell us how they will use important words. They may stipulate a customary meaning or a new one. But when speakers stipulate brand-new meanings without informing us that these are new meanings, we may be misled. Danger lurks in the failure to give us such warning. The semantical tricks used by the Webbs and others were once satirized by a critic in the following lines:

> Semantics will make it clear to you
> That black is white–
> When looked at from the proper point of view.
> And eminent semanticists will undertake to show
> That Yes is but a nearer form of No.

And we are also reminded of Lord Darlington's remark to the Duchess in *Lady Windermere's Fan.* The Duchess: "Do, as a concession to my poor wits, Lord Darlington, just explain to me what you really mean." "I think I had better not," answers the lord; "nowadays to be intelligible is to be found out."

Definitions, then, contain more than meets the eye. The definer's purpose, in other words, may be other than informative.

He may have propagandistic aims, and his definitions may be slanted according to his purposes. Slanting is of course not always done consciously. Unconscious emotional motivations may have been responsible for the following definitions of "fascism" and "communism" which appeared in a well-known dictionary shortly after the second World War:

> FASCISM: Any authoritarian, anti-democratic, anti-socialistic system of government in which economic control by the state, militaristic nationalism, propaganda, and crushing of opposition by means of secret police emphasize the supremacy of the state over the individual.
>
> COMMUNISM: A theory of government and social order according to which property and the instruments of production belong to the people and are held as a common trust and the profits of all labor devoted to the general good.

The definition of "fascism" emphasizes the brutal reality of fascism as it was actually practiced in Germany and Italy, but the definition of "communism" says nothing about realities or practice, but merely mentions the ideal, Utopian, or "Kingdom-in-Heaven" conception of communism. (With one or two changes, such as the deletion of "anti-socialistic" and a special interpretation of "nationalism," the definition of fascism could have served for communism.) But the effect on the unwary reader will be one of creating a favorable attitude toward communism in practice. Definitions such as this one are sometimes called "persuasive definitions": they seek to influence our attitudes rather than to precisely delimit the meaning of a term.

There is also a type of expression which looks like a definition but which really aims at imaginative insight, to capture the "essence" of things. "Architecture is frozen music" is an example. "Poetry is music plus imagination" would not pass muster as an exact definition, although it may be more enlightening for some purposes than a more literal statement. And inventive imaginations have coined many amusing "definitions" which contain sharp social satire: "A politician is a man who sits on a fence with his ear on the ground"; "A wedding ring is a matrimonial tourniquet designed to stop circulation"; "An explorer is a bum with an excuse."

Let us sum up briefly. We have noted the importance of defining our terms in order to facilitate communication. We must make our meanings clear. We have noted some of the pitfalls that arise when definitions are stipulated. In the remainder of this chapter we shall be chiefly concerned with the various methods employed in defining terms.

A definition is a statement that says, "For this word *A*, substitute these words, *X*, *Y*, *Z*." For the word "perjury," substitute its legal definition "the wilful and voluntary giving of false testimony under oath or affirmation, with regard to a material matter, in a judicial proceeding." The single word is substitutable for the long expression, and vice versa. But there are different ways in which a definition may clarify meanings. When we turn to a dictionary for the meaning of an unfamiliar word, we find three kinds of definitions. We find synonyms, examples, and analyses of meanings. For example, if we look up the word "troglodyte," we may get a *synonym:* "hermit." Or suppose we look up "oxymoron." The Funk and Wagnalls dictionary tells us that an oxymoron is "that form of antithesis in which, for emphasis or in an epigram, contradictory terms are brought sharply together." This is an *analysis* of the meaning. But since this analysis is somewhat obscure, our dictionary helps us out by furnishing us with *examples* of oxymorons: "as in the phrase, 'Oh heavy lightness, serious vanity.' " (Other examples are, "To make haste slowly," "His kindness was cruel.")

Definitions, then may consist of synonyms, examples, or analyses. Any one of these will do, provided that it makes the meaning clear, and helps us to understand what the other fellow is trying to say. But the most enlightening type of definition is the analytical. This type is sometimes called definition *per genus et differentiam*, i.e., it states the general class, of things to which a term belongs, and then shows its differentiating characteristics within that class. When we define a triangle as a "plane figure having three sides," we have noted the class of things to which triangles belong: plane figures; and we have noted how they differ from other plane figures, i.e., in being three-sided.

The most important logical problem in connection with analytical definitions concerns the nature of an *adequate* definition of this type. "A triangle is a plane figure having three sides" is a perfect definition of this type because it has the attribute of "convertibility." A convertible definition is one that can be "turned around" and still yield a true statement. Thus, we can say, "Any plane figure having three sides is a triangle." Convertible definitions show an "equivalence" between the definition and the word being defined. Thus, in Aristotle's definition of man as a "rational animal," if we agree that *all* men are rational animals and that *all* rational animals are men, this definition will exhibit equivalence and convertibility. Another way of checking for convertibility is to use the "All and Only" test. Can we say *all* men are rational animals and that *only* men are? If we can, then the definition is convertible.

A definition is inadequate if it lacks convertibility. It is then either too broad or too narrow. "Too broad" means that it covers too much ground, as in a definition of propaganda as "any talk or action which influences anyone toward some predetermined end." This definition covers things it does not mean to cover, as when I say to my neighbor at dinner: "Please pass the salt." I have influenced him; have I thereby become a propagandist? (We cannot say that *only* propaganda involves influencing people or that all influence is propaganda; we may influence people without being propagandists.) On the other hand, a definition may be too restrictive, and not cover enough ground. Any definition of religion which involves the notion of the worship of a Supreme Being would be too narrow, for *not all* religions involve such worship: Buddhism, for example. The only way to save such a definition would be to rule out Buddhism from the list of world religions. Some narrow-minded people, of course, would not regard this as too serious an inconvenience. But most faulty definitions will be found to be too broad. We find some element common to the items we are interested in and hastily define the thing in terms of those common elements without pausing to notice that our net has swept all sorts of other things into our definition.

An example of the search for an adequate definition is illustrated in the following story from *Time* (November 24, 1946):

> Dr. Zilboorg says that present day psychiatry does not possess any satisfactory definition of mental illness or neurosis. To illustrate, he told a story: A psychiatrist was recently asked for a definition of a "well-adjusted person" (not even slightly peculiar). The definition: "A person who feels in harmony with himself and who is not in conflict with his environment." It sounded fine, but up popped a heckler. "Would you then consider an anti-Nazi working in the underground against Hitler a maladjusted person?" "Well," the psychiatrist hemmed, "I withdraw the latter part of my definition." Dr. Zilboorg withdrew the first half for him. Many persons in perfect harmony with themselves, he pointed out, are in "distinctly pathological states."

The heckler's question indicated that the definition was too narrow, for it might exclude a person who was actually well-adjusted. Dr. Zilboorg's criticism was that the definition was also too broad, for it included, according to him, persons who were not well-adjusted. (It should be emphasized here that though an analytical definition may lack equivalence it may nevertheless be satisfactory for most purposes. One should also be aware of the great difficulties in finding exact definitions of words in everyday use, as distinguished from the terms used in technical scientific discourse.)

We noted earlier that definitions by synonym or by example are often quite adequate. This is the case when all we desire is a reference to the sort of thing for which a word stands. But synonyms and examples will be wholly inadequate when an analytic definition is called for. For example: In a discussion of religion, someone may raise the question, "Just what do you mean by God?" An answer like "By the term, God, I mean the Deity" would be inadequate in most cases, for the questioner wanted an explication or analysis of the term. Definition by synonym is often as insufficient as was Polonius' response to the King and Queen when they questioned him concerning Hamlet's strange condition:

> "Your noble son is mad:
> Mad call I it; for, to define true madness,
> What is't but to be nothing else but mad?"

Definition by synonyms is sometimes called "circular" definition, and results in a "begging of the question," a matter to which we will return in Chapter VII. An example: "A morally good man is one who acts virtuously." "Morally good" and "virtuous" are synonymous terms in this context, so that the definition merely repeats the word that is being defined. Circular definitions are of course "convertible equivalents," but they are faulty in that they offer no clarification of the meaning of the word being defined. If we are looking for *clarification* of the meaning of "morally good" so that we may know to what kinds of conduct it refers, it is not helpful to be told that "morally good" refers to "virtuous actions." This is like saying that "virtuous actions are virtuous actions." When Hamlet tells his friends that he brings "wonderful news," namely, that "there's ne'er a villain dwelling in all Denmark, but he's an arrant knave," Horatio answers: "There needs no ghost, my lord, come from the grave to tell us this."

Closely resembling these faults in definition are such things as pleonasms and rhetorical tautologies, as in saying, "He is writing his own autobiography,[1] or "I have one small son, a boy." True, but foolishly superfluous. Even more amusing, usually, is the "Irish bull," a good example of which occurred in the movie, *The Quiet Man:* "He'll regret this to his dying day, if he lives that long." The absurdity of this lies in the fact that it denies a tautology, and a tautology, though vacuous, is necessarily true. And here is one more example, from Pliny, the ancient Roman: "It is better to be idle than to do nothing."

Synonyms, then, do not always satisfy our demand for a definition. "Definition by example" may also be inadequate: "What is

[1] Cf. Charlie Chaplin's *My Autobiography.*

poetry?" "Milton's *Paradise Lost* is an example of a poem." This does not tell us much about the nature of poetry. Or suppose that we are asked to define "free enterprise," and we point to the United States as an example of a nation having free enterprise. We shall give more than we intend by this example of "pointing," for a stranger might conclude that legislation in aid of farmers was an essential part of a free-enterprise system. The vagueness of the reference that may accompany the gesture of pointing is well illustrated by a story that has become a classic among students of language. It is narrated by J. H. Weeks, in his *Among Congo Cannibals:*

> I remember on one occasion wanting the word for Table. There were five or six boys standing round, and, tapping the table with my forefinger, I asked, "What is this?" One boy said it was a *dodela*, another that it was an *etanda*, a third stated that it was *bokali*, a fourth that it was *elamba*, and the fifth said it was *meza*. These various words we wrote in our note-book, and congratulated ourselves that we were working among a people who possessed so rich a language that they had five words for one article.

But later Weeks discovered that

> one lad thought we wanted the word for tapping; another understood that we were seeking the word for the material of which the table was made; another had an idea that we required the word for hardness; another thought we wished a name for that which covered the table; and the last, not being able, perhaps, to think of anything else, gave us the word *meza*, table—the very word we were seeking.

There are of course some situations in which an analytic definition cannot even be attempted, and where only a definition by example (or pointing) is possible. If we are asked what "chrome yellow" means, no words can designate its sense qualities. If this is not obvious, ask yourself how you would explain what any color is, to a person who had been blind from birth. We can explain what sound and light waves are to a blind person, for he can understand these things in terms of his sense of touch, but he cannot understand what we mean by color, for this depends on a sense he lacks.[1]

In concluding our discussion of definition we must issue one final warning. The history of philosophy may be regarded as the record of man's search for adequate analytical definitions of the key terms in human discourse, words such as "truth," "beauty," and "goodness." Let us not hastily assume that "the last word" has been spoken in defining these terms. The "last word" has not been spoken on these matters, and probably never will be. And let us not dogmatically assume that we have adequate definitions of any term whose meaning is a matter of controversy. In the Induction to *Fanny's First Play*, Bernard Shaw cleverly satirizes the type of critic who rigidly applies dogmatic definitions in his criticism. The critic, Trotter, is speaking about "modern" dramatic productions:

> "I think I know the sort of entertainments you mean. But please do not beg a vital question by calling them *plays.* I don't pretend to be an authority; but I have at least established the fact that these productions, whatever else they may be, are certainly not plays . . . Dialogues, if you will. Exhibitions of character, perhaps . . . Fictions, possibly . . . But plays, no. I say NO. Not plays . . . The definition of a play has been settled exactly and scientifically for two thousand two hundred and sixty years. When I say that these entertainments are not plays, I don't mean in *my* sense of the word, but in the sense given it for all time by the immortal Stagirite."[2]

And, finally, let us not demand *precise* definitions of that which lacks precisely determined characteristics. "Art" is in this category. After attending a few exhibitions of "modern art" many

[1] But note that our inability to define a term analytically does not mean that its meaning is unclear. We may have quite clear notions as to what we mean by colors such as "burnt sienna" or "cobalt blue." There are other "indefinable" words whose meanings are familiar: "time," for example. St. Augustine once posed the question: "What, then, is time?" and answered it in this way: "If no one asks of me, I know; if I wish to explain to him who asks, I know not."

[2] Fanny later asks her father: "Who was the Stagirite?'" "'Aristotle,'" he answers, "'but don't mention him to Mr. Trotter.'"

spectators experience a sense of bewilderment, and they are apt to raise the question: "Just what *is* art?" The dictionary will not be very helpful here. According to the Funk and Wagnalls Dictionary: "Art is the embodiment of beautiful thought in sensuous forms, as in pictures, statues, music, or speech, or the works thus produced, as a museum of *art*." Not a very useful instrument for distinguishing art from not-art! There is no definition which can precisely delimit art from that which is not art. And the same problem will be found to arise in connection with many familiar words. To insist on formulating and applying precise definitions in situations in which they are inappropriate is to fail to make sense.

V.

WHAT KIND OF LANGUAGE ARE YOU USING?

A MISUNDERSTANDING may occur because we fail to grasp the meaning of a word, or the thoughts embodied in a sentence. But there is another obstacle to communication: we misunderstand the *purpose* of speech. The most typical form of this mistake is to treat every use of language as if it were intended to convey information. For example, many people read a poem as if it were a scientific treatise. But the criteria of truth and falsity may be irrelevant to the poet's purpose, so far as his actual statements are concerned. He may be trying to evoke a mood, or a state of feeling, or attitude, rather than to give us literal truths. When Shelley writes of the skylark,

> Hail to thee, blithe spirit!
> Bird thou never wert,

he did not really mean to deny that the skylark is a bird. His language was "emotive" rather than scientific in its purpose.

But it is not only poets (in the technical sense) who use language in this way. A purportedly informative book or treatise may be an expression of emotion as well as thought, and the emotional elements may predominate. Justice Holmes, in discussing

Thomas Carlyle, was vividly aware of this distinction: "and dividing mankind around the two poles of emotion and thought—the poets at one end and the philosophers at the other—I don't expect serious thought from Carlyle. . . . Carlyle's interest in truth was mainly aesthetic. His thoughts were rooted in his temperament, his prejudices, and his imagination. He seems to me a poet not a thinker. . . . The interests of explanation and of realizing and feeling are antithetical, and when I have made up my mind to which a given writer is nearer I don't bother much about his relations to the other." And commenting on Goethe, Holmes said, "Goethe could not explain, and so he said that theory was gray."

We are not concerned with the justice of Holmes's remarks concerning Carlyle and Goethe, but his distinction is worth attending to. Holmes's distinction should not be pushed too hard, however. Serious thought that is both clear and accurate may be expressed eloquently, as in many of the Justice's own opinions, and let us not forget that rhetoric and poetry are also intellectual disciplines. What we are emphasizing here is that we shall do well to look for the purposes and intentions of speakers and writers. In this chapter we shall consider the different functions, purposes, and uses of language.

Language, in other words, has more than one purpose. We might say that language operates on different levels, except that the word "levels" suggests higher and lower planes in a scale of value, and this is not intended here. We shall deal with three functions: the informative, the expressive, and the directive. To say that language has these three functions is to say that there are three different reasons for speaking. One reason, or purpose, is to communicate factual information. This is the informative function. We speak also in order to express our feelings, to "blow off steam," or to stir the feelings and attitudes of the person we are talking to. We shall call this the expressive or "emotive" function. And, finally, we speak in order to get people to act. This is the directive function.

Some illustrations are in order. A book on astronomy describes the solar system and the stars. We learn that the diameter of the earth is about 8,000 miles; that of the sun, about 800,000 miles; a ratio of 100 to 1. We learn that the star Betelgeuse has a diameter three hundred times that of the sun. This means that if the earth is represented by a baseball, about three inches in diameter, then Betelgeuse would have a diameter of almost a mile and a half. We may learn that there are as many stars in the heavens as there are grains of sand on all the seashores of the world. . . . I have just been using language to communicate information.

Expressive language is a second type. When I talk about the United States Senator I like least, I may let off some steam, and relieve my pent-up feelings. I may even infect you with my feelings, making you feel as I feel. The poet, of course, is a specialist in expressive language, as in the lines:

> Comes the blind Fury with th' abhorred shears
> And slits the thin-spun life.

These lines give expression to John Milton's feelings and perhaps make us feel as he felt. When we tell our friends a funny story, to get a laugh, we express our feelings too, and affect theirs.

The third type, directive or action-provoking speech, is illustrated by examples like: "Do unto others as you would have others do unto you," or "Praise the Lord, and pass the ammunition!" We say these things to get action. Ceremonial language, such as "I am happy to meet you," "What a beautiful baby!" and conversation about the weather, also have a directive purpose: to establish social rapport, and to get a friendly response.

There are, then, at least three different purposes of discourse. We may also make a somewhat similar classification for words, that is, for words taken by themselves. A basic distinction here is between what we shall call neutral words, and emotive words. Neutral words merely convey ideas to us, as when I say, "The sun rose at six this morning." The words in this sentence do not arouse our emotions. But words like "God," "love," "freedom," and "communism" are so closely connected with our total attitudes to life that they are likely to arouse emotional reactions. This division of words into neutral and emotive, however, is relative to our personal experiences, for there is nothing in the word itself which makes it neutral or emotive. If a word conveys nothing but an idea to you, then it is neutral to you; if it arouses your emotions, then it is emotive to you. The word "bread" is a neutral word to me, but to a "fat boy" or a starving man, it may be fraught with emotion. Nevertheless there are some words which can be counted on to make almost everyone "see red," so to speak, like the word "traitor."

This classification of words is independent of our classification of the functions of language, for those who wish to inform may use either type, as may those who want to express their feelings, or to get action. In general, however, neutral words will be used when we wish merely to inform; emotive words when we wish to be expressive.

Let us return to our classification of the purposes of language. And let us avoid the vice of oversimplification. In life, or living speech, the functions of language are seldom found in a pure or unmixed form. In life things are rarely simple and never pure. Speech and writing usually present mixtures of the informative, expressive, and directive functions of language. Consider the informative item concerning the diameters of the sun and the earth. Though this language informs, and though it is not its primary purpose to stir our emotions, our feelings may nevertheless be stirred when we learn from Sir James Jeans that there are as many stars as there are grains of sand on all the seashores of the world, for this knowledge may make us realize how infinitely vast is space, and how infinitesimally small and feeble is man, crawling for his brief day upon an insignificant planet.

Nevertheless, informative language is the type most likely to be found in a relatively pure form. The writing of scientists is apt to be purely informative, especially in the physical sciences, like physics and chemistry, though less so in political science. But expressive language is rarely, if ever, used exclusively. Expressive language is usually mixed with something else. The lines from Milton's "Lycidas" did not aim primarily at giving us information, but they do say something that has the ring of truth in it. They tell us that men are mortal, and that there are forces beyond our control at work upon us, which give us the helpless feeling that we are the pawns of fate. Alexander Pope's "Essay on Man" is philosophical discourse in rhyming couplets, and contains a developed system of thought, as in the closing lines of the First Epistle:

> All Nature is but art unknown to thee,
> All chance, direction which thou canst not see
> All discord, harmony not understood,
> All partial evil, universal good.
> And, spite of pride, in erring Reason's spite,
> One thing is clear, Whatever is, is right.

The poet may also mix a directive purpose with the expressive one. He may want us to do something, as in so-called "inspirational poetry." Clough's lines are an example:

> Say not, the struggle naught availeth,
> The labour and the wounds are vain,
> The enemy faints not, nor faileth,
> And as things have been, they remain.
>
> If hopes were dupes, fears may be liars;
> It may be, in yon smoke concealed,
> Your comrades chase e'en now the fliers,
> And, but for you, possess the field.

The last line of this poem, "But westward, look, the land is bright!" was quoted very effectively by Winston Churchill during the dark days of the Battle of Britain in 1940. This poem mixes the directive and expressive types of discourse. But one should not expect all poems to give us a moral message, or practical advice, or scientific information. Poets are not necessarily preachers, though some are, and they are not necessarily scientists or philosophers, though some may be. Wordsworth's "Daffodils" should not be read as if it were a botanical treatise on the "Narcissus pseudo-narcissus of the amaryllis family," to use the technical name for the daffodil. The aim of poetry is primarily to communicate feelings and attitudes toward life, to convey to us the poet's feelings concerning his experiences, and to make us aware of life's mystery and wonder.

We shall now examine the directive type of language in some detail. When a speaker wants action from his audience, he may tell them to do what he wants them to do. But, as every parent knows, it is often better to use an indirect approach to get action. Instead of saying, "Johnny, eat your spinach" (or whatever other torture-food happens to be the vogue at the moment), we say, "My, what a gorgeous-looking dish of spinach that is." (The method suggested here cannot, unfortunately, carry a guarantee with it.) Similarly a politician may ask us to work for him, to help him win election; but he may also use an indirect approach. He may stir our emotions by painting a vivid picture of the horrible crimes committed by the opposition party. He arouses our emotions, and these emotions, the psychologists tell us, will demand an outlet. The person thus aroused wants to go out and do something.

Now, this technique of getting action by working on men's emotions has been known to mankind since time immemorial, and has been practiced by politicians ever since they made themselves indispensable. An excellent illustration of this technique is found in Mark Antony's funeral oration in Shakespeare's *Julius Caesar*. Brutus, you will recall, assassinated Caesar because he feared that Caesar had ambitions to make himself dictator of Rome. Brutus is now in power, but graciously permits Mark Antony, Caesar's friend, to make the funeral oration over Caesar's dead body. Antony, however, is not primarily concerned with eulogizing Caesar. He uses the occasion as a step toward seizing power for himself, and seeks to turn the Roman populace from hatred of Caesar to hatred of Brutus and his fellow conspirators. The oration begins with the famous lines:

> "Friends, Romans, countrymen, lend me your ears:
> I come to bury Caesar, not to praise him. . . .
> He was my friend, faithful and just to me.
> But Brutus says he was ambitious;
> And Brutus is an honorable man. . . .
> You all did love him once, not without cause.

> What cause withholds you then to mourn for him? . . .
> My heart is in the coffin there with Caesar,
> And I must pause till it come back to me."

Antony is beginning to awaken the emotions of his hearers. He quotes Brutus, sarcastically. He mentions the sacred bonds of friendship which bound him to Caesar, and which once bound the crowd to Caesar. Antony then goes on to mention Caesar's will, and says that it leaves generous bequests to the people, but, he adds, he cannot possibly read this will aloud. If the people but knew what Caesar had done for them, he says, they would not be able to control themselves, for they are not made of "wood" or "stones" but of flesh and blood. The mob is now inflamed with expectancy and demands that the will be read, but Antony puts them off, first showing them the cloak which Caesar wore when he was killed. He points to the holes made by the stabbing daggers:

> "Look! in this place ran Cassius' dagger through . . .
> Through this, the well-beloved Brutus stabb'd . . .
> And, as he pluck'd his cursed steel away,
> Mark how the blood of Caesar follow'd it . . .
> For Brutus, as you know, was Caesar's angel:
> Judge, O you gods, how dearly Caesar lov'd him.
> This was the most unkindest cut of all."

Tears begin to flow, and Antony now reads the will, with its generous bequests to the people. The crowd leaves Antony in a fury, resolved to destroy Brutus and the assassins who killed their beloved Caesar. As they leave, Antony, knowing that he has accomplished his purpose, mutters to himself:

> "Now let it work: mischief, thou art afoot,
> Take thou what course thou wilt!"

Antony, like other demagogues, is a master of practical human psychology, who knows how to move the masses to his own ends. This kind of psychological insight is often turned to bad uses. But it should also be part of the equipment of anyone who wishes to be effective in moving people to action. Even in the best of causes human beings need some stimulus to action.

In the next chapter we shall distinguish between legitimate and illegitimate appeals to emotion. It should be obvious, however, that emotional appeals are sometimes quite proper, as when the Community Fund and organized charities get us to contribute by appealing to our hearts.

It is well to know when speakers are trying to get us to do something, rather than to inform us. And also—to know when they are trying to get us to do nothing. This is a reverse kind of directive language. And just as ordinary directive language seeks to arouse emotions, so the reverse type seeks to neutralize emotions, or to de-emotionalize a situation. For example, a shocking crime occurs in our city: an important public official is murdered. There will be a great public clamor for drastic action. Those who fear for the status quo will seek to dampen public indignation. We will be told that "the authorities are investigating," etc.

The negative use of directive language often characterizes official government "papers" concerning actions which seem immorally brutal. The actions will be described in a calm, unemotional manner. Neutral words will prevail, and emotive terms will be avoided.

Thus, during the 1930's in the Soviet Union, millions of kulaks, or independent farmers, were killed because they refused to give up their farms to the state. But the Russians never spoke of killings or executions. No, these people were "liquidated." George Orwell once described this use of language very effectively. He was concerned with the many terrible and cruel events that followed the end of the second World War. Millions of peasants were uprooted from their ancestral homes and robbed of their farms. But few people were shocked by these events, Orwell wrote, because they read official accounts of "the transfer of population," or "the rectification of frontiers." In more recent years we have heard of "the pacification of the countryside." This is the name given to the destruction of peasants, their homes and hamlets, by bombers. Neutral language helps to immobilize our emotions. So much for the use of directive language with a "reverse twist."

Our distinctions between types of language may help to clarify some aspects of "propaganda analysis." The meaning of propaganda is extraordinarily vague, at least so far as common usage is concerned. Most people use the word "propaganda" without having any precisely defined meaning in mind. In everyday speech this word may mean anything from "a pack of lies" to "the attempt to influence anyone about anything." But these are inadequate definitions. Not every liar is a propagandist, and we do not usually think of a hostess urging us to have another helping of her culinary specialty as a propagandist. She is trying to influence us about something, but unless the word "propaganda" is more limited in its meaning it will be quite useless, and ought to be dropped from the language. "Trying to influence others" is almost coterminous with speaking.

The usual dictionary definition is better: "Propaganda is a systematic effort for the gaining of public support for a course of action." But even this definition is not accepted by everyone. This lack of agreement concerning the meaning of propaganda may be demonstrated by the following experiment: Go to any library and find twenty books in the fields of government, political science, sociology, and social psychology which contain the word "propaganda" in the indices. You will find twenty different definitions of the word. Some years ago a public-spirited citizen of New York offered a thousand dollar prize to anyone who would define the word in such a way as to win general acceptance. There were no applicants.

We shall not offer a twenty-first definition here. But we can point out some of the things we ought to have in mind when we suspect that we are on the receiving end of propaganda. The word, after all, is of little consequence; it is the thing that counts. Just what is it that we are suspicious of, when we think of propaganda as being in some fashion dishonest, as most people do? This is what concerns us here.

As thoughtful citizens, we want to know the facts, so that we can come to intelligent decisions. We are afraid that there are organized efforts to deceive us so that we will act blindly and unintelligently. What can we do about this? The answer is quite a simple one: become as well-informed as possible. Knowledge is needed to see through a lie, whether a big or a small one, and nothing else will do the job.

In recent years, with the public's increasing awareness that it is being victimized by "propaganda"—understood as a form of organized deception—many writers have sought to help the public in its search for protection against deception. These analysts have sought to give us a method for detecting propaganda and thereby to achieve security against its harmful effects. We are told to watch for such techniques or "tags" as "name-calling," "glittering generalities," "testimonials," "band-wagon appeals," etc. Let us look at the meaning of these categories.

Name-calling, or "labeling," refers to the practice of attaching "bad" names to individuals or groups or ideas: names such as "Red," "Fascist," "reactionary," "totalitarian," "racist." These words stir feelings of fear and hatred for the persons and ideas to whom they are attached. The abusive terminology makes people forget about the necessity for knowing what the facts are. But name-calling, though a popular instrument of propaganda, is not confined to propagandists. We all indulge to some extent, even when we call a man a "name-caller."

We ought not to call names, of course, as a substitute for giving evidence. And the rules of courtesy (not to speak of the laws against slander and libel) tell us that calling names is a boorish as well as an illogical way of making a point. But it is also very easy to exaggerate these warnings. Some people use the category "name-calling" for the use of any uncomplimentary term applied to anyone. But it is not improper to characterize a man as a Communist or a Fascist when these words are adequately defined and there is proof that these statements are true. When a man is called a Communist or a Fascist merely because he espouses views that are more liberal or less liberal than our own, however, we exhibit intellectual irresponsibility.

Similar considerations apply to the other techniques. A "glittering generality" is a smug generalization, illustrated by "Woman's place is in the home," or "What is good for business is good for the country." There is a wisecrack which says that generalizations are always false, and statements like the ones just quoted undoubtedly ought to be qualified. But certainly propagandists have no monopoly on the use of such generalizations. Finally, consider the "testimonial." This may be worthless as evidence, especially when it comes from a non-expert or unqualified source, but the opinions of qualified persons, on the other hand, are worthy of respect. We should always consider the source, i.e., the competence of the testifier, the probability of his being prejudiced, etc. But testimonials are not necessarily illegitimate.

The analysis of these "propaganda techniques" calls our attention to the possibility that we may be permitting emotion to sway us, and we are reminded that we ought to look into the evidence. But language alone does not distinguish propaganda from other forms of discourse. Propagandists may avoid these techniques altogether, and non-propagandists may use them.

What is meant by propaganda in this discussion? Its meaning may be made clearer by contrasting the propagandist and the educator. There are some, of course, who deny the distinction and who tell us that "the advocacy of what we believe in is education; the advocacy of what we don't believe in is propaganda." But this is not what most of us mean by these words. An educator is one who, in the phrase of Robert Hutchins, "seeks to teach people how to think for themselves." An educator wants people to seek the truth. To this end he will present them with facts; he will appeal to their reason; he will follow an argument to whatever conclusions may be warranted by the evidence. An educator will, or ought to, have his own point of view, his own preferences, and he will recommend his personal beliefs to his audience, but he will state the grounds on which he holds these beliefs, and he will state the major objections to them. Thus his students will be able to judge for themselves concerning the validity of his arguments and the truth or falsity of his beliefs.

We have been speaking of an ideal educator, a truth-seeker. But a propagandist, in the strict sense, is not interested in the truth for its own sake, or in spreading it. His purpose is different. He wants a certain kind of action from us. He doesn't want people to think for themselves. He seeks to mold their minds so that they will think as he wants them to think, and act as he wants them to act. He prefers that they should *not* think for themselves. If the knowledge of certain facts will cast doubts in the minds of his hearers, he will conceal or ignore these facts.

It may be said that there are no educators in this ideal sense, and that, really, everyone is a propagandist. "The propaganda with which we agree is called education; the propaganda with which we disagree is called propaganda." If we accept this notion, we are forced to deny the distinction between tricksters and truth-seekers. This confusion of categories may be fostered by those who are afraid of the truth and who therefore want us to disbelieve whatever we read about them. If they can get us to believe that "everything is propaganda," we will believe nothing, including the truth about them. But to accept the wholesale skepticism suggested by the phrase "everything is propaganda" is just as foolish an attitude as to be completely unskeptical. There are two errors we ought to avoid: to be too trusting and to be too skeptical. Some people believe everything they read in the papers, and others believe nothing. We must learn to be discriminating–to distinguish between what it is reasonable to believe, what it is reasonable to doubt, and what we ought to dismiss as probably false.

To sum up. We have noted that there are three kinds of language, or purposes in speaking, and we examined the distinction between neutral and emotive words. We saw how emotion is employed in order to get action. Propaganda, we saw, has a directive purpose, for the propagandist wants us to act. The question, "What shall we do in order to protect ourselves against propaganda?" is misleading. The question assumes that propaganda is bad, and we cannot say that this is so without making certain distinctions. Insofar as propaganda seeks to get us to act by emotional appeals coupled with a concealment of facts–facts that might make us think about the merits of the proposal–it is "bad" *as a method*. It is possible of course that the propagandist may have our best interests at heart, so that his *goal* may be a good one. An illustration of "good" propaganda is found in some of the War Bond posters used during World War II. These posters showed a Marine lying on a foreign beachhead. Underneath the picture was an exhortation to buy Bonds so that our armed forces would not lack ammunition. The real purpose of selling these bonds was to dry up excess purchasing power in the hands of consumers, and thus avoid inflation. This propaganda had a desirable goal, for inflation would have impeded the war effort. And perhaps the truth would not have been so effective, for "Avoid inflation!" has little emotional appeal. We can only hope that propaganda of this sort will some day be unnecessary, even in good causes. This will happen when the people can be trusted to know, and act upon the truth.

Another reason why it is misleading to speak of "protection against propaganda" is that this implies that there is a special kind of defense against propaganda. There is no magic amulet whereby one may exorcise its evils. The only defense against harmful propaganda is to add to our knowledge and to sharpen our critical abilities. We shall then know how to protect ourselves against the various forms of hokum.

The Chinese have a proverb which says that there are three sides to every question: my side, your side, and the right side. Though the right side is hard to find, to seek for it is legitimate, and we should have the confidence that we may find it if we try hard enough.

VI.

HOW NOT TO ARGUE

In the spring of the year 399 B.C., a famous Greek philosopher was put on trial for having committed two crimes. One was impiety to the gods of the state; the other was the corruption of youth, by teaching them impiety. The penalty for a conviction on these charges was a severe one, possibly death. The prisoner's name was Socrates, and he was seventy years old at the time.

There were other reasons, political reasons, for trying Socrates. He had been associated with the old aristocratic regime, now overthrown by the democracy, and he was held in suspicion as a critic of the democracy. Among other things, he became unpopular for his strange doctrine that even politicians ought to know what they are doing.

Socrates was reputed to be the wisest man of his time. This reputation surprised him, he said, for he considered himself to be an ignorant man; ignorant of the answers to the supreme questions concerning human happiness and human destiny. But he was also sure that no one else knew the answers to these questions, and this furnished him with an explanation of his reputation as a wise man. Though he was ignorant, he alone *knew* that he was ignorant, whereas other ignorant men did not know that they were, thinking they had all the answers.

The court which tried Socrates was made up of 501 of his fellow Athenians, the 501st man being added in order to avoid a tie vote. As Plato reports the trial in his short masterpiece, "The Apology," Socrates vigorously denied that he had done anything wrong. He denied that he was guilty of impiety to the gods and he denied that it was wrong to carry on free and open discussions with young men. He was convinced that he was right in what he was doing, and he was sure that he could convince his judges, by logic and reason, of the justice of his cause. Throughout his life he acted on the principle that clear thinking is indispensable for right living, and that human life without the joy of thinking is a life not worth living. Let us look at one passage from his speech to the judges at his trial:

"Perhaps some of you," he says to his judges, "when you appeared before the judges in a similar situation, begged and besought the judges with many tears, and perhaps you brought your children into court to arouse the compassion of the judges. But I will do none of these things, though I am in peril of losing my life. I too have children, but nevertheless I shall not bring any of them into court to beg you to acquit me. This is not because I am stubborn, my fellow Athenians, or because I lack respect for you, but because I think it disgraceful for respected people to act in that manner. But, apart from the question of reputation, gentlemen, I think it is not right to implore the judge or to get acquitted by begging; we ought rather to inform the judge and convince him. For the judge is not here to grant favors in matters of justice, but to give judgment; and his oath binds him not to grant favors according to his pleasure, but to judge according to the laws."

Socrates, in other words, used a rational and logical approach in presenting his case to the jury. This was the speech of a rational man. Socrates presented the evidence, and refused to indulge in an emotional harangue in his own defense. In other parts of his speech, however, he did present an eloquent defense of the free pursuit of truth, and he also goaded his accusers with withering sarcasm. Socrates' spirit of reasonableness and, incidentally, his sense of humor, did not desert him even after he heard the sentence of the court that he be condemned to die by drinking a poison made of hemlock. An anecdote bears witness to this. After the verdict of guilty was returned, one of his disciples, Apollodorous, who was at the trial with him, exclaimed, "But what I find it hardest to bear, Socrates, is that I see you being put to death unjustly." Socrates replied, "Was it your preference, Apollodorus, to see me put to death *justly?*"

The question may be raised: Was Socrates' rational approach the proper one under the circumstances? Should one use a "logical" approach, or should one use an emotional appeal in presenting a case to a jury? We are all of us familiar with that favorite of the cartoonists, the glamorous blonde witness who sits in the witness chair with her beautiful legs crossed provocatively. This, one might say, is the proper technique for presenting a case to a jury, especially when the jury is an all-male one.

Before we try to answer our question, it will be instructive to compare Socrates' approach with that of Mark Antony. The Funeral Oration was an emotional appeal. Antony achieved the goal he sought. Now, can one say that Socrates used the wrong technique, and Antony the right one? If Socrates had had you as his lawyer, would you have advised him to appeal to the emotions of the court, consisting as it did, of a large crowd? It all depends, of course, on what one is after. The question, "Did Socrates use the proper approach?" is somewhat ambiguous. "Proper approach" has at least two meanings. "Proper" may refer to an efficient technique for achieving a goal, whatever it may be, or it may mean what we ought (in a moral sense) to do.

Taking people as they are, and desiring to mold them to one's purpose, an emotional appeal may be more effective than a rational one. Unscrupulous demagoguery may get results. One might wish it were otherwise, but in the real world, as distinguished from an ideal society, such is often the case. But talk also has a moral aspect. There is a moral obligation to tell the truth. And there is also the element we call "honorable conduct." Though few would have condemned Socrates if he had obtained an acquittal by an appeal to the court's emotions, he preferred death to what he considered dishonorable conduct. His sense of moral integrity did not permit him to compromise with his principles and he became a martyr to the principle of unswerving devotion to the truth. To the truth, that is, as he saw it.

Thus the question, "Who used the proper approach?" depends upon the meaning we give to "proper." But there is also a larger issue. Logic has its proper place, and so has emotion. A purely intellectual approach to life is as insufficient as a purely emotional one. The activities of life may be divided into two broad categories, the logical and the non-logical. By "non-logical" we do not mean "illogical," but rather activities that have nothing to do with logic. There are times when we reason, and argue, and draw inferences. But, for the most part, we are engaged in non-logical activities, like eating and sleeping, or narrating the events of the day, and so on. Logic enters only when we give reasons for our beliefs.

When we give reasons for our beliefs, we are reasoning. Reasoning is either logical or illogical. *Il*logical reasoning is bad reasoning, but the *non*-logical has nothing to do with reasoning. When we seek to prove that something is or is not the case, then we engage in argument, in which we say: This is true because that is true, or This is so because that is so. When the reasoning is adequate we say it is logical; when not, illogical.

When we assert beliefs which may be questioned, then we have an obligation to be rational. This common human obligation may be stated in the form of a "law of rationality" or "law of argument," that *we ought to support our beliefs by adequate evidence*. When we say that we know that something is true, we ought to be able to justify our belief by adequate evidence. What is adequate evidence? This term is best defined by example, and we shall give examples as we go along, but we shall assume here that we agree pretty well as to the distinction between evidence that is good and sufficient, and that which is not. In the end there is only one court of final appeal in settling a problem concerning what is rational and what is not: the community of reasonable men. Fortunately, the human race has always agreed pretty well on which of its members are reasonable and which not.

Logic is not all, then, but we have a common obligation to be logical when logic is relevant. In the last chapter we saw how emotional language is used to get action and we raised the question as to when emotional appeals are appropriate and when not. An emotional appeal under circumstances like those portrayed by Shakespeare is highly improper. For the mob did not know what the facts were. They came believing that Caesar was an evildoer, and they left convinced that Brutus was. But they did not revise their judgment on the basis of evidence. When the facts are in dispute, we ought to demand information and evidence rather than emotion. The Roman mob thus fell short of the human obligation to be rational. Before acting they should have asked themselves some questions concerning the facts: Did Caesar really aspire to be a dictator? Did Brutus seek to save their freedom? What evidence is there for or against the issues involved in these questions? But Antony foreclosed the inquiry by substituting emotion and passion for reason. And when we act on emotion without concerning ourselves with the facts, we are likely to rush into disaster.

Usually, when a politician does what Antony did, that is, when he substitutes emotional appeals for proof, propaganda for rational persuasion; when he inflames rather than informs, we shall find that he does so for one of two reasons. Either he has a contempt for the people, treating them as if they were children, incapable of understanding the issues, or he doesn't want them to know the truth.

We are not saying that emotional appeals are never appropriate. On the contrary. When the facts are not in question, and action is desired, then an emotional appeal is appropriate, even indispensable. In the critical days during the "Battle of Britain," Prime Minister Winston Churchill made his great "blood, toil, tears, and sweat" speech to the British people. He inspired his people and spurred them to heroic efforts. Emotion is the best fuel for this kind of energy, and this kind of stimulus is needed even in the best of causes.

Let us pause for a moment to get our bearings. The law of rationality is the central core of the rational approach: When we assert that a belief is true, we should be prepared to support our belief by adequate evidence. But the law of rationality is frequently violated, and it may be evaded. All of us hold many beliefs that are unsupported by evidence, and we sometimes argue as if evidence were unnecessary. One of the most common violations of the law is one that we have been discussing in this chapter: to make an emotional appeal at a time when evidence is required. We have not condemned emotional appeals under all circumstances, but only when we substitute emotion for proof when proof is required. The latter form of behavior is the essence of what is meant by "How Not to Argue." Let us look at some further illustrations.

Some years ago, when Mr. David Lilienthal was nominated as the first Chairman of the Atomic Energy Commission, the senior Senator from Tennessee attacked his fitness for the job. The Senator considered Mr. Lilienthal a dangerous man, he said, because his parents were born in Hungary, a country "now dominated by the Communists" (1947). Since Mr. Lilienthal's parents came to this country about fifty years before Hungary was taken over by the Communists, the fact cited by the Senator was grotesquely irrelevant. But it was not cited as evidence. Its purpose was to stir the emotions. The Senator believed that the mere mention of "Communists" would so inflame his audience that they would completely forget about asking for evidence concerning Mr. Lilienthal's fitness for his post.

The appeal to emotion sometimes takes the special form called "the appeal to laughter." If one is unable to refute an opponent's arguments by evidence, it is always possible to make him the butt of a joke and thereby evade the necessity of presenting evidence. A notorious example of this sort of thing, which apparently misfired, occured in a celebrated debate over the theory of evolution in 1860. Bishop Wilberforce scored when he asked Thomas Huxley, who was defending the Darwinian theory, whether it was through his grandfather or his grandmother that he claimed descent from a monkey? Huxley, who was in no mood to appreciate the Bishop's humor, retorted that he preferred descent from a monkey to descent from a man who used his great gifts and versatile intellect to distract the attention of his hearers from the real point at issue by eloquent digressions and skilled appeals to prejudice.

We have been discussing bad logical behavior on the part of speakers and writers who try to divert our attention from the need for evidence by working on our emotions. They fool us in this way. But we also fool ourselves. We rationalize; we engage in "wishful thinking"; we may accept unfounded beliefs because they satisfy us emotionally. For example: Do we find ourselves saying, "I believe thus and so because it makes me feel good so to believe"? Or do we say, "I *must* believe as I do because I just couldn't bear to think my belief false"? We deceive ourselves if we believe that our emotions guarantee truth. A beautiful passion, which makes its object appear not only handsome or beautiful, but also good, reliable, noble, and intelligent, really guarantees nothing of the kind. This is an insight, however, that many young persons acquire too late, to their sorrow. Perhaps it is not wholly undesirable to use a little logic even in love.

When one says, "This must be true, because I feel so strongly about it, and if it were not true I could not feel as I do," he may be misleading himself. For alas, wishes are fathers to thoughts that just aren't so. The fact that we want something very strongly apparently does not guarantee that it will come our way. This would be a much nicer world, of course, if our wishes could make things come true. There would then be no broken hearts, unsatisfied ambitions, or even lack of the wherewithal to own yachts, including the cost of the upkeep.

Our emotions, in other words, may interfere with our logic, and prevent us from seeing the truth. This is why we fail to see ourselves as others see us. "I am firm; you are stubborn; he is pigheaded." And do you know women whose attitude might be expressed in the following way: "*I* am beautiful; *you* have quite good-looking features; while *she* isn't bad-looking, if you like that type"?

It is our emotions that make us adopt a double standard of intellectual morality; one for ourselves, another for the other fellow. The Democrats are naturally enraged when they are unjustly attacked by Republican speakers; the Republicans may candidly acknowledge that the spokesmen of their party have been guilty of some exaggerations, but they will say that such attacks are justified in political debate. The Republicans, on the other hand, find unjust Democratic charges unbelievably vicious, while the Democrats will say of their own speakers that though they may have made it a little strong, nevertheless all's fair in love and politics.

And then there are those who think that they have transcended their emotions, who "see both sides," but all too often what they tell us is, in the words of an unknown poet,

> In matters controversial,
> My perception's rather fine.
> I always see both points of view,
> The one that's wrong, and mine.

So much for one of the major ways in which we evade what we have called the "law of rationality" or the "law of argument." We should aim to support our beliefs by adequate evidence. The form of the evasion we have been discussing is called the "appeal to emotion." There are of course many other ways in which the law of rationality is evaded. To draw an analogy from ethics: Aristotle once said that good men are good in one way, but the evil are evil in many ways; that is, good men resemble each other in their actions, but there is great variety in wickedness. Perhaps that is why we read so much more crime fiction than stories about virtuous men. Variety is more interesting. Aristotle also uses the image of the archer shooting his arrow at the target: there is just one way to get a bull's-eye, but many different ways in which to miss.

So with arguments. A good argument must hit the point exactly, but there are many ways in which we can miss. Logicians have catalogued many types of errors of reasoning, but it would be impossible to list every possible kind of error, for there are an infinite number of ways in which we can miss the target. In arguments, too, it sometimes seems as if the archer has turned his back on the target and shot in the opposite direction!

In the remainder of this chapter we shall discuss one other

major evasion of the law of rationality, the "argumentum ad hominem." This term, from the Latin, means "an argument directed to the man." To the man, that is, as distinguished from the point at issue. For example: Let us suppose that we disagree with what a speaker says. Now, we may try to disprove what he says by presenting contrary evidence. But sometimes we don't bother to present the evidence. Instead, we simply attack the speaker, verbally, that is.[1]

If we believe that a statement is false, we ought to attack the statement, not the man who utters it. A speaker, let us say, attacks the so-called "Right-to-Work" laws, which forbid compulsory union membership. He argues that the law unfairly discriminates against unions, on the ground that workers who benefit from union activities ought to pay for these benefits. Now, if you disagree with the speaker, you should support the position that the law does not unfairly discriminate against labor. But suppose, instead, you say to the speaker, "By the way, you're a union man, aren't you?" The question implies that the speaker's views must be false, on the ground that his union membership makes him so biased and prejudiced that it would be a waste of time to take his remarks seriously—they simply must be false.

As another example of this sort of thing, let us examine some remarks made by the German philosopher Arthur Schopenhauer in his "Essay on Women." In this famous, or perhaps we should say monstrous essay, Schopenhauer has some hard things to say about those delightful creatures. In reading what follows, it may be helpful to remember that Schopenhauer was a pessimist who believed that life is a painful and very sad affair. Here are a few lines from the essay:

> It is only the man whose intellect is clouded by his sexual impulses that could give the name of the fair sex to that undersized, narrow-shouldered, broad-hipped and short-legged race: for the whole beauty of the sex is bound up with this impulse. Instead of calling them beautiful, there would

[1] "Ad hominem" is sometimes used in a different sense—for an argument based on an appeal to a person's private prejudices: "You, as a businessman, will surely oppose legislation which will require higher taxes. . . ."

> be more warrant for describing women as the unaesthetic sex. Neither for music, nor for poetry, nor for fine art, have they really and truly any sense or susceptibility; it is a mere mockery if they make a pretence of it in order to please. Hence, as a result of this, they are incapable of taking a purely objective interest in anything.

Schopenhauer continues on and on in the same vein. He tells us that women are interested only in acquiring husbands, and that to this end they develop their *real* interests: in cosmetics, in clothing, and in jewelry, to the exclusion of all higher interests.

Perhaps at this point I should emphasize, as strongly as I can, that I happen to disagree with Schopenhauer. I am using this example for illustrative purposes only. The point is this: How do many women react to these remarks? Do they present evidence to disprove what he says, as required by the fundamental law of rationality? No. Rather, they attack Schopenhauer himself, with remarks like these: "That fellow must have had very little success in his love life"; "He must have been refused by every woman he proposed to"; "He must have been psychologically frustrated, and suffered from an anxiety neurosis"; "He should have been psycho-analyzed."

Now, these remarks give us an example of the argumentum ad hominem, for the argument attacks the man instead of disproving what he says. But even an unpleasant fellow like Schopenhauer may be stating the truth, so if you disagree with what he says, present the evidence. It certainly is not true, for instance, that all women have short legs.

Perhaps we ought not to take Schopenhauer's remarks so seriously, for they are of the nature of an emotional diatribe. His purpose may have been merely to express his splenetic feelings. The point is that a man's statements are logically independent of who the man is, or what he is, and that we do not disprove what he says by raising doubts concerning his parentage. Logically, a statement stands or falls on its own merits, regardless of who makes it. Truth and falsity are determined only by evidence. Personalities do not determine logical issues, and discussions should not degenerate into name-calling.

The reader may have a question at this point: Is it always wrong to attack the speaker personally? Is it wrong to cite the speaker's history, background, and associations in order to discredit what he says? This question requires a distinction between the argumentum ad hominem and a different kind of attack against a speaker. A witness testifies in a courtroom and the other side believes that he is lying. If they cannot directly disprove his alleged eyewitness testimony then they will seek to attack his character. They show that he was once convicted of perjury, after giving testimony in another trial. Now, what effect should this have on a jury? The jury learns that the witness once lied under oath, but this does not prove that he is lying now. He may be telling the truth. To say that his conviction for perjury *proves* that he is lying now would be to commit the argumentum ad hominem. But, though there is no proof that he is lying now, he has been shown unworthy of trust, and the jury should therefore refuse to give much weight to his testimony.

In other words, it is quite legitimate to show that a speaker is unworthy of trust, or that he is prejudiced, or biased, or that special interests have paid him to say what he is now saying, that he is insincere, and so on. "What you are," we say, "speaks so loudly that it is difficult to hear what you are saying, even though what you are saying may be true." The important thing, however, is that we should clearly distinguish between convicting a speaker of prejudice, on the one hand, and disproving what he has specifically said, on the other. We customarily give a speaker our trust and faith; we assume that he is telling the truth as he sees it. But if the speaker has open or concealed affiliations, such as paid or unpaid connections with propaganda organizations, or other special interests, which make it impossible for him to tell the whole truth, then we should not give him our trust. He *may* be telling the truth, but we should not rely on anything he says merely because he says it, since we do not believe in his sincerity.

The history of warfare shows that every new offensive weapon encourages the development of new defensive weapons. The same is true of arguments. The ad hominem is an attack, and this attack often calls forth a counterattack. Logicians call this counterattack, or defensive weapon, the "tu quoque." Translated into less dignified language, this means "You're another." This counterattack is appropriate only when one has been unjustly and irrelevantly attacked with an ad hominem. Here is a simple example: In the days before the United States instituted the peacetime drafting of members of the armed forces, there were many debates as to the desirability of the draft. A man in his forties argued that the draft was desirable, since it would make the United States ready for any emergency in the dangerous world situation. A young man, instead of trying to prove that the draft law was unnecessary, used the ad hominem attack. He said to the speaker, "You favor the draft because you are past the draft age and won't have to serve." This ad hominem approach calls for an obvious tu quoque. The older man replied, "By the same token, the only reason you are against the draft is because you are afraid you will have to serve." But the real question should have been, "Is the draft in the best interests of our country?" The answer to this question does not depend on who says what. An attack against the speaker proves nothing concerning the merits of what is being discussed.

There is a variant of the ad hominem which furnishes a useful clarification of the tu quoque. Speakers sometimes try to discredit theories by calling them old-fashioned. Now, "old-fashioned" may be a devastating criticism in the field of the exact sciences, when experiments have disproved an old theory. But in the field of social and political ideas, most theories have some merit, regardless of their age. Let us assume that a speaker wishes to refute the theory of "free-enterprise." "That idea is old-fashioned," he says. "It goes back to the eighteenth century." Two answers are possible. One may point out that this "criticism" is like the ad hominem approach, for the date of a theory is irrelevant to its validity. Only evidence can disprove a theory. Or one may use the tu quoque here. "If the theory of free-enterprise is discredited because it goes back to the eighteenth century," we may say, "then the theory of government regulation is even more conclusively discredited, for it goes back to the seventeenth century."

We have seen that there is a fundamental law of rationality, or, as we have also called it, a "law of argument," which tells us that we ought to justify our beliefs by adequate evidence. We evade this law when we ignore the requirement of presenting evidence, and instead make an appeal to emotion, or attack the speaker instead of what he has said. These evasions furnish no evidence, either for or against the point at issue. These evasions, then, are the fundamental things to avoid, when we concern ourselves with how not to argue.

VII.

ON STICKING TO THE POINT

IN GILBERT AND SULLIVAN'S *Mikado*, there is a famous song about the flowers that bloom in the spring. But Ko-Ko, who is required to marry the unattractive Katisha, sadly reflects that the flowers that bloom in the spring have nothing to do with the case. And that suggests our topic in this chapter. We shall be concerned with distinguishing between things that do and that do not have something to do with the case.

One of the rules of a good discussion is that the participants should stick to the point, and not wander away from it. Their remarks should be relevant and pertinent to the matter at hand. We shall not attempt to define "relevance" except to note that it means something like "connected with." The connection may be a cause-and-effect relationship, or it may have to do with a logical proof, or explanation in general. Illustrations are in order.

Is the fact that a certain Senator parts his hair in the middle relevant to the question as to whether he is an authority on free trade? Should scientists investigating cancer examine the fabrics worn by victims of the disease? If a historian is investigating the causes of the downfall of the Roman Empire, should he note the date of the building of the Great Wall of China? Does a decision as to guilt in a trial for murder depend on a belief in capital punishment? These questions involve different aspects of relevance (or irrelevance).

When we say that the way in which a certain Senator parts his hair is irrelevant to the soundness of his views on free trade, we mean that no one has ever established a connection between coiffure and economic insight. Nor is there any causal connection between clothing and cancer. But there does appear to be a cause-and-effect relationship between the building of the Chinese Wall and the downfall of the Roman Empire. The Chinese built the Great Wall to protect their borders against invasion. After the Wall was built the Huns advanced on China but found their path blocked by the Wall. Thwarted in their eastward motion, they turned west and finally reached the Roman area where they contributed mightily to the fall of that once majestic empire. What appears at first sight to be an irrelevancy, then, may actually have a significant relationship to the end-result. There are some very old verses which tell us how, for the want of a horseshoe, a battle was lost. The chain of causal connection is often made up of very subtle links.

The last remark suggests that it is safer to say "no apparent connection," rather than "no connection." This is a matter of great importance in science. Anything whatsoever may turn out to be relevant, but in the meantime, with limited funds for research and limited time, scientists must explore along the avenues which appear most likely to be successful in solving a problem. The number of "e's" which appear in the words of *New York Times*' editorials may have something to do with the forecasting of economic conditions, but it is so unlikely that we think we can safely ignore this approach. Experience bears out our judgment that some things are irrelevant.

We shall be concerned with relevance in the sense of logical rather than causal connection. For example, suppose that I should say that the great majority of Americans enjoy, on the average, the highest living standards of any people in the whole world. An objector says that my statement is false, and that he can disprove it. He points to the fact that there are many people in the United States who are quite poor, having yearly incomes of less than $2,500 per year. Now, the facts cited by the objector are logically irrelevant. They are not to the point. Why not? Let us grant the truth of the facts he cites. There *are* many poor people in the United States. But I did not say that every American was "well off." Nor did I say that there were no poor in the United States. I said only that the majority of our people have the highest living standards, on the average, in the world. To disprove my statement, the objector would have to cite a country in which the masses of the people enjoy a higher living standard. There may be such countries, but it is irrelevant to point to poor people in our country as a disproof of a statement which refers to comparative average living standards.

To argue in the manner of the objector involves a slipping away from the point. The objector has committed a "diversion." He has diverted the issue from one question to another. This practice is also referred to as "drawing a red herring across the trail of an argument."

A speaker may also slip away from his own point and thus create a diversion. This usually happens when a speaker has undertaken to support a difficult case. He may seek to create the impression that it is sufficient if he proves a point that can more easily be established. But the latter may represent a quite different issue. For example, a Senator may speak in behalf of a bill requiring "one hundred per cent parity prices" for farmers. He may dwell at length (or even exclusively) on the economic suffering of the farmers before the days of government-supported farm prices. But instead of answering the question, "Is one hundred per cent parity desirable?" he answers one that may be stated as "Is some form of government aid to farmers desirable?" It is much easier to support the latter question than the former. When speakers set out to prove the obvious, look for a diversion.

Let us look at more examples. In 1940, when Congress was debating the question as to whether we should send Lend-Lease materials to Britain to help her in her lone stand against Germany, a college president who opposed the proposed aid asked the following questions: "Are we to help the British Empire whenever it goes to war?" and "Do you think that a victory for the

British Empire will result in the disappearance of all the ills which afflict us at home?" These questions were diversions. The real problem, aside from moral considerations, was whether it was in the best interests of the United States to give Britain armed aid in 1940. The quoted questions refer to different problems. Their irrelevance may be seen in this way: Even if we answer the questions with "No's" (as we are expected to), the fundamental problem: Ought we to give Britain *this* aid *now?* would still be unanswered. Thus, we might say, "No, helping Britain will not solve all of our problems, but we ought to help them, because it is in our interest to do so."

A somewhat different type of diversion occurs in the following. Assuming that the laws of a State impose capital punishment for murder in the first degree, is the State justified in executing a man found guilty on circumstantial evidence alone? An answer such as "No, because capital punishment is always wrong" would be an irrelevancy. Perhaps capital punishment ought to be abolished, but the question here is whether the law should be applied when the evidence is wholly circumstantial, assuming that it would be applied where the act is seen by witnesses. Incidentally, it is desirable to learn the art of working out the logical consequences of assumptions that we consider false. The anti-executionist in this case should have said, "I don't believe in capital punishment, but if you accept it, then I see no justification for drawing a line between circumstantial and testimonial evidence," or: "Even if you assume that capital punishment is sometimes justified, this is not the appropriate kind of case for its application," etc.

Diversions are traps for the unwary, and one should be constantly on the alert for them. Let us imagine a conversation between a pacifist and a non-pacifist. The pacifist argues that "all wars are morally evil, no matter for what purpose they may be fought." "No war," he goes on, "is ever justified, so we should sternly refuse to distinguish between just wars and unjust wars. It is always wrong to a kill a fellow human being." His opponent then asks him whether it would be immoral for a man to fight in defense of his country in the event his country is invaded. To this the pacifist responds, "I can assure you that no one is going to invade us." His opponent then proceeds to argue that there is a real danger that their country may be invaded.

Let us analyze what happened here. The pacifist was asked whether his principles require that a man should refuse to fight to repel an invader. The pacifist slipped away from the point when he said there will be no invasion. This was a diversion. But his opponent did not notice it and fell into the trap, arguing the irrelevant issue as to whether there might be an invasion, and the original question was forgotten.

And here is another example of a snare for the innocent: A man says that he favors compulsory military training in a time of emergency. His adversary says, "As for me, I'm against it. I'm opposed to anything that violates the Constitution. I believe in complying with the Constitution at all times." The speaker then says, "In an emergency we must do whatever is necessary for survival, Constitution or no Constitution." This is of course a foolish example, but it illustrates the point. Compulsory military training does *not* violate the Constitution and so there was no need to justify the "violation." Before you accept the assumption on which an objection is based, ask yourself whether the assumption is a true one. If it is false, you will not have to answer or evade its possibly embarrassing implications, and a possible diversion will be avoided.

The diversion sometimes takes the special form called "extension." A speaker says that some corporation executives sympathize with the aims of organized labor. A critic argues that it is false to say that all corporation executives are friendly to labor. But the critic is not attacking the speaker's statement, which said "some." The critic has extended "some" into "all" and attacked his own extended version of the original statement. Similarly, if the issue in debate were, "Are all corporation executives opposed to labor unions?" it would be irrelevant to prove the *falsity* of the statement that all executives are friendly. For even if it is false that all executives are friendly, this would not necessarily mean that all were unfriendly. Some are and some are not.

And the fact that some are unfriendly does not prove that none are friendly. Debaters use this trick of extension because it is so much easier to disprove an extreme statement than a moderate one.

So much for one type of irrelevancy in argument. But before we discuss another type of failure to "stick to the point," we shall discuss an error which may be called an "overdoing" of this business of sticking to the point. This new error, in fact, is opposite in form to the error of slipping away from the point. In this new error we *never get away from* the point. We merely repeat it, over and over again. Examples: "Why do I say that every human being believes in God? How do I know that? The proof is that the belief is universal in the human race." Now, this is sticking to the point with grim tenacity. But it proves exactly as much—no more, no less—as we prove when we argue that a rose is a rose. The speaker says that everyone believes in God, and when asked for proof tells us that everyone *does*. "How do I know that it is so? Because it is so." In an argument a reason should be given for a belief, and the reason should be a fact from which the belief can be inferred. But in this "argument" the reason (or proof) is exactly the same as the original belief. The reason ("The belief is universal in the human race") merely repeats the original statement in different words. This is not *proof*. This kind of "reasoning" is on the level of the child's response to the question "Why?" The child responds with a "Because," and nothing more. The demand for a reason is unsatisfied.

This fault in reasoning is called "begging the question." Its older Latin name is "petitio principii." The error consists in our pretending to prove something when actually we *assume*, in the "proof," that which we are supposed to prove. "Why do I believe that the Russians can't be trusted? Because they can't be." (Am I doing all right or am I doing all right?) Now, no formal logical error is committed in these examples, for we do not infer conclusions unwarranted by the facts. We infer no conclusion at all—we merely make an assertion. If the belief in God is universal, then it is surely the case that everyone believes in God.

But the repetition of a belief is not the same as proof that it is true.

Here is another simple example. A guardian (self-appointed) of the public morals tells us that it is morally wrong for women to wear tiny bikinis. We ask, "Why is it immoral?" and receive the answer, "Because it isn't right." The answer begs the question. It repeats, in different words, what was supposed to be proved. And if we now asked, "But why isn't it right?" the answer we should expect to receive would be, "Because it's wrong."

When we beg the question we make a pretense of proving a point, but actually merely repeat it. Nietzsche once said that all mankind was corrupted, and when challenged for a proof answered, "The mere fact that you disagree with me is in itself proof that you are corrupted." And here are two passably humorous illustrations. The first is a little story about two men who approached a teller in a bank. One of them wished to cash a check. The man was unknown to the banker, who asked if someone could identify him. "Yes," the man said, "my friend will identify me." "But I don't know your friend, either," the banker objected. "Oh, that's all right," the man replied, "I'll be glad to introduce you to him." The second illustration, a very old tale, is about two medieval Jews who were engaged in a dispute concerning the respective spiritual gifts of their rabbis. To clinch his case, one of them said, "And now I'll give you proof positive that my rabbi is the most wonderful rabbi in the whole world. Is there another rabbi who dances with angels every night after he falls asleep?" The other was somewhat skeptical of this. "But how do you know," he asked, "that your rabbi really dances with angels?" "Why," replied the other, "because he told us so himself." "But can you believe him?" "What!" the other retorted in indignation, "would a rabbi who dances with angels every night tell a lie?"

"Reasoning in a circle" is a "drawn-out" form of begging the question. It contains intermediate steps. A man says that classical music is better than modern music. Challenged for proof, he answers, "The best critics agree that this is so." Who are the best critics? "Those who prefer classical to modern music." And here is a more complex example: The founder of a new religion tells his followers that he is inspired, so that they may believe whatever he tells them. Now, in the unlikely case that he should be challenged for proof of his inspiration, he might answer, "Because I am inspired." That would be the simplest form of begging the question. But if he "reasoned in a circle," the argument might go like this: "Why do I say that I am inspired? Because here is a Book which says that I speak in God's name." "Why should we believe this Book?" he is asked. "Because it comes from God," he answers. "How can we know this?" "Because you can take my word for it." "And why should we take your word?" "Because I am inspired." If we now ask, "How can we know you are?" the circle will start all over again.

The so-called "argument by definition" is a special form of begging the question. Jones asserts that all Christians are good men. Brown disagrees, and points to Thwackum, who is a Christian, but whose conduct falls very much short of that of a model of virtue. "Ah," answers Jones, "Thwackum may attend church regularly, but he is no real Christian, for if he were, then he would be a completely virtuous man. I reiterate, all *Christians* are virtuous men." This argument begs the question. What Jones meant was this: "I *define* a Christian as a good man. Thus I can assert without fear of contradiction that every Christian [defined as a good man] is a good man." Jones' original statement cannot be proved false, for it is not a statement about facts, but a "stipulative definition." A stipulation, insofar as it is nothing but a declaration of intention as to how a word is going to be used is neither true nor false. The question, "Is this statement true?" can be raised only with respect to assertions that purport to describe facts. Observation or experiment may confirm or disprove factual statements—they are true or false—but we cannot raise the question of truth or falsity concerning a man's declaration of his intention to define a word in a certain way. If Jones had said that every *churchgoer* is faithful to his spouse, that statement would be true or false. But Jones merely tells us that he is going to use the words "Christian" and "virtuous man" interchangeably. By definition, then, no bad man can possibly be a Christian. (If we stipulate a definition of a square as a four-sided figure, it is senseless to ask, "Can a square have more than four sides?") Jones' statement, that "all Christians are good men" is thus tautological. He is saying that all good men are good men. But this is not what Brown took him to mean. Brown understood him to say that a Christian, defined as a member of a church that worships Christ, can always be depended on for his trustworthiness. This might conceivably be false. But a definition taken as a stipulation concerning word usage cannot be false.

Similarly, the members of a certain religious sect believe that none of their true believers will ever die. When it is noted that the mortality rates for the members of the sect do not differ significantly from the rates for the general population, the answer is: "Those who died were not true believers, for if they were, then they wouldn't have died." And here is another of the same type: Black says that nowadays no educated person believes in the devil. White disagrees, and points to Reinhold, a college graduate, who does believe in the devil. Black: "But Reinhold isn't really an *educated* man, though he has a degree, for if he were really educated, then he wouldn't believe in the devil."

These examples of arguing by definition give only the pretense of proof. They really say nothing about facts; they merely tell us how a word is going to be used. A man says, "I pay no attention to newspapers which criticize the administration, for they are prejudiced." When asked for proof of their prejudice, he answers, "The proof is that they criticize the administration." A more vicious form of this trick in reasoning is one in which we try to twist facts by definition. For example, the Chinese Communist General Wu appeared before the United Nations Assembly to deny the charge that China was an aggressor in Korea. "This cannot possibly be so," he said, "because my government is, by definition, a peace-loving nation." And here is an even cruder example: "Communist countries have real freedom, and capitalistic countries have no freedom. What proof do I have? Because, by definition, capitalism enslaves the workers."

Yes, and if we define Communism as a system which creates irrational human beings, then it will be impossible to carry on a rational discussion with a Communist.

And here is one more variety of question-begging: the "question-begging epithet." The previous varieties were cast in the form of arguments, with a pretence at giving proof. Repetition was substituted for evidence. Our new variety merely uses epithets. For example, expressions like "the stupid conservative point of view," or "wild-eyed radicalism," contain question-begging epithets which assume something that may require proof, without even a pretense at proof. Instead of proving, first of all, that Moriarity is a crook, we ask: "What do you think of that crook?" A ready-made conclusion is put into the hearer's mind. This variety of question-begging is perhaps more dangerous than the other forms, for it operates on our reluctance to question a positive assertion that is "unquestionable," especially when asserted in a strong manner. The intimidated listener may also be at a loss to know just what it is that he should question.

We beg the question, in other words, when we proceed on the basis of an unquestioned assumption, without examining the evidence for that assumption. This is a particularly vicious practice when it results in judging men guilty without trial. All too often we find the attitude which is satirized in the frontiersman's judicial procedure: "We're going to give this here hoss-thief a fair trial. Send to town for a good, strong rope." When the community is aroused over a series of monstrous crimes, people are apt to be impatient with the slow processes of legal proof. Lurking in our hearts there is often the desire to put into practice the theory of a famous prosecutor of witches, who had a unique method of determining guilt. When women were accused of witchcraft, this prosecutor advocated that their hands and feet be tied, and that they then be thrown into a tank filled with water. "If they sink and drown," he argued, "that would prove that they are innocent of witchcraft. But, if they float and do not drown, that should be regarded as proof that they are really witches, and they should then be fished out and burned." But the modern reader is more conscious of the inadequacy of the evidence ("She floats.") to support the conclusion: "She is a witch." We suspect that the prosecutor was begging the question.

This type of question-begging without argument is most difficult to detect when it is put into the form of a question. Logicians use the term "complex question" for such "question-begging" questions. To illustrate: "Will the farmer benefit by the increased wages which labor will receive if we raise our tariffs?" The most likely response to this question is "Of course he will!" The only problem here seems to be: "Will the farmer benefit or will he not?" But we may fail to notice that the question contains the false assumption that labor *will* receive increased wages if we raise our tariffs. Or consider the question, "How do you account for the fact of mental telepathy?" This assumes that it *is* a fact. It may or may not be. And when the salesperson in a department store deals with a customer who has difficulty in making up her (his) mind, the tactful complex question, "Shall I wrap it up or will you have it delivered?" may swing the sale.

We should be on the lookout for complex questions. If we do not we may find ourselves making admissions against our own interests. The danger here is illustrated by the famous question hurled at a witness: "Have you stopped beating your wife? Answer Yes or No!" Whether the witness answered Yes or No, his answer would be damaging to him. The same kind of difficulty confronts us when we are on the receiving end of a question like: "Are you for the Republocrats and prosperity for everyone? Answer Yes or No!" One may want to break this question into two parts. Complex questions may also contain self-contradictory assumptions, as in the question: "What happens when an irresistible force meets an immovable object?" This assumes that you can have both simultaneously, which is obviously impossible, since one precludes the other.

But we are suggestible creatures, and the next time someone asks us a question such as, "Why is it that businessmen are so much less concerned with the general welfare than are labor leaders?" our response is apt to be something like this: "Well, you know, I wonder why that is so too, though I hadn't thought much about this problem. It must be because they are interested only in their own profits." When a question begins with "Why?" it asks for an explanation, and assumes a state of affairs that needs justification. We must stop to ask: "Is the assumption actually true?" Well, then, how would *you* answer if you were asked whether you have any explanation for the sparing of the Krupp Works when the Allied flyers bombed Germany during World War II?

One final point concerning complex questions. The assumption, of course, may be true. The question concerning the alleged sparing of the Krupp Works is a perfectly fair one, *if* it is really true that these works were spared. But is it? What are the facts? The point is that we should watch for these "slumbering" assumptions and not take the false ones for granted.

Let us sum up before proceeding further. We have noted two vices that come under the category of "sticking to the point." One is slipping away therefrom; the other is *not getting away from it.* Our evidence, in other words, should be relevant to the point, and it should not merely repeat the point over and over again. We have examined diversions from the issue, and the begging of questions. Our last topic in this chapter concerns a mistake commonly made with respect to the burden of proof in an argument, a mistake called the "argumentum ad ignorantiam."

As the name suggests, the argumentum ad ignorantiam means an argument based on ignorance, or on an appeal to our lack of knowledge. For example, a man states his belief that God selected Mohammed as the final prophet of His Word. When challenged for a justification of this belief, he asks: "Can you disprove it? If you deny what I say, it's up to you to disprove my statement." Or let us say that an atheist denies the existence of God. When asked for evidence, he answers: "Can you prove that God exists?" But just as failure to disprove is not proof of the opposite (the Mohammed example) so failure to prove is not equivalent to disproof. It all depends on who has the burden of proof. If a man makes the claim that God does not exist, then the burden is on him to prove his point. Atheism is quite different from agnosticism, which merely says, "I don't know." Similarly the person who argues that God *does* exist, has the burden of proof for that thesis.

This, then, is the appeal to ignorance. Instead of proving a statement by positive evidence in its favor, we appeal to the fact that our opponent hasn't disproved it. But the law of rationality tells us that we should furnish positive evidence for our beliefs. To say that we are ignorant of the disproof is not equivalent to proof, nor vice versa. A political speaker alleges that there are thousands of secret Communists working in government bureaus in Washington. When asked for proof he says, "Well, you can't disprove it, can you?" By the same logic we can assert that this speaker himself is a disguised Communist, who is trying to undermine confidence in our government. I can't prove this, but that is unimportant. By his own logic it is up to him to *disprove* it. But of course his inability to do this will not prove that he is himself a Communist.

Our system of criminal law rejects the ad ignorantiam argument in that it does not require an accused man to prove his innocence. The State must prove that he is guilty. A failure to prove that a man is guilty does not mean that he has been proved innocent, of course, though it is sometimes accepted as such. The rule means exactly what it says: a man is assumed to be innocent until *proved* guilty.

An amusing variant on the ad ignorantiam argument is the old story about the justice of the peace who heard a case concerning a man who was accused of stealing a horse. Two witnesses testified that they saw the accused unhitch the horse from a post and lead it away, but five witnesses testified that they had *not* seen the defendant steal the horse. The J.P. said that since there were more people who had *not* seen the alleged theft than there were persons who claimed to have seen it, and since he believed that the majority were always right, he was forced to dismiss the case.

VIII.

PUTTING UP AN ARGUMENT

IF YOU WANT to make friends and influence people, a well-known public relations expert assures us, then you should never get into an argument, for you are sure to lose. If you win the argument, the loser will be unhappy and angry, and you will have lost a friend, or a possible friend. Dale Carnegie's advice is probably sound if you wish to "keep the peace." The most popular people are not the most skillful arguers. But the reader may be assured that he will not necessarily lose his friends if he continues with this chapter.

The word "argument" has several senses. Mr. Carnegie had the popular sense in mind: a contest in reasoning in which one person wins and another loses. In contentious arguments one person tries to prove another wrong. An argument in this sense is often contrasted with "discussion," an interchange of ideas in which there is no attempt to defeat an opponent.

Arguments, in the popular sense, often become verbal slugfests, in which one person tries to beat another down. All too often contentious arguments are wrangles in which tempers rise and in which the arguers often put up a mule-like resistance against anything their opponents may say. But we shall not be concerned here with such arguments.

By "argument" we shall mean the *basic unit of reasoning*. The proof of any statement or belief is always presented in the form of argument, defined as "a unit of discourse in which beliefs are supported by reasons." Our interest henceforth is in argument not for purposes of contention, but insofar as arguments are an indispensable element in the quest of truth. Argument in this sense is the heart and soul of the rational enterprise.

Arguments, then, are not things that are either lost or won, but units of proof (or attempted proof) that something is or is not the case. Here is an example: "Only citizens who have registered can vote, and you haven't registered, so you can't vote." In this argument the speaker seeks to prove that "you can't vote." This statement is supported by reasons. A statement supported by reasons is known technically as the "conclusion" of the argument. This is its "point," what it is "driving at." The statements which support the conclusion (the reasons) are called the "premises" of the argument. The premises are the evidence, or facts, or assumptions, or reasons, on which the conclusion is based. Note that a statement is a premise only in the context of an argument. The mere assertion, "Dust thou art," becomes a premise when it is used in an argument: "Dust thou art; therefore the body is inferior to the spirit." A statement becomes a premise by virtue of the role it plays in an argument.

In an argument, then, we say, "This, because of that," or "This is so, therefore that is so." This process is called "inference." But before we engage in further analysis of argument, let us contrast an argument with what we shall call a "mere assertion." Here is an example of the latter: "There are thousands of persons on the federal payroll who don't earn their pay, but are kept on until they retire. The committee studying this matter may recommend that these workers be let off with adequate severance pay."

By a "mere assertion" we mean any statement for which no "justifying reasons" are given. In an argument there are several statements, one of which is supported by others. The supported statement is the conclusion; the supporting statements are the reasons or premises. In the "federal payroll" quotation there are no supported and supporting statements. And when you read, "Dust thou art, and unto dust shalt thou return"—period, this too is an unsupported statement, thus a mere assertion.

The argument, in the sense of "discourse containing inference," is the central core of logic. *Only arguments* can be called logical or illogical. Not all discourse is argument; perhaps most is not. We ask of a friend, "What's new?" and he tells us. Narration is not argument, and so there is little argument in newspaper reporting and historical writing. But when we read a newspaper editorial, we are likely to find argument. The writer will be trying to prove something, such as the error in present public policy or the desirability of a new course of action. We support our beliefs by argument when we expect to be met with a challenging "Why?"—"Why do you believe that?" "Why do you think so?" "Why ought we to?" We said earlier that it was the mark of a rational man to support his beliefs by adequate evidence. This is especially the case when his beliefs are of a controversial nature.

Now, when we read argumentative discourse it is well to know how to "take it apart" with the critical eye of logic. There is perhaps no more important lesson for skilled reading than this: When you read argumentative discourse, find and identify its conclusion, and then note its supporting reasons, or premises. There are two questions which should always be in the forefront of the reader's mind: (1) What is the writer's point, exactly what is he trying to prove, or disprove; what is he trying to "put across"? (2) What reasons does he present to persuade me that he is right, on what basis am I expected to agree with or accept the conclusion? These two questions, of course, constitute only the first lesson in logical analysis. The next lesson will take up the question as to whether the argument presented by the writer of the editorial is sound or unsound. But one thing at a time. What we are now concerned with is the analysis of an argument into its parts, and the reader who makes the two questions part of his normal response to argumentative discourse is already on the road to becoming a more critical and intelligent reader.

An argument, then, has two parts: the premises (or premise) and the conclusion. The premises may be stated before the conclusion, or they may be stated after the conclusion. There are certain words, called "logical indicators," which connect the premises and the conclusion. When the premises are stated first, the word "therefore" (or a synonym) will be used: "You haven't registered; *therefore,* you can't vote." The word "therefore" always precedes the conclusion of an argument, and it always follows the premises. On the other hand, when the conclusion comes first, we use "because" (or a synonym) to connect the parts of the argument: "You can't vote, *because* you haven't registered." The word "because" always precedes a premise. The conclusion may also be sandwiched in between two premises: "Only those who have registered can vote, so you can't vote, for you haven't registered." If you are henceforth in doubt as to what the conclusion of an argument is, look for the logical indicators. They may of course not be present in expressed form (they may be understood) and one should then look to see where they can be inserted.

There are many synonyms for "therefore" and "because." For example, if you substitute words like "so," "hence," and "consequently" for "therefore" you will see that they have the same meaning. Sometimes the logical indicator is spelled out more fully, as in "which shows that," "which indicates that," "and so we may conclude that," etc. Synonyms for "because," are "for," "since," or phrases like "in view of the fact that," or "for the reason that," and so on.

In an argument, then, we find the two elements, premises and conclusion. There is no rule as to whether we should state the premise before the conclusion, or vice versa. In an extended argument which aims at persuasion, however, certain strategical considerations may influence the positions of the premises and the conclusion. For example, let us suppose that you are going to argue in behalf of a conclusion which will sound reasonable to your audience. It will then be well to state your conclusion at the outset, before giving your reasons for accepting it. You will have won the confidence of your hearers by the "soundness" of the conclusion which you are going to prove. On the other hand, let us assume that you wish to attack the popular view. Now, if you were to state your conclusion at the outset, this would arouse strong opposition and perhaps resentment. Many hearers would regard you as so unreasonable that they would not listen carefully to the rest of what you had to say. In this case, then, it may be advisable to build up the evidence with facts that your hearers accept, and then show how these facts logically require a conclusion different from the one they accepted previously. But these strategical considerations have nothing to do with the logic; they relate solely to the strategy of the argument.

Arguments may have more than one premise, and they may also have more than one conclusion. "I believe that Police Captain Blue takes bribes. He associates with gangsters and has become very wealthy." Two premises for one conclusion here. Note that there are no explicit logical indicators in this argument, but the sense indicates the structure. "The farmers voted for quotas. This will increase government expenditures, and it also signals the end of free enterprise." Two conclusions drawn here from a single fact.

In a "serial argument," we find a conclusion drawn from a reason, and this conclusion then serves as a reason for drawing a second conclusion. The final conclusion is the main point of the argument. Here is an example: "I am not as wealthy as I used to be, because of the decline in the stock market. And, since I am not as wealthy as I used to be, I shall be unable to buy that new house."

An argument has been defined as "discourse containing inference." Inference is used in *proof*, which we shall now consider. Proof may be used in a broad or in a strict sense. In the broad sense proof means "enough evidence" to justify a conclusion, as in the legal expressions "proof by preponderance of the evidence" or "proved guilty beyond a reasonable doubt." In the strict sense, as used in the proof of a theorem in geometry, proof means "demonstration," i.e., the logically necessary relation between axioms and theorem. We shall use the broader sense unless otherwise noted.

"Proof" also covers "disproof," for a disproof is simply proof that a statement is false. This must be distinguished from "failure to prove," just as a verdict of "not proven guilty" differs from proof of innocence. (We suspect that many guilty defendants have been acquitted in criminal trials.) Disproofs (or refutations) often take a characteristic pattern which resembles the "reductio ad absurdum" (reduction to an absurdity). The principle of the reductio is that if a statement implies absurd (or false) consequences, then the statement must be false. As an example, consider the following: It is said that wealthy people control the U. S. Congress. If this were true, then we would expect the income tax laws to favor the wealthy. But our income tax is steeply progressive, at one time rising to 91% of net income over $200,000. Hence the wealthy do not control the Congress.

And here is a more complex sample of the reductio ad absurdum:

> It is a common notion that morality simply means conformity to the customs of one's group. But this cannot be the case. If it were, we could never criticize and improve the morals of our group, at least we would have no moral basis for doing so. However superstitious, or stupid, or cruel the customs of our community are, they would be, by definition, morally right–for us. The unthinking conformist would be the moral man, the moral reformer the immoral man. There would be no moral progress. But no one really believes this. We all constantly criticize the morals of our group. (Adapted from an argument by Durant Drake, in *Invitation to Philosophy*.)

This argument seeks to disprove the theory that morality means conformity to the customs of one's group. The theory is disproved by showing that it entails absurd or false consequences. If this theory were true, the argument runs, then we could never be justified in criticizing the morals of our group, and it would be senseless to speak of "improving" them. But, as the last sentence in the argument notes, we do criticize the morals of our group, and assume that we are justified in doing so. The consequences being false, the theory must be false.

The last two arguments may raise some unanswered questions: Are these arguments sound? Do the conclusions really follow from the facts cited? But such questions must be postponed until the next chapter. What we are here concerned with is simply to illustrate the *structure* of an argument, not to assess its validity. The criticism of an argument for faulty reasoning must come after we understand exactly what the argument says. To understand what it says we must know what to look for. Thus the understanding of an argument often requires a great deal of co-operation from the reader. It is the duty of a writer to make his meanings clear, and also to make the argumentative structure clear, but there are bad readers as well as bad writers.

Sometimes we are not sure whether a unit of discourse contains an argument or not, as in the next example. In it G. M. Trevelyan, in his *History of England*, is commenting on the execution of Mary, Queen of Scots. Many have felt a sense of moral revulsion toward Elizabeth for ordering the execution of her cousin. But Trevelyan gives us a different line on this:

> . . . The execution of Mary Queen of Scots was the volition of the people rather than of their sovereign. Elizabeth long resisted the outcry, but her subjects forced her hand when the discovery by Walsingham of Babington's plot to murder her revealed Mary as acquainted with the design. Mary's prolonged existence raged like the fever in men's blood, for if she survived Elizabeth, either she would become Queen and the work of the Reformation be undone, or else there would be the worst of civil wars, with the national sentiment in arms against the legitimate heir backed by the whole power of Spain. The prospect was too near and too dreadful to leave men time to pity a most unhappy woman. Parliament, people and Ministers at length prevailed on Elizabeth to authorize the execution.

Trevelyan may not appear to be trying to prove anything. He

is narrating what purport to be historical facts. But his narrative is interpretative, and he gives reasons for his assertions. Thus he is presenting an argument. He has a main thesis, that the execution was not the desire of Elizabeth, that her hand was forced. This thesis is found at the beginning and end of the selection. In between we are given items that make it reasonable to believe the main thesis: The people wanted Mary out of the way, etc. And so these items constitute the reasons for his conclusion. (We are not concerned here with the truth of the cited facts, but with the structure of the argument.) We also note a subsidiary argument, in the line, "Mary's prolonged existence raged like the fever in men's blood, for if she survived Elizabeth. . . ." The word "for" in this line separates the conclusion from the premises of this subsidiary argument.

The structure of the argument, then, goes something like this: If Mary survived Elizabeth, then grave troubles would ensue. Therefore the people demanded that Mary be put out of the way. Elizabeth long resisted their demands, but when Mary's co-operation with Babington's plot was discovered, the people insisted on Mary's death and forced Elizabeth's hand. Therefore Mary's death was the will of the people rather than of their sovereign.

We shall now analyze the formal structure of the syllogism, a common form of argument. A syllogism is an argument consisting of two premises and a conclusion: "Only those who have registered can vote, and you haven't registered, so you can't vote." The most famous syllogism of all time is one used in logic texts for the past two thousand years:

All men are mortal
And Socrates is a man;
Therefore, Socrates is mortal.

The syllogism has two premises, one major and the other minor. The major premise is simply the premise which contains the "major term," which is defined as the "predicate of the conclusion." "Mortal" is the predicate of the conclusion, so "All men are mortal" is the major premise. The subject of the conclusion is called the "minor" term: Socrates. There is one more term, which appears in both premises but not in the conclusion. This is called the "middle" term: men. The "middle term" is so-called because it is the connecting link between the other two terms. "Man" connects Socrates and mortality.

The syllogism we have just analyzed is only one type of syllogism. It is sometimes called the "Aristotelian" type, because Aristotle was the first logician who analyzed syllogisms having this type of structure. Later logicians have examined other kinds of syllogisms. Here is a different type: "If prices continue to rise, then the unions will ask for further wage increases. Prices *are* continuing to go up, so we may be confident that the unions will demand further wage increases." And another: "Either a world government with an international police force will be established, or the world will continue in a state of tension. But there are no signs that such a government will be established, hence we can expect tension to continue." Now these last two arguments are syllogisms, for each has two premises leading to a conclusion. But they do not contain major, minor, and middle terms. Different kinds of analyses are required for these types, as we shall see in Chapter X.

There are many confusions concerning the role of the syllogism in thinking. We are sometimes told that "the syllogism is artificial, and outmoded," or that no one ever reasons in accordance with the form of the Socrates example above. But the logician does not present the syllogism as a model to be imitated. His point is, rather, that it is a form we actually do use in our reasonings. This may seem surprising to the reader, for no one would normally think in the pattern of the Socrates example. This example is truly in an artificial form, but it is deliberately put into that form for purposes of analysis, so that we may get a clear picture of what we are talking about. In "real life" this is the way the reasoning might look: "Socrates must die: we must lose him some day. For he is but a man, and mortality is a doom which none of us can escape." If we eliminate the rhetoric here, we shall find the familiar syllogism, which gives us only the bare bones of the argument.

A syllogistic pattern may sometimes add more to our knowledge than the Socrates example does. The American philosopher, W. P. Montague, once described how, many years ago, he had puzzled over whether women should have the right to vote. He was also a firm believer in that famous historical slogan: "No taxation without representation." He suddenly saw the answer to his problem: Taxpayers should have the right to vote, and women pay taxes, so women obviously should have the right to vote. He had found his middle term!

There is another reason for our surprise when we learn that we reason in syllogisms. This is because few syllogisms are stated completely in everyday talk. The obvious should not be belabored, and so, to avoid boredom and tedium, we leave something to the imagination of the listener. When what is clearly indicated is too obvious to mention, we may omit a premise from a syllogism, or we may even omit the conclusion. The following example is typical of ordinary reasoning: "Joe must be doing well this year, for he took his family to Florida this winter." This is a syllogism, but it is incompletely stated. There was an additional premise in the speaker's mind: "People who take their families for winter vacations in Florida are 'doing well.' "

Incompletely stated syllogisms are called "enthymemes" (rhymes with "Bentham-eems"), from the Greek *en* (in) and *thymos* (mind). Here are some more examples: "Naturally I consider him an intelligent man; he's an independent voter, isn't he?" This assumes that all independent voters are intelligent. "Our police should not carry guns. This type of police practice has worked well in England." This argument may sound more plausible in its incomplete form than it does when spelled out. For the missing premise would be something like "What works well in England will work well in the U.S." This last argument closely resembles the next one: "This cough medicine ought to be good for my cough, for, according to the advertisement, it helped a man in Minneapolis." Will whatever helps one man in Minneapolis help you?

Sometimes the structure of the argument is not quite so obvious. During the French Revolution, Robespierre headed the Reign of Terror for a time. Many thousands of "enemies of the State" were guillotined. During one of the proceedings at the Convention, Robespierre's enemies accused him of identifying the "enemies of the State" with his personal enemies. To this he responded, "I deny the accusation, and the proof is that you still live." The missing assumption here is not too obvious. This enthymeme is of course an incomplete syllogism, but it requires a flash of wit to state an argument in this way. Robespierre is of course assuming that his critics are his personal enemies, and that all of the enemies of the State are dead. Spelled out, then, the argument reads: "The enemies of the State are dead. But since some of my personal enemies still live, it follows that some of my personal enemies are not enemies of the State."

And here is an enthymeme with its conclusion missing: "An old Abbé, talking among a party of intimate friends, happened to say, 'A priest has strange experiences; why, ladies, my first penitent was a murderer.' Upon this, the principal nobleman of the neighborhood enters the room. 'Ah, Abbé, here you are; do you know, ladies, I was the Abbé's first penitent, and I may promise you my confession astonished him!' " (From a story by Thackeray.)

We shall note one further type of structure here. This is the "chain argument." A chain argument is a serial argument (mentioned earlier) in which a conclusion becomes a premise for a further conclusion. Let us look at a fairly complex example taken from Leibniz:[1]

> The human soul is a thing whose activity is thinking. A thing whose activity is thinking is one whose activity is immediately apprehended, and without any representation of parts therein. A thing whose activity is immediately apprehended without any representation of parts therein is a thing whose activity does not contain parts. A thing whose activity does not contain parts is one whose activity is not motion. A thing whose activity is not motion is not a body.

[1] "*Confessio Naturae Contra Atheistas,*" translated by H. W. B. Joseph, in *An Introduction to Logic,* The Clarendon Press.

> What is not a body is not in space. What is not in space is insusceptible of motion. What is insusceptible of motion is indissoluble (for dissolution is a movement of parts). What is indissoluble is incorruptible. What is incorruptible is immortal. Therefore, the human soul is immortal.

There are several variations in chain arguments, but this sample will indicate the general idea. The *validity* of arguments of this type, to anticipate the subject of the next chapter, depends on a property of what logicians call "transitive relations." A transitive relation is one such that, if A has it to B, and B has it to C, then A must have it to C. "Ancestor of" is a transitive relation. If A is the ancestor of B, and B is the ancestor of C, then A is the ancestor of C. When we speak of one class of things as being "included in" another class of things, we are also dealing with a transitive relation, for if class A is included in class B, and B is included in C, then A must be included in the class C. If the "class" of whales is included in that of mammals, and the class of mammals is included in that of warm-blooded creatures, then whales must be warm-blooded. In the Leibniz argument we find this relation of class inclusion. Each sentence can be interpreted in terms of the relations of two classes to each other: The class of "souls" is included in the class of "things whose activity is thinking." The latter class is included in the class of "things whose activity is immediately apprehended," and so on. The argument is valid because "class inclusion" is a transitive relation.

Not all relations are transitive, of course. Some are "intransitive," such as "being the father of." An intransitive relation means that if A has a certain relation to B and B has it to C, then A *cannot* have it to C. "Ten per cent larger than" is another such relation. Then there are "non-transitive" relations, such as "being a friend of": If A has a relation of this kind to B, and B has it to C, then A may or may not have it to C.

Logicians also classify relations as "symmetrical," "asymmetrical," and "non-symmetrical." A "symmetrical" relation is one such that if A has it to B, then B must have it to A: "equal to." (If A equals B, B equals A.) An "asymmetrical" relation is one such that if A has it to B, B *cannot* have it to A: "mother of." A "non-symmetrical" relation, obviously, is one where B may or may not have the relation to A, when A has it to B: "lover of." The reader may find it amusing to discover additional examples for the nine possible combinations of the relations of transitivity and symmetry:

1. Transitive-symmetrical: equal to
2. Transitive-asymmetrical: greater than
3. Transitive–non-symmetrical: included in the class of
4. Intransitive-symmetrical: polygynous spouse of
5. Intransitive-asymmetrical: father of
6. Intransitive–non-symmetrical: nearest blood relative of
7. Non-transitive–symmetrical: cousin of
8. Non-transitive–asymmetrical: unrequited lover of
9. Non-transitive–non-symmetrical: lover of

In this chapter we have been concerned with understanding what an argument is, how to identify one, and how to break it up into its parts. Two questions should be asked whenever we find an argument: What is its conclusion? What reasons are presented in support of the conclusion?

But there are other questions we must ask. These new questions center around the goodness or badness of the argument. What kinds of arguments do you consider good ones? When you say that an argument is "good," do you mean that you agree with the conclusion? Does it make a difference, in your estimate of an argument, whether or not you agree with the premises? Can you refuse to grant the truth of the premises, and yet accept the truth of the conclusion? Can an argument be a good one though every statement in it is false? Can it be a bad argument though every statement in it is true? In the next chapter we shall examine the principles which will help us in answering these questions.

But before we leave these questions let us note an ambiguity in the word "good" when applied to arguments. A "good" argument may mean one which is *valid* in form, i.e., an argument whose structure is such that *if* the premises are true, the conclusion must necessarily be true. Such an argument is *valid* even if the premises are not true. On the other hand, "good argument" may mean one that is completely satisfactory: valid in form and containing true statements. A valid argument, then, may not be completely satisfactory.

IX.

PUTTING UP A LOGICAL ARGUMENT

ARE THERE TWO PERSONS in the city of Chicago who have exactly the same number of hairs on their heads? Perhaps you think this highly unlikely, or perhaps you think it likely, but can we *prove* it one way or the other? It would be highly desirable if we could decide the issue without having to count the hairs on thousands of heads. Logic comes to our aid here. There are two well-known facts that make our answer certain. First, we must acknowledge the fact that a human head can have, as a maximum, about a quarter of a million hairs. A second fact is that there are close to four million persons in Chicago. Now, let us put these facts together, and we see that there must be two persons with the same number of hairs. For suppose that we actually did start counting the number of hairs on people's heads. And suppose that in the first 250,000 heads we counted, each head had a different number of hairs, so that no duplication occurs in the first 250,000 heads. In other words, there will be one head with one hair, a second with two, and so on up to 250,000, the maximum possible. We then come to the 250,001st head, i.e., the first head beyond a quarter of a million. *We must now duplicate* one of the numbers of the earlier subjects, since no one can have a number greater than 250,000. How useful logic is in sparing us tedious investigations!

This was an example of a logical proof. Let us now look at a different kind of "proof," the kind we find in a law court. A man is tried for the murder of his business partner. The accused was the beneficiary of a large insurance policy made out by the victim, and an additional motive is established in the fact that the victim was in love with the accused's wife. Ballistics experts establish that the bullet which killed the deceased was fired from the defendant's gun. The accused man claims that he is innocent, but cannot establish an alibi. His only defense is his claim that he is innocent. The jury must weigh his denial against the evidence presented by the State. The jury finds that the State has proved his guilt beyond a reasonable doubt.

We have examined two arguments, each of which uses the term "proof." But there is an important difference between them. If it is true that there are x numbers of hairs on a human head and more than that number of persons in Chicago, then it must necessarily be true that there are two persons with the same number of hairs. This is a formally valid, or necessary argument. But in the second case, if we grant the truth of the premises (the evidence given), the conclusion—that the accused is guilty—may or may not be true. There is a probability that he is, but he is not *necessarily* guilty. There is a possibility that he is innocent.

In the strictest sense, "proof" means an argument in which the conclusion *necessarily* follows from the premises. This is "formal" proof, or "demonstration." If we accept the premises in the hair-counting argument, we *must* accept the conclusion of that argument; if we grant the truth of the premises of that argument, then we must accept the truth of its conclusion. On the other hand, when we say "proved beyond a reasonable doubt," we do not mean that the conclusion *must* be accepted, or that it necessarily follows from the premises, but only that it would be "unreasonable" to accept the premises and not accept the conclusion. This is "proof" in a less precise sense of the term. We shall use the word "proof" in both senses, but we should recognize the difference between the strict and the looser sense of the word. We shall also use the term "valid" for an argument that involves logical necessity, and we shall call the other type a "probable argument." The distinction depends on the relationship of the premises to the conclusion. Granted the truth of the premises, *must* the conclusion be true? If it is impossible that the conclusion should be false when the premises are true, then the argument is a valid one. If it is true that all reformers are idealists, and that all idealists are nonconformists—if these premises are true, then it is impossible for "all reformers are nonconformists" *not* to be true, and so this is a valid argument. But if the premises can be true while the conclusion can be false—as in the murder example above—then the argument is not valid, though the premises may make the conclusion highly probable. In a "probable argument," of course, the degree of the probability, whether high, low, or moderate, will depend on the quantity and quality of the evidence.[1]

Logicians use the word "necessarily" in the strict sense indicated above. Thus, "not necessarily" covers a lot of ground, from an argument in which the evidence is grotesquely irrelevant to one in which the premises establish a high degree of probability, even though no certainty. In the following example, the speaker uses "not necessarily" to convey the impression that he is straining at a gnat, when he is really swallowing a camel: "Mr. A. attended a social gathering about twenty-five years ago at the home of Mr. B. Mr. C., a Communist, attended that party. Now, I do not say that Mr. A's presence at this party necessarily proves that he is a Communist, but . . ." "Not necessarily" has a pleasant sound here. It conveys the notion that the speaker is a cautious and fair-minded man who does not jump to unwarranted conclusions, for he is willing to grant the possibility that Mr. A. is not a Communist. But this is an odd usage, as odd as it would be to say, "The fact that John published his first novel last year does

[1] Recent logicians distinguish these as deductive and inductive arguments. In deductive arguments we say "If P (or P and R, etc.) are true, then Q is necessarily true" (the reformers argument); in inductive arguments: "If P (or P and R) are true, then Q is probably true" (the law-court argument).

not necessarily prove that he is now a multi-millionaire." To say, "Mr. A. is not necessarily a Communist" is to draw an insinuation based on the flimsiest kind of evidence. We ought to use "not necessarily" for arguments in which the evidence is not quite sufficient, rather than frightfully inadequate.

Thus far we have been discussing the distinction between a necessary and a probable argument. We shall now discuss the relationship between truth and validity. The main point is this: The truth or falsity of the premises (or the conclusion) has nothing whatsoever to do with the validity of the argument. This point is perhaps the most important lesson that one can learn about logical thinking: the distinction between the logical structure of an argument, on the one hand, and the truth or falsity of its evidence, on the other.

In connection with this distinction it is well to bear in mind the precise definitions logicians give the terms "truth" and "validity." *Statements* are true or false: A true statement is one which describes the facts correctly. *Arguments* are valid or invalid: A valid argument is one in which the conclusion is necessitated by the premises. Note in particular that *only statements* are true or false; *only arguments* are valid or invalid. Thus logicians never (or almost never) say, "A true argument," or "A valid statement."

Let us illustrate the distinction between truth and validity. "Human beings can't live on the moon, for there is no oxygen on the moon, and human beings can live only in places that contain oxygen." This is a valid argument, for *if* the premises are true then it would be impossible for the conclusion to be false. But we may question the truth of the second premise: Astronauts can bring their own oxygen with them when they land on the moon. So, though formally valid, this is not a satisfactory argument.

Further, an argument may be valid though all its assertions are preposterous: "If Eskimos were Cubans, and if every Cuban was an atomic scientist, then every Eskimo would be an atomic scientist." Validity is concerned with form or structure alone. If we symbolize Eskimos by E, Cubans by C, and atomic scientists by A, the form of the argument is: If E's are C's, and C's are A's, then E's are A's. The content of the substitutions for E, C, and A are irrelevant to validity. The rules of logic in relation to the substance of an argument are like the rules of arithmetic in relation to examples of application: "If you had 12 purple cows and 7 of them were kidnapped, you would then have 5 in your possession." It would be an irrelevance, insofar as we were interested in the correctness of the *arithmetic* here, to tell us that you, speaking for yourself alone, never saw a purple cow.

Let us now apply the same considerations to a probable, or inductive argument. Another murder trial. The prosecution presents three witnesses who testify that they saw the accused murder the victim. A motive is established, opportunity is proved, and other incriminating circumstances weigh heavily against the accused. The jury brings in a verdict of guilty beyond a reasonable doubt. We say that the jury acted reasonably, that is, they reasoned quite soundly in returning the verdict of guilty. But later we learn that the three witnesses were conspiring against the accused; they had framed him with his own gun, etc. The logical question: Does this new information affect our previous decision that the jury acted reaonably? It does not. It was reasonable to believe that the accused was guilty on the basis of all the evidence known at the time of the verdict. The quality of the reasoning, then, is independent of the truth of the assertions on which the conclusion is based.

Let us refer back to the Trevelyan argument for another illustration. We might say: "Trevelyan has proved his point if his facts are correct; that is, the logic of his argument is unimpeachable. But *are* his facts correct? Did Elizabeth really resist the demands of the people? Was Mary really cognizant of Babington's plot? On what evidence does he base these statements?" So far as I know, most historians would agree with Trevelyan, but these are legitimate questions which have nothing to do with the logical structure of the argument.

We see, then, that the truth or falsity of the premises is irrelevant to the "logic" of an argument. Just as an argument may be valid though its premises are false, so a conclusion may be probable on the basis of accepted premises, even though these premises turn out to be false or questionable.

The principles we just discussed will perhaps explain some familiar experiences, in which we listen to arguments in which each step follows from the preceding one without a logical flaw —but in the end we are "of the same opinion still," unconvinced. This sort of thing often happens when someone is trying to convince us of the errors of our political or religious ways. These unconvincing arguments may actually have been quite sound from a purely logical point of view. But this means only that the conclusion did actually follow from the premises *assumed* by the speaker. Your refusal to accept his conclusion, then, indicates that you refuse to accept the truth of his premises, and if you examine the premises carefully, you will be able to spot the place where your disbelief or doubt arises. (We are assuming that the argument is understandable.) Arguments of this kind are obviously unsatisfactory, for a completely satisfactory argument is not only correctly reasoned in the purely logical sense, but it is also one in which the premises are acceptable to us.

If the reader will turn back to the chain-argument quoted from Leibniz on page 102, he will find that the logical form of this argument is impeccable. You may or may not agree with Leibniz' conclusion that the soul is immortal. But if you do accept the truth of his premises, you *must* accept the truth of his conclusion, for the argument is valid. It is not the mark of a rational mind to say, "Your argument is valid, and your premises are true, but I refuse to grant the truth of your conclusion." This statement would be self-contradictory for it first grants the validity of the argument and then denies it. It is like saying, "This is a square but it has five sides." *If* an argument is valid, *and* the premises are true, the conclusion *must* be true, for this is what validity *means:* a structure such that if the premises are true, the conclusion must also be true.

But let us suppose that a reader disagrees with Leibniz' conclusion that the soul is immortal, or that he remains uncertain of its truth, although he does see that the argument is a valid one.

This must mean, then, that he disagrees with, or is at least uncertain concerning the truth of at least one of the premises. He may be able to point to the premise he disagrees with. But a reader untrained in metaphysics may find the meaning of the premises in Leibniz' argument obscure, or even unintelligible. A properly worded objection to the argument, in this case, might go like this:

"I am unconvinced of the truth of the conclusion, even though it follows logically from the premises. I must therefore be unconvinced of the truth of a premise or premises. I can't tell you which I consider wrong, for I don't understand them well enough to criticize, but I feel that there *must* be one premise that I would consider uncertain even if I understood it, for I don't accept the conclusion."

Now, this is not an unreasonable position to take, for, just as it is the mark of a boor to criticize an argument he doesn't understand, so it is the mark of an intellectually irresponsible person to *accept* an argument he doesn't understand. If we wish to make friends and influence people we may find intellectual irresponsibility less irritating to others than candor, but an *intellectually responsible* person will refuse to agree or disagree until he understands.[1]

We have devoted a good deal of attention to the distinction between validity and truth, for this is a much misunderstood point. And there is a special kind of confusion concerning the matter of accepting an unproved premise "for the sake of the argument." Suppose someone says, "If the need for large military expenditures should diminish within the next year—" and an objector breaks in at this point. "Stop right there," he says. "There's no point in your going on with your argument, for I don't accept your basic premise, and therefore can't accept whatever conclusion you will draw." But this is a refusal to be rational, for it may be very enlightening to deduce the logical consequences of uncertain, or even false premises. What the

[1] But the premises in Leibniz' argument *may* be true. In that case the result of our lack of understanding will be the refusal to accept a true conclusion.

speaker was going to say was: "If the need for military expenditures should diminish within the next year, and we are not prepared with plans for immediate tax reductions and other stimulants to the domestic economy, then we shall have a severe depression." It is worthwhile considering the logic of this argument even if we do not admit the truth of its major assumption. For *if* the premises should turn out to be correct, it is certainly useful to know the consequences they entail, and thus prepare ourselves accordingly.

The good thinker, then, must often entertain unproved or even false assumptions "for the sake of the argument." Scientists do this as a matter of course. Sir Isaac Newton's "first law of motion" tells us that if a moving body is not influenced by outside forces it will continue in motion forever. The first part of this law contains an assumption which is contrary to fact, for there are no bodies which are "not influenced by outside forces." But physicists find this law useful, for it implies that a body will continue in motion for a longer and longer period as friction is reduced.

Our basic distinction is between the truth of the premises or conclusion on the one hand, and the logical validity of the form, on the other. The distinction may be put in another way. It is like the difference, in an audit, between the soundness of the evaluations of items and the arithmetic used in adding up the totals. I may evaluate a pretzel factory building at $50,000, the machinery at $50,000, and the pretzels on hand at $900,000. Total assets: $1,000,000. The arithmetic is faultless, but the evaluations may be unrealistic.

The significance of what the logician means by validity may become clearer when we understand the meaning of an "invalid argument." A formally invalid argument is one which is deductive in form, but in which the conclusion is not necessitated by the premises. The conclusion does not "follow" from the premises. This is the meaning of "non sequitur." Two examples:

(1) Cats climb trees
And Squirrels climb trees;

Therefore, Cats are squirrels.

(2) Manitobans live in the northern part of North America
And Canadians live in the northern part of North America;
Therefore, Manitobans are Canadians.

Note that these arguments are similar in form. In each, the premises compare two things, cats with squirrels, and Manitobans with Canadians. In both, the compared entities have common characteristics. In (1) the common characteristic is tree-climbing, in (2) it is living in the northern part of North America. The conclusions are similar in that each tells us that one of the compared entities is identical with, or at least included within, the other.

Both of these arguments are invalid. In neither case does the conclusion follow from the premises. The relevant principle of logic is this: The mere fact that two things have one or more characteristics in common does not justify us in concluding that the two things are identical, or even that one is included within the other.[1] The fact that cats and fox terriers suckle their young does not justify the inference that cats are fox terriers; the fact that the Chinese and Japanese eat rice does not justify the inference that the Chinese, after all, are nothing but Japanese.

Note that the conclusion in (1) is false; that in (2) true. Many people will think that (2) is a better argument than (1), but the arguments are equally bad from a *strictly formal* point of view. The second appears more plausible because the conclusion is true, but in order to see how bad the logic is, let the reader substitute the word "Alaskans" for "Manitobans" in (2). The new premise: "Alaskans live in the northern part of North America." The new conclusion: "Therefore, Alaskans are Canadians."

The error we have just described may appear to be a very simple one, too obvious to mention, but we commit it often. The

[1] The logician's name for the error which involves a violation of this principle is "the fallacy of the undistributed middle term." The meaning of this technical term will be explained in the next chapter.

error occurs most often in complex contexts, and in subject matter that involves our emotions. We are particularly apt to overlook the badness of an argument when we believe the conclusion to be true, and particularly so when we derive emotional gratification from it. Consider the following: Joe Doakes must be a Communist, for he believes that Communists should be permitted to speak on University campuses, and we all know that Communists are in favor of permitting them to speak. This argument will sound plausible to many.

But, once more, the same error as above. Joe agrees with the Communists in one respect, we are told: both believe that Communists should have permission to speak. A common characteristic! But this does not prove that Joe is a Communist, for "the fact that two things have a characteristic in common does not prove that they are identical." Joe may be a good American, violently opposed to communism, but one who believes that students should be permitted to hear *all* points of view. Joe, by the way, may also be in favor of comparable privileges for students in Communist countries, something that Communists *are* opposed to.

But a warning signal should be posted at this point. Though an argument is invalid, it may have considerable merit. An invalid argument is one in which the conclusion does not necessarily follow from the premises. We remarked earlier that the phrase "not necessarily" covers a lot of ground. The conclusion that cats are squirrels does not follow necessarily from the premises we noted above. Nor does the conclusion follow necessarily in this argument: "True theories are confirmed by careful experiments, and Einstein's theory has been confirmed by careful experiments, so his theory must be true." This argument, like the cats and squirrels argument, is invalid, and for the same reason. The premises tell us that Einstein's theory shares a characteristic with true theories, namely, that both are confirmed by careful experiments. But this does not guarantee that Einstein's theories must be true, for the sharing of a characteristic does not prove identity. Scientists will agree that this is a correct analysis of the argument. For it is a well-known fact that many theories have been confirmed by experiments, only to be disproved by later experiments. This is the basic reason why scientists disclaim absolute certainty for their findings.

We are not of course singling out Einstein's theory as a special case, but are using it only as an illustration. Every experimental proof in science takes the same form. Nor are we casting the doubt of skepticism over scientific findings, for though the argument we just considered is invalid from a technical, formal point of view, it differs from the foolish arguments considered in this chapter as sense differs from nonsense. This point requires careful consideration.

"Invalid" means that the conclusion does not follow necessarily from the premises. But in some cases the premises of an invalid argument seem to make the conclusion highly probable, as in the Einstein example; in others they do nothing of the sort. Why this difference? It all depends on the nature of the characteristic in which the two things agree. We say that the sharing of a common characteristic does not prove that two things are identical, or that one of these things is included within the other, but we come nearer to proving this inclusion in some cases than in others. For example, anarchists eat food, and so does Joe. Agreement in "eating food" proves absolutely nothing concerning the political similarities of food-eaters. But if we say, "The anarchists believe in abolishing all government controls, including the police force, and so does Joe," here the shared characteristic is highly significant. The argument is invalid, if we conclude that Joe is necessarily an anarchist, for the premises may be true and the conclusion false. Joe may merely be a "rebel without a cause." But the probability is high that he is an anarchist.

In other words, if the shared characteristic is one that is possessed *only* by anarchists, or if there is a high probability that anyone having the shared characteristic is an anarchist, then we can translate our invalid argument into a valid one. If we can say, "Anyone who believes in the abolition of all government controls, including the police force is probably an anarchist," and we find that Joe so believes, then obviously Joe is probably an anarchist. This argument is valid for the conclusion necessarily follows from its premises.

If we return now to the argument that led to this discussion, the premise "True theories are confirmed by careful experiments" can be translated into "If a theory is confirmed by careful experiments then it is probably true." (Note that we did not say "necessarily.") And thus, since Einstein's theory was so confirmed, we can derive the valid conclusion that it is probably true. But this kind of translation is possible only when the shared characteristics are of such a nature as to make it probable that one thing is included within another. We cannot translate our "cats and squirrels" argument in this way, for "Cats climb trees" can't be translated into "If it climbs trees it probably is a cat" (or a squirrel). Thus the conclusion of this argument is not a probable one. The point is this: When we note an argument based on shared characteristics hereafter, let us also note the significance of the shared characteristics. Some shared characteristics may yield a probable conclusion. To repeat, "not necessarily" covers a lot of ground, from a highly probable conclusion to a worthless one.[1]

The fallacy of the "shared characteristic," known technically as the fallacy of the "undistributed middle term," resembles the idea of "guilt by association." Just as the sharing of a characteristic does not prove identity, so the fact that a man *knows* a Communist does not prove that he is one. But just as the significance of the characteristic—or characteristics—is important in establishing probability, so with one's associates. If a state's attorney has gangsters as his constant companions, there may be a justifiable suspicion as to his honesty, and we may want state's attorneys

[1] It is a rule of logic that sentences of the form "If–Then" or beginning with "All" cannot be formally "converted." Thus, "All dogs are animals" cannot be converted into "All animals are dogs." We can say only that some animals are dogs. This is called a "partial converse." And some "All" sentences can be partially converted into "Most," as in the "significant shared characteristics" discussed above. These yield probability statements. Also note that when we have equivalent definitions, the converses will be true as a matter of fact: "All men are rational animals" and "All rational animals are men." But the rule holds: *formally*, we cannot convert "All A is B" into "All B is A."

who are not only unconvicted of crimes, but also above suspicion.

In concluding our discussion of validity and its relation to the truth of assertions—the subject-matter of "deductive" logic—we shall sum up the matter schematically. There are four possible combinations of premises and conclusion with respect to their truth and falsity:

(1) the premises may be true, and the conclusion true
(2) the premises may be false[1] and the conclusion true
(3) the premises false and the conclusion false
(4) the premises true and the conclusion false.

We shall now illustrate these combinations with examples of invalid and valid arguments, respectively.

In arguments which are *invalid*, we can find each of the four combinations listed above:

(1) The invalid Manitobans argument. (Page 114.)

(2) "Socialists are capitalists, and those who wish to abolish private property are capitalists, so Socialists wish to abolish private property." (The sharing of characteristics does not prove identity.)

(3) Too obvious to illustrate.

(4) The "cats are squirrels" argument. (Pages 113-4).

In *valid* arguments, on the other hand, only the first three of these combinations of truth and falsity can be illustrated:

(1) The familiar "All men are mortal" syllogism.

(2) "Socialists are capitalists, and capitalists favor the abolition of private property; therefore, Socialists favor the abolition of private property." This is a valid argument, for *if* the premises are true, then the conclusion would have to be true. It may be helpful to compare this illustration of a *valid* argument for combination (2) with the illustration of the *invalid* argument for combination (2) given above. Each has false premises and a true

[1] If one premise is false, and one true, then we count "the premises" as false.

conclusion. But in the invalid argument the conclusion is not necessitated by the premises; that is, acceptance of the premises as true would not require us to accept the conclusion as true. The conclusion of that argument happens to be true, but we cannot say: *If* these premises are true, then the conclusion *must* be true. But this is precisely what we must say of the *valid* argument illustrating combination (2) in this paragraph.

(3) The valid Eskimos argument on pages 109-10.

(4) This combination is impossible when an argument is valid. For consider the meaning of the term "valid argument": one in which the truth of the premises requires us to accept the truth of the conclusion. If we say that an argument has true premises and a false conclusion, we thereby declare that it is not a valid argument.

The main points of this chapter may be summed up. (a) By formal logic alone we cannot prove the truth of any assertion. What formal logic tells us is that if we start with true premises and reason logically from these premises, then our conclusion must be true. (b) If our premises are false, or even uncertain, then even when we reason logically our conclusion has not been proved to be true. (c) When the logical form is invalid, that is, when the reasoning is illogical, then even true premises cannot guarantee a true conclusion. (d) In arguments like the Einstein example, we found that some invalid arguments can be translated into valid arguments yielding probable conclusions.

We also recall our earlier discussion of the ambiguity of "good" as applied to arguments. A completely satisfactory argument, we said, was not only valid in form, but also contained true premises. A bad argument, then, is one which is either invalid or which lacks truth. We have also seen that true conclusions may be supported by either true or false premises in invalid arguments.

A final point. A bad argument, i.e., one invalid in form or containing false premises, cannot prove a true thesis. But it is also important to remember that a bad argument does not discredit a true thesis, though it may sometimes appear to, as when a weak premise is attacked in a debate. The refutation of the premise may then seem to be a refutation of the thesis. An illustration:

In a TV debate on tariffs, a Congressman argued for lowering our tariffs. The reason we should do this, he said, is that it is our moral duty to make sacrifices for our friends and allies in Western Europe and elsewhere. Now this was a bad argument for it assumed that lower tariffs will involve sacrifices by the general public in the United States. The Congressman's opponent seized on this point and appealed to the self-interest of the audience: "Why should we make further sacrifices for ungrateful foreigners, etc." The audience decided that it would be unwise to lower tariffs.

But most economists tell us that lower tariffs will *benefit* the American consumer and hurt only the inefficient American producers. Thus lower tariffs will involve benefits to the public, rather than sacrifices. If the economists are right, then a foolish argument like that of the Congressman may weaken the good cause it supports, for it promulgates the false notion that low tariffs call for sacrifices by the public. And so bad arguments operate to discredit good causes. In general, it is better to present a few good arguments for a thesis, rather than a great many, one or more of which may be weak, for the opponents are apt to seize on the weak premise, and, by discrediting it, appear to discredit the conclusion.

Similarly, many foolish and intemperate friends of good causes, such as Civil Rights, will cast doubts on the justice of their cause by their witless actions and arguments. But the logical person will consider the merits of ideas regardless of the bad arguments used to support them.

X.

SOME PATTERNS OF REASONING

In the last two chapters we have been discussing arguments, and we noted some of the differences between a logical and an illogical argument. It is time now to examine the notion of validity somewhat more closely and to explain why some structures of reasoning permit us to draw valid deductions whereas others do not. In carrying out this task we shall have to indulge in a technicality or two.

We begin by considering a lion, his cage, and a zoo. We shall construct four very simple arguments which reveal some of the basic patterns of reasoning:

1. The lion is in his cage, and the cage is in the zoo. We draw the conclusion: The lion is in the zoo. Obviously this conclusion follows necessarily from the premises. The argument is valid.

2. The lion is in his cage, but the cage is not in the zoo. The conclusion: "The lion is not in the zoo" follows necessarily from these premises. Valid.

3. The cage is in the zoo, but the lion is not in his cage. Now, can we conclude with *certainty* concerning the whereabouts of the lion? Obviously not, for the lion may or may not be in the zoo. If we draw either one of these conclusions: "He is in

the zoo" or "He is not in the zoo," we will draw a conclusion not warranted by the premises, and the argument will be invalid. Neither conclusions follows *necessarily* from these premises.

4. The cage is in the zoo, and the lion is in the zoo. We cannot draw a necessary conclusion concerning the lion's relationship to his cage. He may be inside it and he may not be. To draw either conclusion as following from the information given would be illogical.

In these simple examples we find four basic patterns of reasoning, two of which are sound, and two unsound. The information given to us by the premises permits us to draw valid conclusions in Patterns 1 and 2; not in 3 and 4. We shall now draw diagrams to illustrate these patterns in order to get a visual picture of the difference between valid and invalid structures of reasoning. We shall combine the *premises* of each argument in diagrams, in order to see why the conclusions are necessitated by Patterns 1 and 2 and not by 3 and 4.

1. Premises: The lion is in his cage and the cage is in the zoo.

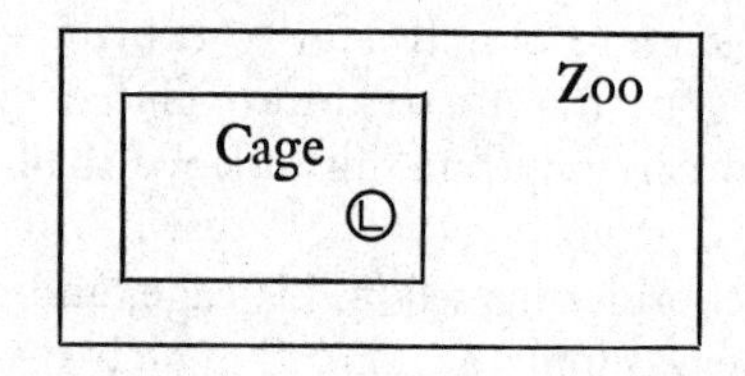

This diagram exhibits the premises: the lion in his cage and the cage in the zoo. The conclusion: "The lion must be in the zoo" is unavoidable.

2. Premises: The lion is in his cage but the cage is not in the zoo.

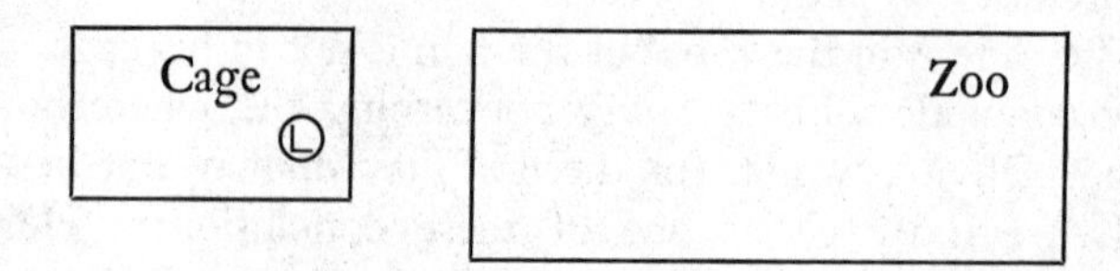

This is the only way in which it is possible to diagram the information given by the two premises. The conclusion: The lion cannot be in the zoo.

3. Premises: The cage is in the zoo, but the lion is not in his cage.

Difficulties arise when we try to diagram these premises. Let us start with the first premise:

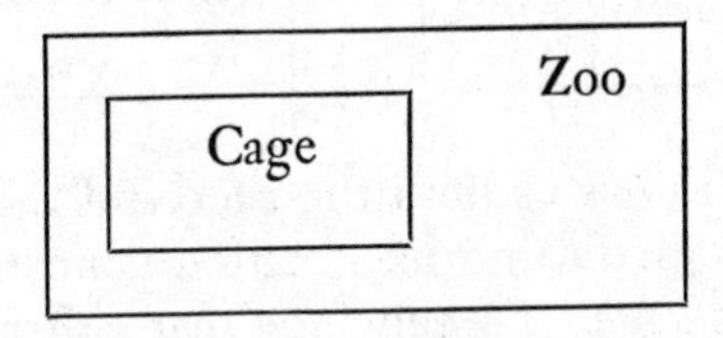

We must now show "the lion is not in his cage." There are two ways of showing this, in conjunction with the first premise:

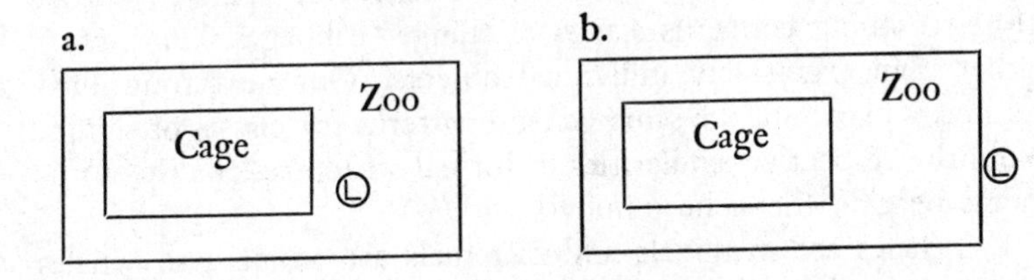

Diagrams "a" and "b" are both faithful to the premises, but neither one is necessarily required by the premises. Diagram "a" shows the lion in the zoo; "b" shows him outside. An argument which drew either conclusion would be invalid.

4. Premises: The cage is in the zoo and the lion is in the zoo. Similar difficulties arise. We begin by diagramming the first premise:

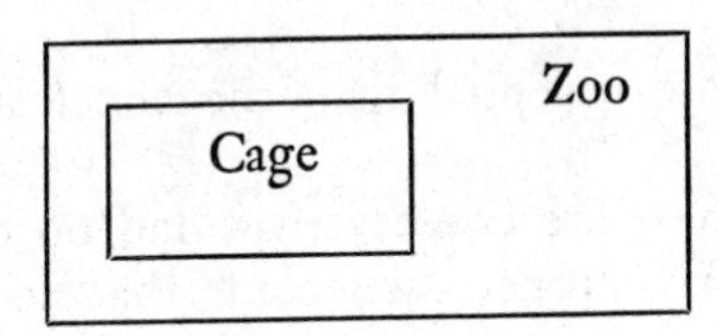

The second premise tells us that the lion is in the zoo. Two ways to show this:

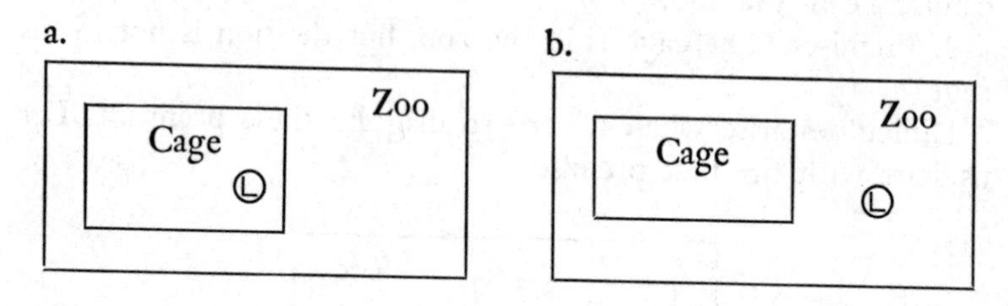

Each diagram shows us both the cage and the lion in the zoo. But the premises give us no information concerning the relation of the lion to his cage. To conclude that either "a" or "b" necessarily follows from these premises is to draw an unjustified inference.

Our first set of illustrations is oversimplified, for we were talking about a particular lion, a particular cage, and a particular zoo. Most reasoning concerns *classes* of things (cabbages, kings, etc.) rather than exclusively individual objects. Our next four illustrations will exhibit the same general patterns for classes of things. Note the respective similarities in formal structures for the arguments bearing the same numbers:

1. Whales are mammals and mammals are animals, so whales are animals. Diagram to illustrate the premises:

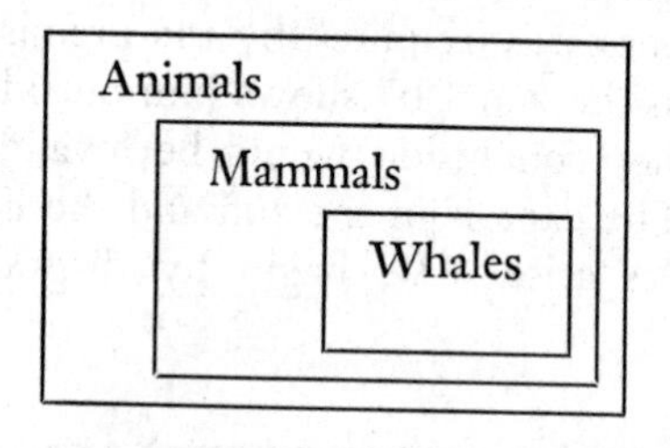

If the premises are accepted then the conclusion must be accepted. Valid.

2. All monarchists are conservatives and no conservatives are Utopians. We may properly conclude that no monarchists are

Utopians. The diagram shows that the argument is valid:

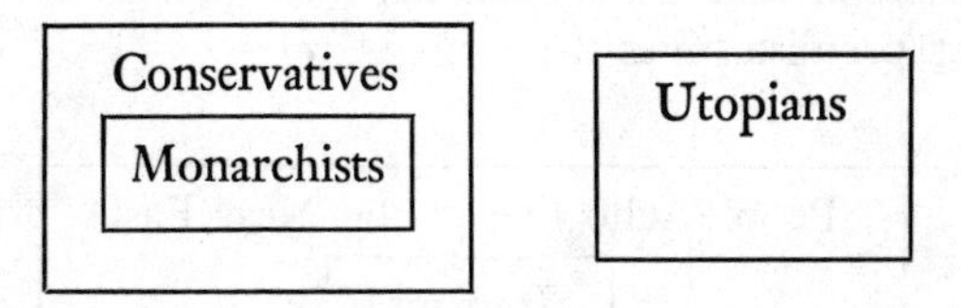

3. All Hindus are vegetarians, and no Sikhs are Hindus, so no Sikhs are vegetarians. The conclusion "No Sikhs are vegetarians" is not justified by the evidence presented. The argument is invalid. As before, we draw a diagram for the first premise:

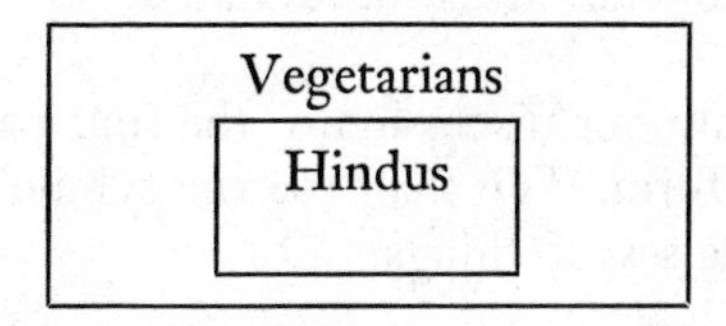

The second premise tells us to draw Sikhs outside of Hindus, but it tells us nothing about the position of Sikhs with respect to vegetarians. We can draw at least two diagrams to show the possibilities:

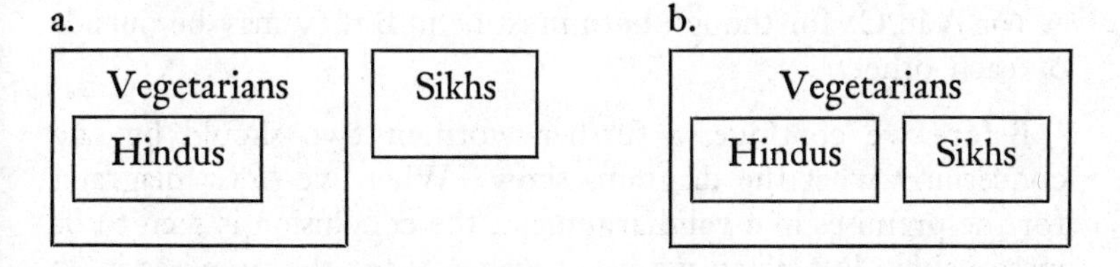

Diagram "a" shows Sikhs outside the class of vegetarians. This was the conclusion of the argument. But "b" is also a possibility, and "b" shows Sikhs inside the vegetarian box. To say that "a" (or "b") follows necessarily from the premises is to draw an unjustified inference.

4. Iranians live in the Near East, and Kurds live in the Near East, so Kurds must be Iranians. Invalid. From the information

given in the premises, Kurds may or may not be Iranians. We cannot conclude that they must be.

The first premise gives us:

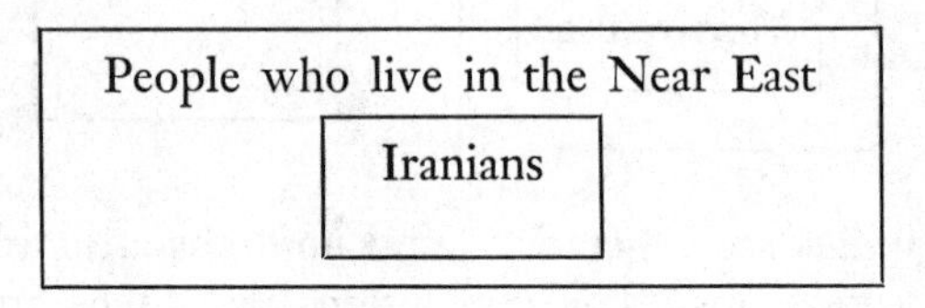

We must now draw Kurds inside the box "People who live in the Near East." But they may be inside the Iranian box or outside. Neither conclusion is necessitated, so the argument is invalid.

We may sum up our discussion of the four patterns of reasoning in symbolic form. We shall use the symbols "A," "B," "C" for any three classes of things:

1. A is in B and B is in C. That A is in C follows necessarily.
2. A is in B and B is outside of C. A must be outside of C.
3. A is in B and C is outside of A. We cannot conclude that C must be outside of B, for C may be outside of A and inside of B. Nor does any other conclusion follow necessarily.
4. A is in B and C is in B. We cannot conclude that C is in A (or A in C) for though both must be in B they may be outside of each other.

Before we continue, a further word or two should be said concerning what the diagrams show. When we draw diagrams for the premises in a valid argument, the conclusion is seen to be inescapable. But when we draw diagrams for the premises in an invalid argument, we see that no definite conclusion is necessitated. We can draw the premises of an invalid argument without exhibiting the particular conclusion which the argument drew. In other words, in an invalid argument we need not accept the conclusion even though we accept the premises. The conclusion *may* be true, but it is not proven true by the premises.

Let us sum up for a moment. Arguments 1 and 2 were valid in

each set; 3 and 4 were invalid. Let us now examine the technical rules of logic violated by Patterns 3 and 4. Argument 3 is an example of the fallacy called "illicit distribution," and Argument 4 illustrates the fallacy of the "undistributed middle term." These are two of the most frequently encountered errors in reasoning. In order to understand the meaning of these fallacies, let us examine the technical logical term known as "distribution."

The logician speaks of the "distribution" of words that designate classes of things (apples, mortals, emotions). To say that a term is *distributed* means that we have said something about *all* members of the class to which it refers; that we have asserted something about each and every member of that class. Thus, in "All dogs are animals," "dogs" is a distributed term, for we said *all* dogs. But we did not say anything about *all animals* in this particular sentence. Dogs constitute only part of the class of animals, so our sentence refers only to *some* animals. "Animals" is an undistributed term in this sentence. Similarly, if we had said "Some dogs are hunters" both dogs and hunters would be undistributed.

In the sentence "No men are angels" both terms are distributed. The sentence asserts that each and every man is outside the class of angels, and it also says that each and every angel is outside the class of men.

To sum up. The distribution of the *subject* term in a sentence depends on whether its quantifier is "All," "No," or "Some." The distribution of the *predicate* term in a sentence is dependent on whether the sentence is affirmative or negative, and this distinction in turn depends on the *copula* of the sentence. The copula, a form of the verb "to be," connects the subject and predicate. When the copula is "is" or "are," the sentence is affirmative (S *is* P); when it is "is not," the sentence is negative (S *is not* P). "No S are P" is classified as negative, since it states that S *are not* P, i.e., all of S are excluded from all of P. The sentence "All non-S are non-P" is affirmative, since the copula is "are."

The distribution of the *predicate* term may now be summed up in two rules: (1) Affirmative sentences *never* distribute the predicate term (P): All S are P, Some S are P; (2) Negative sentences *always* distribute the predicate term: No S are P, Some S are not P.

The distribution of S and P in the four possible types of subject-predicate sentences are shown below:

All S (distributed) are P (undistributed)
No S (distributed) are P (distributed)
Some S (undistributed) are P (undistributed)
Some S (undistributed) are not P (distributed).

This discussion of "distribution" by no means exhausts the subject, but it is sufficient for our purposes. We are now ready to explain the fallacies of "illicit distribution" (illustrated by No. 3) and "undistributed middle term" (illustrated by No. 4). Let us take No. 4 first since this fallacy is already familiar to us. The reader will recall the many examples of this error—the error involving "shared characteristics"—in the last chapter: the arguments concerning cats and squirrels, both being tree-climbers; the argument that told us that Chinese must be Japanese since both eat rice; that Manitobans must be Canadians since both live in North America; that Einstein's theory must be true since it has been confirmed by careful experiments, and all true theories are so confirmed. We shall see, in a moment, how we may apply this particular technique of logic—the "distribution" idea—to these arguments.

Just one further preliminary comment: the "middle term" of a syllogism is the term that appears in the two *premises,* serving as a connecting link between the other two terms.

The fallacy of the "undistributed middle term" refers to a rule of logic which tells us that the middle term of a syllogism must be "distributed at least once" in order to permit the drawing of a valid conclusion. This means that if the middle term is not distributed at all, no valid conclusion is possible. Argument 4 illustrates this fallacy. Let us examine it:

(All) Iranians *live in the Near East* (middle term)
And (All) Kurds *live in the Near East* (middle term)
Therefore, Kurds are Iranians.

"Live in the Near East" is the "middle term" (defined as the term which appears in both premises). This term was distributed in neither premise. "Kurds" and "Iranians" were distributed in their respective premises, for we assume that "all" was understood for each, but the premises refer only to "some" people who live in the Near East. Thus this syllogism violates a rule of logic. The reader will find the same technical error in the other examples of this fallacy in the last chapter. The diagrams a and b on page 124 and the diagram on page 126 show us the sense of the rule.

In the patterns of reasoning illustrated on pages 124–126, only No. 4 violates this rule. In argument No. 1 the middle term is "mammals." This term is not distributed in the premise, "All whales are mammals," but it is distributed in "Mammals are animals," for "All mammals" is intended here. So the rule is satisfied. In argument No. 2 the middle term is "conservatives." It is distributed in "No conservatives are Utopians." In argument No. 3 the middle term is "Hindus." This term is distributed twice. This argument, then, does not violate the rule concerning the distribution of the middle term but it violates a different rule involving distribution. Let us examine it.

A second rule of logic tells us that "if a term is undistributed in the premises, then that term must not be distributed in the conclusion." This is the sense of the rule: when a term is distributed, information is given concerning *each and every* member of the class referred to. When a term is undistributed, information is given only about *some* of its members. From information concerning "some" we can draw no conclusion concerning "all." For example, if experience teaches me that *some* women are fickle, I cannot logically conclude that *all* are. We commit the fallacy of going from "some" to "all" when the conclusion distributes a term that was not distributed in the premises.

Let us restate No. 3:

	All Hindus are vegetarians
And	No Sikhs are Hindus
Therefore,	No Sikhs are vegetarians.

We examine the distributed terms in the conclusion to detect a possible violation of the rule against illicit distribution. If a term is distributed in the conclusion then it should have been distributed in the premises. We find that *both* of the terms in the conclusion are distributed. Now examine these terms in the premises. "Sikhs" was distributed in the second premise. But "vegetarians" was not distributed in its premise, and so the rule is violated. When we conclude that "no Sikhs are vegetarians" we assert something about *all* vegetarians; "All of them," we say, "are outside the class of Sikhs." But the premise gave us information only about *some* vegetarians.

Here is another example of the same fallacy:

(All) Senators have traveling privileges
And (All) Senators are politicians
Therefore, (All) politicians have traveling privileges.

"Politicians" was undistributed in the second premise and distributed in the conclusion.

Let us examine the conclusions of arguments 1, 2, and 4, on pages 124–126 in which this second rule is *not* violated. No. 1: Whales are animals. Whales is distributed in the premise as well as in the conclusion.[1] No. 2: No monarchists are Utopians. Both terms distributed in the premises as well as in the conclusion. No. 4: All Kurds are Iranians. Kurds is distributed in the premises. This last argument, however, violates the rule concerning the distribution of the middle term.

So much for two of the basic rules of validity for syllogisms. There are also three additional rules, each of which concerns negative premises or a negative conclusion: A valid conclusion cannot be drawn from two negative premises; a negative premise requires a negative conclusion; and a negative conclusion requires a negative premise. These five rules are like the axioms in Euclidean geometry. They are necessary and sufficient to test the validity of any syllogism involving subject-predicate sentences in ordinary language.

[1] Though we did not say *all* whales, "all" is obviously meant.

Symbolic Logic

We shall discuss some patterns of reasoning in modern symbolic logic in this section. This is a vast and complex field and we cannot hope to do more than to suggest some of the procedures of the new logic.

We begin with a new set of elements, and a new vocabulary. Previously we have dealt with subject-predicate sentences: S is P, Men are mortal. We shall now work with *compound* sentences, i.e., sentences which are formed by joining complete sentences to each other in specific ways. There are three types of compound sentences: the "hypothetical," the "alternative" (sometimes called "disjunctive"), and the "conjunctive." We shall deal with these in order.

(1) The hypothetical takes the form "If– Then–": "*If* prices continue to rise, *Then* the unions will ask for wage increases." Note that the four words following "If" make a grammatically complete sentence. This is the "antecedent" of the compound hypothetical. The sentence which follows "Then" is called the "consequent."

We shall symbolize the antecedent by "p," and the consequent by "q," so that "p" will stand for "prices continue to rise," and "q" for "The unions will ask for wage increases." Letters such as p, q, r, etc. will always stand for complete sentences, not for classes of things such as men or mortals. Note further that "p," asserted by itself, means "p is true," and that "not–p," taken by itself, means "p is false." We may symbolize the hypothetical sentence above by "If p then q." Obviously this does not say that p is true, or that q is true. It merely says that *if* p should be the case, then q will occur.

Let us now see how hypothetical sentences may be used in constructing syllogisms. A common form of such syllogisms will have a hypothetical "major" premise and a subject-predicate sentence as the "minor." The minor premise will either "affirm" or "deny" the antecedent or consequent. Thus there will be four possible "figures" in such syllogisms, viz.:

1. If p then q	2. If p then q	3. If p then q	4. If p then q
p	Not-p	q	Not-q
(affirms antecedent)	(denies antecedent)	(affirms consequent)	(denies consequent)
∴ q	∴ Not-q	∴ q	∴ Not-p

In each figure the major premise "If p then q" stands for "If prices continue to rise, then the unions will ask for wage increases." In the "minor" premise, "p" stands for "Prices continue to rise," and "Not-p" stands for "Prices do not continue to rise," or "It is false that prices continue to rise," and similarly with "q."

The validity or invalidity of these figures follows from the *meaning* of the hypothetical major premise. The meaning of "If p then q" is that if p occurs, then q must occur. In Figure 1, p occurs, so q must occur. Another way of stating the meaning of "If p then q" is that if q does not occur, then p could not have occurred. (If p *had* occurred q would have also.) This is shown in Figure 4. Thus both Figures 1 and 4 are valid arguments.

Figures 2 and 3, on the other hand, are invalid forms of reasoning. Since "If p then q" does not state that p is the *exclusive condition* for q, but only that q is a necessary consequent of p, then the fact that p does not occur does not tell us that q could not have occurred. Thus Figure 2 is invalid: the fact that prices did not rise (Not-p) does not tell us that the unions will not ask for wage increases (Not-q). And similarly, in Figure 3, the fact that the unions asked for wage increases does not mean that prices necessarily rose.

Figures 1 and 4, then, are valid, and Figures 2 and 3 are invalid argument-forms. The valid Figures 1 and 4 are known to logicians as *modus ponens* (the *affirming* mode) and *modus tollens* (the *denying* mode). When people argue in the manner of Figures 2 or 3, on the other hand, they are said to be guilty of the fallacies of "denying the antecedent" or "affirming the consequent." The reader may also find it interesting to note the parallelism between these four patterns and the patterns shown on page 126: two valid and two invalid.

(2) Alternative sentences take the form "Either–or–": "*Either* X is a fool *or* X is a knave." The two sentences, "X is a fool" and "X is a knave" are called the "alternants." Substituting the symbols p and q for the two alternants we have "Either p or q." The logician interprets this as meaning that either p is true, or q is true, and possibly both are true; i.e., at least one alternant is true, and possibly both.

An alternative syllogism will be valid if the minor premise denies one of the alternants, for if at least one of the alternants is assumed to be true, and we learn that one is false, then the other must be true. (If X is either a fool or a knave, and he is not a fool, then he must be a knave.) But if we learn only that one of the alternants *is* true, we can draw no necessary conclusion concerning the truth or falsity of the other. If we learn that X is a fool, it is possible that he may also be a knave, since both alternants may be true. But he may not be. Thus no valid conclusion may be drawn when an alternant is affirmed.

(3) A conjunctive sentence merely joins two (or more) sentences together by the conjunctive "and": "We shall continue to build atom bombs *and* there will be no third world war." We symbolize again by "p *and* q." This is interpreted to read: Both p and q are true. Thus, if either p or q is false, the whole sentence will be considered false, since it asserts that *both* are true.

Conjunctive sentences can be used in syllogisms when they are negated, or declared to be false. We then have a "negated conjunct." Example: "*Not both* can we continue to build bombs *and* avoid a third war." Such sentences assert that at least one of the two conjuncts is false, and possibly both are. The rule of validity will now be opposite to that in the alternative syllogism. A valid argument requires that the minor premise *affirm* one of the conjuncts, and we can then deny the other. Since one at least is false, if one is true, the other must be false.

Let us now symbolize these new concepts. There is no official set of symbols in modern logic. We shall use what is perhaps the most common notation, based on Whitehead and Russell's *Principia Mathematica.* "If–then–" will be symbolized by the horseshoe "$\supset$"; "Either–or–" by the caret "v," and the conjunctive "and" by a dot "." The concept of negation, "not," i.e., "It is false that . . ." will be shown by the tilde "$\sim$." Parentheses will indicate that an expression is to be taken as a unitary whole.

The hypothetical, alternative, conjunctive, and negated conjunct sentences, then, are symbolized as follows: $p \supset q =$ If p is true then q is true; $p \vee q =$ Either p is true or q is true; $p \cdot q =$ Both p and q are true; $\sim(p \cdot q) =$ Not both p and q, i.e., It is false that both p and q are true.

These symbolic functions can be defined in terms of the other functions. For example, $p \supset q$ is equivalent to $\sim p \vee q$. ("If p then q" is equivalent to "Either p is false or q is true.") In words, the hypothetical "*If* x is a man *then* x is mortal" is equivalent to the alternative sentence "*Either* x is not a man *or* x is mortal." A simple way to test equivalence is to check whether the translation of a true statement will be true under all possible conditions. Let us check to see whether "Either x is not a man or x is mortal" is true under the assumptions that x is a stone, or that x is a man, or that x is an animal which is not a man, say a dog.

If we make the first assumption, that x is a stone then the first alternant ("x is not a man") will be true. An alternative sentence is true if either alternant is true. The second assumption, that x is a man, denies the first alternant, but the second ("x is mortal") will be true. And if x is a dog, then both alternants will be true.

This analysis may be compared with the results that would have ensued if we had made the incorrect translation of "$p \supset q$" into "$p \vee \sim q$" (Either x is a man or x is not mortal). For a stone, the second alternant would be true; for a man, the first. So far, so good. But for a dog, both would be false. This being so, the alternative sentence is false, and cannot be the equivalent of the true sentence "If x is a man then x is mortal."

Another functional equivalence: $p \supset q$ is equivalent to $\sim(p \cdot \sim q)$. The hypothetical "If x is a man then x is mortal" can be translated into the negated conjunct "It is *false* to say that *both* of the following are true: x is a man and x is not mortal." This asserts that at least one of the two conjuncts is false, and possibly both are. In the stone example, "x is a man" is false. Applied to a man, "x is not mortal" is false, and for the dog both conjuncts are false. Since at least one conjunct will be false under any possible assumption, and this is exactly what the negated conjunct asserts will be the case, the negated conjunct is a true sentence.

Let us summarize the equivalences we have just discussed. The lower line gives the equivalents of the functions on the upper line:

$p \supset q$	$p \vee q$	$p \supset q$	$\sim(p \cdot q)$
$\sim p \vee q$	$\sim p \supset q$	$\sim(p \cdot \sim q)$	$p \supset \sim q$

Note that when we go from the hypothetical to alternative (or vice versa) we negate the first sentence. In going from the hypothetical to the negated conjunct (or vice versa) we negate the second sentence. In making these translations also remember that the negation of a negation yields a positive.

We shall now show how these equivalences may be used in analyzing arguments. Consider the following:

Not both can a nation be at war and not have its resources strained

Either a nation's resources are not strained, or prices will rise

∴ Not both can a nation be at war, and prices not rise.

We begin by symbolizing the sentences. "A nation is at war" will be symbolized by P; "A nation's resources are strained" by Q, and "Prices will rise" by R. We now symbolize the entire argument:

$$\sim(P \cdot \sim Q)$$
$$\sim Q \vee R$$
$$\therefore \sim(P \cdot \sim R)$$

The validity of this argument will be seen very clearly if we translate it into a purely hypothetical syllogism. To do this we must translate each of these sentences into If–Then–sentences. Using our table of equivalences, $\sim(P \cdot \sim Q)$ gives us $P \supset Q$.

(The original second conjunct $\sim Q$ must be negated when we translate the premise into the If–Then–form. This gives us $\sim \sim Q$, and the double negation is equal to the positive Q.) The second premise is equivalent to $Q \supset R$, and the conclusion, $\sim(P \cdot \sim R)$, is equivalent to $P \supset R$. The argument now reads:

$$P \supset Q$$
$$Q \supset R$$
$$\therefore P \supset R.$$

This argument form is called a "pure hypothetical syllogism" since it uses nothing but If–Then–sentences, as distinguished from the "mixed" forms of the four figures analyzed earlier. The validity of a pure hypothetical syllogism is based on the fact that the relation symbolized by "$\supset$," a type of "implication," is a transitive relation.

And now for a more interesting example, in which we shall employ other procedures that we have learned in this section. The argument we shall consider is a proof that the groom was the murderer of the chauffeur. We shall assume that the following facts or premises have been established: (1) The cook does not know who committed the murder, (2) It must have been either the maid or the groom, (3) It is impossible both that the butler would know and that the cook would not know, (4) Either the maid did not do it, or the butler would know. Therefore, the groom is guilty.

We symbolize: C, the cook knows; M, the maid did it; G, the groom did it; B, the butler knows. Replacing the sentences by symbols, we then have:

1. $\sim C$ (The cook does not know who did it)
2. $M \vee G$ (Either the maid did it or the groom did it)
3. $\sim(B \cdot \sim C)$ (It is false that both the butler knows and the cook does not know)
4. $\sim M \vee B$ (Either the maid did not do it or the butler knows)

Therefore, G (The groom did it)

We wish to show that these premises necessitate the conclusion. A little ingenuity and some trial-and-error experimentation may be necessary. Premises 3 and 4 contain the letter "B." Let us see whether we can join them in a purely hypothetical syllogism. Premise 4 is equivalent to $M \supset B$, and premise 3 to $B \supset C$. When we join these we get the conclusion $M \supset C$. The importance of this step is that we now have an additional premise, since any sentence implied by premises 3 and 4 will itself be a premise. We number it 5:

5. $M \supset C$.

We now use 5 as a major premise and 1 as a minor. This combination is that of Figure 4 of the hypothetical syllogism, and yields the conclusion $\sim M$. This will now be premise 6.

6. $\sim M$

Combining premise 2 with 6 we derive the conclusion G, by the rule of validity of the alternative syllogism: when one alternant is denied the other may be affirmed. Thus we have shown that G (the groom did it) is necessitated by the premises.

We have indicated some of the ways in which symbolic statements and rules of transformation may aid us in the analysis of arguments. This discussion, however, has touched on only a few of the most elementary elements of a vast and complex subject. In its more advanced techniques this new symbolic language not only furnishes a theoretical basis for logical and mathematical science but it also has many practical applications. It gives us a powerful instrument for systematizing large numbers of complicated statements, and helps to detect internal inconsistencies. Insurance companies, for example, write complex policies covering all sorts of contingencies, and questions may arise as to whether there are any inconsistencies in the various clauses. Engineers use symbolic logic in analyzing switching circuits. These new techniques in logic have also contributed toward the simplifying of the electrical circuits in computers, the "thinking machines," or "electronic brains."

Perhaps we have indicated something of interest concerning this very important development in modern logic. Some remarks on the relation of the new logic to the traditional, or "Aristotelian" logic will be found in Chapter XII.

XI.

EITHER-OR

DURING THE FIRST World War, when the casualty rate for aviators was very high, the flyers developed a somewhat cynical philosophy concerning their prospects. This philosophy was expressed in a series of Either-Or propositions which sought to prove that there was really no need to worry about anything at all. The series went something like this:

If all goes well, then there's nothing to worry about. On the other hand, if all does not go well, then there are just two possibilities: Either you'll crash or you won't. If you don't crash, there's nothing to worry about. If you do crash, there are just two possibilities: Either you'll be badly hurt or you won't be. If you're not badly hurt, there's nothing to worry about. If you are badly hurt, there are just two possibilities: Either you'll recover or you won't. If you recover, there's nothing to worry about. If you don't, then you *can't* worry.

These two little words, "either" and "or" make trouble for us unless we watch them carefully. They were not used carefully in the "Airman's Philosophy." They are useful tools in thinking, but a great deal of bad and confused thinking falls into an Either-Or pattern. The worst of these vices is the assumption that there are only two possibilities in a situation, or only two choices, when there are in fact more than two. This can be a very serious matter, indeed. Consider, for example, an application of this assumption to our international problems. There are people who say, "Either other nations are for us or they are against us; either they will take sides with us against our enemies, or they are taking sides with our enemies against us." But this ignores the possibility of neutrality. Other nations may be neither for us nor against us, and they may lean toward us without wishing to announce this fact. The U.S., of all nations, should not engage in this kind of Either-Or thinking, for we have often been neutral in world conflicts in the past. What is dangerous about this mistake is that it may lead us into treating other nations as our enemies when such is not the case at all.

Or we may reason in this way: *Either* we must establish a World Government *or* a thermo-nuclear war is inevitable, or *Either* we will have general disarmament *or* we are sure to have a war which will destroy civilization. But these are not the only possibilities. The cold war, or an armed truce, may continue indefinitely. This, then, is a dangerous trap into which Either-Or thinking may lead us: to assume that there are only two possibilities when there are more than two. We shall call this "the error of insufficient options" (or "insufficient alternatives"). The color of an automobile may be neither red nor yellow.

Too frequently, also, we set up two extremes and say that everyone must be one or the other. We assume that the two extreme positions account for all of the possibilities when, as a matter of fact, they may not: Either you are a capitalist or you are a Communist. Either the labor unions are always right in their disputes with management or they are always wrong. But perhaps they are sometimes right and sometimes wrong. We often assume that there is no middle ground between All and Nothing. But it is not the case that "a man either believes that our present social system is perfect or he is a Communist." One may want to correct certain imperfections in our present system without being a Communist. It is not the case that "I am either for you one hundred per cent or I am against you." I may be for you ninety-nine per cent, or I may be neither for you nor against you. There is a middle ground between love and hate called indifference, just as between indifference and hate there is a region called dislike. We cannot say of a man that he is either an angel or a devil, either a god or a beast. As Aristotle said long ago, we are in between, superior to the beasts and inferior to the gods. Let us stop using just two categories for people: the saints and the devils. Many of us are middle-of-the-roaders.

The kind of thinking we have just described is sometimes confused with a law or principle of logic called the "law of the excluded middle." This law tells us that a thing *either* has a particular characteristic *or* it does not have that particular characteristic: A man either has a million dollars or he does not; he either owns a home of his own, or he doesn't. Anything, the law tells us, is either A or it is not A; either it has characteristic A or it does not. These alternatives do exhaust the possibilities; the options are *sufficient*. Note that the examples of "insufficient alternatives" we considered above do *not* illustrate the law of the excluded middle. It is false that a car's color must be either red or yellow; it may be black, or blue, or green. But the law of the excluded middle says only that a car is either red or it is *not red*. A chemist analyzes a solution to determine the presence or absence of arsenic. Either at least one molecule of arsenic is present or no arsenic at all is present. This is in accordance with the law.

The most interesting and troublesome problems involving the use of Either-Or, however, concern a type of application in which the law of the excluded middle is not violated—the two alternatives actually do exhaust the possibilities—but in which the Either-Or may be misleading, or unrealistic. This type of thinking requires a more extended discussion. One of the most striking illustrations of this sort of thing is found in the bad habit of thinking which we shall call "moral perfectionism." The perfectionist sets up an ideal or standard of moral perfection, and then thinks in terms of only two alternatives, "Either you are a good man, or you are not." Though the perfectionist does not always say so, he usually implies that he himself has achieved perfection and that the rest of the world has not, and he judges everyone else as falling short of the standard. The perfectionist thinks of every man as falling into one or the other of the two classes, the good, and the not-good.

There are many illustrations of this kind of perfectionism. To the ancient Stoics there were no degrees in vice; you were either perfectly virtuous or you were not virtuous at all. The theft of a piece of firewood, they said, is just as much a violation of the moral law as ruining a man in a swindle. As one of them put it, "The man who is a hundred miles from Canopus, and the man who is only one mile from Canopus, are both equally not in Canopus." A similar thought is expressed in the New Testament, in the words of James: "For whosoever shall keep the whole law, and yet offend in one point, he is guilty of all." In other words, for the perfectionist you are either good or you are not good—and there is no middle ground. This kind of thing is also illustrated by the uncompromising attitude which once characterized the leaders of the Communists toward members of the party. If a member deviated in the slightest degree from the party line that was being followed at any given moment, he was cursed with the awful charge of being a "deviationist," and purged.

This kind of thinking permits of no compromise. Either you fulfill the moral law completely or you do not fulfill it completely. Either you are perfectly good or you are classed undiscriminatingly with all the backsliders. And herein lies the most serious fault of this attitude. Though the perfectionist says, "All—or Not-All," *in practice* he means, "All—or Nothing," for the man who falls just short of perfection is regarded as being in the same class as the most vicious and hardened criminal. The perfectionist is not interested in the degree in which one falls short. He has no sympathy with the point of view expressed by Edward Young, the English poet:

> The purpose firm is equal to the deed:
> Who does the best his circumstance allows
> Does well, acts nobly; angels could do no more.

The perfectionist attitude is discouraging for those of us who cannot achieve perfection.

To the perfectionist an action is either right or wrong; there is no in-between. If it is wrong to tell a lie, then it is always wrong, and never right. Extenuating circumstances are irrelevant; one must never fall short of perfection. The German philosopher Fichte, who held that lying was never justified, was once asked whether he would not tell a lie to his sick wife if the truth might mean her death. Fichte, the perfectionist, answered thunderingly and uncompromisingly, "If my wife must die by the truth, then let her die!"

The perfectionist attitude is found in all sorts of places. Consider the perfectionist's attitude toward philanthropic benefactions. Either a person is a "perfect giver," they say, or he is not. A perfect giver always gives anonymously, for if it is known that he has made a contribution, then we must assume that he expects to receive applause for what he has done. And if he desires public acclaim, then he deserves no credit for giving, for he didn't give solely for the joy of giving. Those who don't give at all are apparently no more ungenerous than the donors whose names appear in the lists. But surely we should distinguish between the man who gives, hoping for some expression of gratitude, and the man who refuses to give anything at all.

And here is another example. It is sometimes said that there are no impartial human beings, that everyone is biased in one way or another. This is a more tolerant type of perfectionism, for everyone without exception is put into one class. The so-called unbiased man, it is said, is always "unbiased in favor of his side." Now of course there is a great deal of truth in this view. We may think we are "fair-minded," but how we wring our hands in horror at the baseness of the dirty politicians on the other side, and how complacent we are about *our* scoundrels. An error in judgment is excusable when committed by our side, but unforgivable when committed by the other side. And how easy it is to settle a dispute by giving away the other fellow's property; how hard to give away one's own.

This denial of the possibility of impartiality also expresses a perfectionist attitude, for it assumes that there are just two possibilities: you are perfectly impartial or you are not, and the conclusion is that no one is. "For whosoever shall keep the whole law, and yet offend in one point, he is guilty of all." The All—or Nothing attitude once more. But aren't there *degrees* of impartiality? And isn't this, after all, the important thing? Aren't there some persons who are capable of appreciating another's point of view to some degree, whereas others fail to do this at all? Is there no difference between the kind of man we think of as highly prejudiced, on the one hand, and the man we consider relatively fair-minded? The latter may not be completely impartial, but he is more impartial than many. There are people who cannot vote other than as Republicans or Democrats, but there are also independent voters. Most political scientists are more impartial than most politicians. In other words, we should not divide all of mankind into just two classes: the perfectly impartial and all the rest, the former constituting what logicians call a "null class," a class without any members. It is unrealistic to set up just two classes: the one-hundred-per-centers and all the rest.

So much for perfectionism, which uses the Either-Or to formulate unrealistic dichotomies. Let us now restate the three types of usage of the Either-Or formulation that we have considered. There is first the "Either A or B" statement, in which one says, "He is either a member of the bourgeoise or he is a member of the proletariat. He must be one or the other." This is the error of "insufficient options." He need not be either; there are other possibilities. This type of usage is characteristically at variance with the facts. The second usage is in the form of the law of the excluded middle: "Either A or not-A." Here we can properly say, "It must be one or the other, A or not-A," for these exhaust the possibilities; either he has a particular characteristic or he does not have it. We then drew a distinction between realistic and unrealistic applications of the law of the excluded middle. "Either A or not-A," we noted, is quite adequate where *degrees* are not involved, as when the chemist says, "Either arsenic is present or it is not present." But when degrees are involved, then the expression "Either A or not-A" may be unrealistic and misleading. This is the third type of usage we discussed: "He is perfect or he is not perfect." Now, this statement is in accordance with the principle of the excluded middle, and so not incorrect when we understand it as a precise formulation concerning those who have a characteristic and those who do not. Nevertheless, the statement is misleading because the important thing about human conduct is the *degree* with which conduct approaches a standard of perfection. "He is either perfect or not-perfect" makes us lose sight of the degrees of imperfection.

Let us look at some further illustrations of the application of "Either-Or" to cases involving degrees. Where there is a continuum of degrees—as in rating the intelligence of human beings—the subjects do not divide into two sharply contrasted opposites: the intelligent and the unintelligent. It would be misleading to use the principle of the excluded middle here, to say, "Every human being is either intelligent or unintelligent," as if there were just two classes, into one of which every human being falls. Or at least this would be a very arbitrary thing to do. But—and this is the other side of the coin—there are occasions when it is necessary to make such arbitrary distinctions between the two classes, the intelligent and the unintelligent, as in the Armed Forces Qualification Tests. It may even be necessary to draw a sharp and arbitrary distinction between sane and insane, as in a trial for murder. Our criminal law draws a distinction between offenders who are sane and those who are not, on the principle that we ought not to treat the two classes in the same manner. And judges need clear-cut definitions, or at least some kind of arbitrary dividing line. In the State of Illinois, for example, the statutes define sanity as the ability to distinguish between right and wrong. Though most psychiatrists consider this definition inadequate, it is at least workable, in a rough sort of way, and gives us an arbitrary dividing line.

Or consider the matter of academic grades. In our schools we use an Either-Or for passing or not-passing. Passing means that a student has mastered the subject-matter to the required degree. Thus we can say of any student, "Either he has mastered the course or he hasn't." But, you may protest, this is unrealistic, for mastery is a matter of degree, and it is wrong to divide all students into only two classes. The differences between students lie in a continuum of almost imperceptible differences in degrees.

Let us say that a grade of sixty-five per cent is set as the minimum passing grade. But how much difference is there, after all, between the student who makes sixty-five and the one who makes sixty-four? The latter fails the course, and it seems grossly unfair that a one per cent difference should have such enormous consequences. Shall we pass the sixty-four-per-center? But now, the sixty-three comes to claim equal justice. We pass him too. The logic of this procedure is that we must finally pass even the person who makes zero, for zero is only one per cent below 1. The grades from zero to 100 are connected by small gradations in degrees. But school administrations need a dividing line, and they arbitrarily set it at sixty-five per cent or some other definite figure. If there were no such dividing lines there could be no definite standards of competence. There could be no bar examinations, or C.P.A. examinations. Though we recognize the dividing line as arbitrary, still we must have one. And even the kindest-hearted teacher, who passes the sixty-fours and the sixty-threes and the sixty-twos, must draw a line somewhere. Certainly the twelves and thirteens should not pass.

We shall consider two further illustrations to bring out the many-sided complexity of this problem. One illustration concerns the continuum of colors ranging from white to black; the other concerns a beard. Pure white is defined as a surface which reflects one hundred per cent of the light which falls upon it, and pure black is a surface that reflects none. Pure whites and blacks are rarely, if ever, encountered. What we call whites and blacks, then, are really shades of gray, though they are "whiter" or "blacker" than what we call "gray."[1] If we put two different "whites" alongside each other, we will see that one is grayer than the other. Try this with the pages in two books. The same is true for blacks. It is said that the human eye is able to distinguish

[1] Arthur Koestler once used a black and white analogy in contrasting the communist world and the "free world" with respect to basic liberties. "We should not think of our differences as those of white against black," he said. "It is true," he added, "that they are black, but we are not white. We are a shade of gray."

40,000 different shades of gray running from pure white to pure black.

If we spread out these 40,000 shades next to one another in a continuum of colors, the differences between any two adjoining shades will be almost imperceptible. It is of course easy enough to distinguish the differences when we skip several "degrees." But suppose someone asks us where white ends and gray begins, or where gray ends and black begins. We could not say, for at no point do we find anything but an almost imperceptible difference. The dividing line, then, is purely arbitrary.

The beard illustration is a very old one. It is in the form of a puzzle: How many hairs on a man's face constitute a beard? Now everyone would agree that one thousand hairs would make a beard, but that ten would not. We agree further that 999 would make a beard, but that eleven would not. Well, then, how about 998? Yes, that would make a beard. Twelve? No. Now we try 997 and thirteen, and then 996 and fourteen. Do you think we will finally find a number, say 104, of which we could say: 104 hairs constitute a beard, but 103 do not? Will the addition of one hair make the difference, like the one straw that broke the camel's back? We simply do not make such fine distinctions in practice, and it would seem absurd to set up an arbitrary dividing line for beards, just as it was in the case of whites and blacks.

We have been discussing some of the difficulties which arise in saying "Either a color is white or it is not-white," or "Either a collection of hairs is a beard or it is not a beard." These are the difficulties that arise in matters of degree, for there are no distinct classes in a continuum. These difficulties raise the interesting logical problem: Is the law of the excluded middle (either A or not-A) applicable to these examples?

The law of the excluded middle presupposes that our terms are precisely defined. "White" and "beard" are vague terms. But if it is necessary to do so, we can set up an arbitrary dividing line and we will then have two distinct classes: the whites and the not-whites. For most purposes this is unnecessary. But if we were manufacturers of shirts, using a popular shade of gray cloth, and our supplier sent us an off-shade, it would be important to define the exact shade of grayness we required, just as it is necessary to specify the exact degree of competence required of students. Temperature is also a continuum, and we do not usually divide all temperatures into "hot" and "not-hot." But we *can* arbitrarily define the word "hot" as a specific degree of temperature, and each of us carries an arbitrary standard with him when he orders coffee in a restaurant. There is a certain minimum degree below which coffee is not hot enough for our taste, regardless of the continuum.

There is another point worth mentioning here. Though there is no natural dividing line in a continuum—the items do not naturally fall into two distinct classes—nevertheless the extremes do form distinct classes. We all know when to say "Beaver," as in the old game, and we cannot fail to recognize the difference between a clean-shaven and a bearded Ernest Hemingway. We have no difficulty in detecting the difference between a black tie and a white one. The print on this page is black, the paper white. And some people are competent surgeons; others, completely unqualified. It is only in the "twilight zones" that we find difficulty in drawing dividing lines.

There are two extremes to avoid with respect to the continuum. One is the danger of making too sharp divisions in reality, of thinking that all people can be divided into just two classes: into capitalists and Communists, or into the good and the not-good. The other extreme is to deny the existence of all distinctions simply because one class passes into another by imperceptible degrees. This leads to a fuzzy-mindedness, which says that the good are really not-good, for they are connected by imperceptible degrees to the not-good, or, conversely, that the not-good are really good, for exactly the same reason. In making the first error we think in terms of two sharply divided natural classes; in the other we see no classes at all. Justice Holmes once referred to the question "Where are you going to draw the line?" as "the tyro's question." We *must* draw lines, he added, for all life involves "the marking of grades between white and black." There *are* classes of things even though they merge into each other by imperceptible degrees. The mistake we too often make is in thinking that there can be only two.

There are times when we must make *decisions*, and the etymology of the word is instructive. It comes from the Latin, meaning "to cut off." We make a sharp break when we decide, for we must decide in one way or another, no matter with how many qualifications. In an election we must decide whether an officeholder has or has not satisfied our standards. Though our minimum standards of decency are vague and ill-defined, they are there. There are times also when we cannot evade a Yes or No answer: when we must choose between alternatives. People who dislike Yes or No answers dislike saying "Everything is either A or not-A." Some people would even like to "abolish" the law of the excluded middle. We shall deal with some of their criticisms of the law in the next chapter.

This chapter has emphasized a fundamental paradox, which may be called the "it is and it isn't" situation. There are no sharp divisions between white and black, and yet there are. There are continuities and there is also the necessity for arbitrary standards. The lesson of this chapter, if there is one, is this: Let us not deny or forget the facts of continuity, and let us not make sharp divisions where these are inappropriate. And let us not deny the distinctions between classes of things.

Perhaps at this point we ought to mention one example of the "Either-Or" construction not considered in this chapter. Some years ago, in the Li'l Abner comic strip, Daisy Mae was expecting a baby. The creator of the strip, cartoonist Al Capp, concealed the sex of the baby for quite a spell. He was finally put on the grill by a question, "Is it a boy or a girl?" Capp grinned, and answered, "Yes."

XII.

SHALL WE EXCLUDE THE EXCLUDED MIDDLE?

IN THE FOLLOWING PUZZLE, C. L. Dodgson, the eminent author of *Symbolic Logic*, *Alice in Wonderland*, *The Hunting of the Snark*, and other works, shows us how easy it is to contradict ourselves:

> Which is better, a clock that is right only once a year, or a clock that is right twice every day? "The latter," you reply, "unquestionably." Very good, now attend.
>
> I have two clocks; one doesn't go *at all*, and the other loses a minute every day: which would you prefer? "The losing one," you answer, "without a doubt." Now observe: the one which loses a minute every day has to lose 12 hours or 720 minutes, before it is right, whereas the other is evidently right as often as the time it points to comes round, which happens twice a day.
>
> So you've contradicted yourself *once*.
>
> "Ah, but," you say, "what's the use of its being right twice a day, if I can't tell when the time comes?"
>
> Why, suppose the clock points to 8 o'clock, don't you see that the clock is right *at* 8 o'clock? Consequently, when 8 o'clock comes round your clock is right.

"Yes, I see *that*," you reply.

Very good, then you've contradicted yourself *twice*: now get out of the difficulty as best you can, and don't contradict yourself again if you can help it.

You *might* go on to ask, "How am I to know when 8 o'clock *does* come? My clock will not tell." Be patient. You know that when 8 o'clock comes your clock is right; very good; then your rule is this: Keep your eye fixed on your clock, and the *very moment it is right* it will be 8 o'clock. "But–," you say. There, that'll do; the more you argue, the farther you get from the point, so it will be as well to stop.

Let us pause for a moment while the reader mentally catches his breath and recovers from his desire to continue arguing with that arch-sophist, Lewis Carroll. But our interest in this item is directed toward its assumption that a contradiction is intolerable. A rational being does not wish to contradict himself. He may change his mind, and say, "What I once thought true I now think false," but he will not, in the same breath, say, "I prefer clock A to clock B, and vice versa," if he uses "prefer" in exactly the same sense. Nor will he say, "I was born in the U.S. and I was not born in the U.S.," using "born" in the same sense. He will not talk in this way if he is rational and knows what he is saying. Rationality requires consistency.

Our recognition of the impropriety of an inconsistency is the reason we find humor in the story about the justice of the peace who doubled as guide and counsellor in marital difficulties. One day a neighbor's wife complained to him about her husband, and, after she narrated the facts in a particular dispute, the J.P. assured her that she was absolutely right, and her husband wrong. Later in the day the husband came in, and narrated the same set of facts. Now the J.P. told the husband that he was absolutely right and his wife wrong. The J.P.'s wife had overheard both conversations and she now lodged a vigorous protest. "How," she asked her husband, "can you do a thing like that? First you tell the wife that she is right, and then you tell the husband that he is absolutely right. But they can't both be right." The J.P.

pondered for a moment, and then answered, "My good wife," he said, "you are absolutely right."

To contradict onself is to place oneself in an impossible situation. If we have asserted two contradictory statements, we must abandon one, or abandon all claims of rationality. Thus it is impossible (rationally) to say, "He is breathing" and "He is not breathing," at any given moment, or to say, "There are irresistible forces and there are immovable objects." We do not make sense when we utter self-contradictory statements such as "There are no words," or "Some triangles, i.e., three-sided figures, have four or five sides." Rational thinking assumes that nothing can *be* thus and so, and also *not be* thus and so—always adding the provisos of course: "in the same sense and/or at a given moment."

The assumption that a contradiction represents an "impossible situation" is found in a "law" or principle of logic called the "law of contradiction": "Nothing can be both A and not-A." (Nothing can be an aardvark and not be an aardvark.) By "law" here we mean, not a command issued by a legislative body, nor a scientific description of actual behavior, but simply a principle assumed whenever we reason. If a creature should ever come to us from outer space and tell us that he comes from a region called Betelgemania but that he does not come from Betelgemania, we could not proceed in conversation with him, for he asserts something while simultaneously withdrawing it. He cannot both come from that region and not come from there.

The close relationship of the law of contradiction to the law of the excluded middle (anything is either A or not-A) should be readily apparent. The thought expressed in the last paragraph can also be put into the form: "Either the creature comes from Betelgemania or he does not." According to the law of the excluded middle, a trace of arsenic is either present or not present in a solution; according to the law of contradiction, it cannot be both present and not present. There is also a third law usually associated with these two: the law of identity, which tells us that A is A, i.e., that "anything is itself." "A rose is a rose," "The present President of the U.S. is the present President of the U.S." We assume this law also whenever we reason. We assume that anything is what it is and not some other thing.

We shall deal more fully with the laws or principles of "identity," "excluded middle," and "contradiction"—traditionally called the three "laws of thought"—in a moment. But first, let us be clear as to the role of these principles in thinking. They are basic *assumptions* of rational thinking. They are not statements that we can prove, but they are principles we use whenever we prove other things. They are indispensable conditions of rational thinking. There are of course other basic principles assumed in ordinary reasoning: for example, "If one class is included in another, any member of the first class must be included in the second." Logic, insofar as it is a science, investigates, analyzes, organizes, and systematizes the principles assumed in rational thinking. In this chapter, however, we shall be concerned only with the three "traditional" laws of logic. Let us now become better acquainted with them by considering certain objections that have been lodged against the assertion that these laws are necessary assumptions of all rational discourse.

Since most of the critics we shall quote are identified with the school of thought called "General Semantics," a few words concerning this school may be helpful. General Semantics should be distinguished from semantics-in-general. Count Alfred Korzybski, its founder, developed a theory concerning the nature of "reality" —fundamentally a metaphysical doctrine—and sought to apply his theory to human problems. What concerns us here is that he believed that our reactions to language—conceived of as reactions of our nervous systems to words—lie at the root of individual and social maladjustments, and that a "re-training" of the nervous system's reactions would eliminate these maladjustments.

In his *Science and Sanity*, Count Korzybski tells us that the "Aristotelian" point of view is responsible for most of our difficulties, so that therapy must consist largely in eliminating this point of view. In particular, he holds the three laws of logic noted above as prime offenders against "proper evaluations," and he singles out the law of identity as the chief culprit lying at the root of most of the ills which afflict modern man. The mistaken belief in identity, he thinks, is responsible for such ills as "unrest, unhappiness, nervous strain, irritability, lack of wisdom, and absence of balance, the instability of our institutions, the wars and revolutions, the increase of 'mental' ills, prostitution, criminality, commercialism as a creed, the inadequate standards of education, the low professional standards of lawyers, priests, politicians, physicians, teachers, parents, and even scientists. . . ." (*Science and Sanity*, 1948 ed., p. 304.)

These are the ills that will be cured if we eliminate the belief that A is A! This apparently trivial law is obviously less innocuous than it appears to be.

What Korzybski and the General Semanticists want to eliminate from our thinking are such bad habits as prejudice, rigid and inflexible patterns of thinking, and fixed reactions to changing situations. They want us to think more carefully and precisely. These are aims with which all reasonable men will agree. But is the law of identity responsible for our failure to achieve these goals?

We shall consider three objections to the law of identity: that it requires the identification of words with things, that no two things are identical with each other, and that we live in a changing world (so that nothing is the same from one moment to the next). We shall deal rather briefly with these objections, and then consider objections to the laws of the excluded middle and contradiction.

As an illustration of the identification of words with things, Korzybski uses the example: "Smith is a man." Korzybski regretfully notes that even great modern philosophers like Bertrand Russell and A. N. Whitehead are guilty of making statements of this kind. The statement is "false to facts," he says, for Smith is not identical with man! We agree that Smith is not, and we agree also that the word "steak" is not identical with the real thing. But this is not the way any logician or philosopher has ever interpreted the law of identity, so the first objection is a rather pointless one.

The second objection: no two things are identical with each other. But when we say "A is A": "A rose is a rose," we do not mean that this rose is identical, in a physical sense, with that rose. No two things are exactly alike, neither any two leaves on a tree nor any two fingerprints. But when I say "fingerprints" this is what I *mean* and not footprints or anything else. The law of identity as a law of logic simply refers to the fact that fixed meanings are presupposed in scientific discourse. We must therefore reject Mr. S. I. Hayakawa's assertion, in his *Language in Thought and Action*, that "no word ever has exactly the same meaning twice." When I say, "The F.B.I. collected fingerprints in 1933 and they collected fingerprints in 1968," the word "fingerprints" has exactly the same meaning twice. It is one of the conditions of rational discourse that our words must retain the same meanings throughout a single conversation or single unit of discourse, though of course words may change their meanings gradually with usage over long periods of time. So much for the second objection.

Nor, when we say that A is A do we mean that things never change. In his *Tyranny of Words*, Stuart Chase interprets the law of identity as meaning that things never change. This is the third objection. "The rose," he says, "withered now and lovely a week ago"–is it the *same* rose? But Mr. Chase has misinterpreted the meaning of the law. It asserts only that we mean what we mean, and not some other thing. If I say "A," I mean "A"; if I say "a rose" I mean "a rose." Chase's criticism is based on a metaphysical rather than a logical doctrine. Metaphysical, in the sense that it presupposes a theory about the nature of the universe. In answer to Mr. Chase's metaphysical point, we may say, "True, the rose has changed, but it is *this very rose* that has changed." You, the reader, have changed since you began reading this chapter: you are at least several minutes older than you were when you began to read. But unless you retain your personal identity during this change–unless you are still the same person you were earlier–we could not say that *you* have changed.

Chase's objection to the metaphysical principle of identity is not new. Its earliest exponent was the ancient Greek philosopher Heraclitus, who taught that we live in a world of flux and change, and that "it is impossible to step into the same river twice, for fresh waters are ever flowing in upon you." The Greeks disposed of this point in an amusing anecdote. Heraclitus, they said, lent several drachmas to a friend, who failed to repay the debt. When Heraclitus dunned the debtor, he denied that it was he who received the money, and he supported his denial by citing Heraclitus' philosophy of change, which asserts that no man is the same from moment to moment!

We turn now to the law of the excluded middle. Before we consider objections, however, let us carefully note the correct formulation of this law. It asserts that anything is either A or *not-A*. It does *not* assert that anything is either A or *B*. Critics of the law often confuse these utterly different statements, which involve two quite distinct logical relations known as "contradiction" and "contrariety" (con-tra-rī′e-ty). Definitions of these relations are in order.

Bill and Jim go on a hunting trip, and they take along a gift bottle, carefully wrapped. Before opening it, they play a guessing game. Bill: "It's Scotch." Jim: "It's bourbon." Now, obviously, both Bill and Jim may be wrong. The bottle may contain wine, or water. But the logical point is this: Jim's statement does not *contradict* Bill's statement, as logicians define the term "contradiction."

"It's Scotch" and "It's bourbon" are *contraries*, not contradictories. Contraries are statements so related that if one is true, the other must be false, but *both can* be false. Contradictories, on the other hand, are illustrated by the following pair: Bill: "It's Scotch." Jim: "It's not Scotch." With respect to this latter pair, we find that if one is true, the other must be false, but *both cannot be false.* If Bill's statement is false, Jim's must be true, and vice versa.

Now, the law of the excluded middle refers exclusively to statements that contradict each other. A beverage must be either Scotch or not-Scotch (contradictories), but it need not be either Scotch or bourbon (contraries). There is no "middle ground" between "Either A or not-A" ("This beverage is Scotch whiskey" or "This beverage is not Scotch whiskey"), but there is a "middle ground" between "Either A or B" ("This beverage is Scotch" or "This beverage is bourbon"). Similarly, the law does not justify our saying "Either All or None," as in "*All* women are fickle or *No* women are fickle," for there is a middle ground here: some are and some aren't. Thus these statements are contraries. The contradictory of "All women are fickle" is "At least one is not."

When critics of the law of the excluded middle tell us that it is "false to facts," and that it encourages what they call "vicious two-valued orientations" ("You must be an atheist if you are not a member of any church"), what they have in mind, of course, is the "error of insufficient options." The law, however, does not say, "Either you are a church member or you are an atheist," but "Either you are a church member or you are not." The law provides options that are sufficient and exhaustive.

In an article in the magazine *Etc* (Summer Issue, 1952), Mr. Hayakawa gives us the following illustration of the law: "You are either for us or against us." But this confuses "A or not-A" with "A or B." "For us" and "against us" are contraries, for you may be neither. In terms of the law one should say: "You are either for us or not for us." And here is another example, from an article originally written by Mr. Hayakawa for the *New Republic,* and later reprinted by the Institute for General Semantics:

> All people tend to think of things in terms of good and bad, black and white, hot and cold, God and Satan, rich and poor, etc. . . . Since this two-valued orientation underlies most of our thinking except in technological matters, the outcome of almost all disagreements is that both sides are pushed to irreconcilable extremes. . . . Illiterates and "uneducated" people are by no means alone in their two-valued orientation; controversialists in intelligent magazines and in learned journals are similarly conditioned . . . there is no middle ground between black and white; it is *all* or *none.* This is what is meant, of course, by the "excluded middle" of Aristotelian logic. . . .

Though we certainly agree with Mr. Hayakawa's strictures against the kind of extremist thinking which divides all things into "black" and "white," nevertheless this is not the kind of thinking that is referred to in the law of the excluded middle. For good and bad, hot and cold, etc., are *contraries,* not contradictories.

Nor were exponents of the "Aristotelian logic" ever guilty of the kind of thinking to which Mr. Hayakawa properly objects. Aristotle went to great pains to distinguish contraries from contradictories in his formulation of the law of the excluded middle. Mr. Hayakawa's misinterpretation of this law is characteristic of most General Semanticists. If the law were what they think it is, their criticisms would be justified, but the law is quite different from what they think it is. The General Semanticists have been tilting at windmills, thinking that they were monstrous giants.

Count Korzybski has also attacked the law of the excluded middle, which he refers to as the law of the "excluded third." But in a list he presents of "two-valued" orientations, we find the following:

> We deal with day and night, land or water, etc. On the living level we have life or death, our hearts beat or not, we breathe or suffocate, are hot or cold, etc. Similar relations occur on higher levels. Thus, we have induction or deduction, materialism or idealism, capitalism or communism, democrat or republican, etc.

Note the indiscriminate lumping together of contraries and contradictories. Our hearts must either beat or not, but it is not necessary that we must be either capitalists or Communists. And we need not be Democrats or Republicans—we may be Prohibitionists.

In Stuart Chase's *Tyranny of Words* we find a more complex and interesting misinterpretation of the law of the excluded middle. The law is false, says Mr. Chase, and so is its counterpart, the law of contradiction:

> The law of the excluded middle might read: "Every living thing is either an animal or a plant." It was so employed by biologists for centuries. We still play the game of twenty questions on the animal, vegetable, mineral basis. In recent years a number of organisms have been studied which defy the distinction. A class of living things has been observed whose metabolism under certain conditions follows the clas-

> sification of "plant," under other conditions that of "animal." Thus "Euglena," a little unicellular water organism, becomes green in abundant sunlight and behaves like a "plant." Remove the light, the green color disappears, and Euglena proceeds to digest carbohydrates like an "animal," rather than synthesizing them like a plant. . . . The law of the excluded middle is an unreliable guide to knowledge. The law of contradiction: Nothing is both A and not-A is equally unreliable. Euglena is both "plant" and "animal."

Mr. Chase has given us an excellent criticism of the statement that "every living being is either a plant or an animal." But he has not given us a criticism of the law of the excluded middle. A statement formulated in terms of the law would say: "Every living being is either an animal or it is not an animal," or "Every living being is either a plant or not a plant." These statements must be true, no matter how the biologists define the terms "plant" and "animal."

Obviously Mr. Chase has not formulated the law of the excluded middle properly. But the reader may raise the question: May it not be the case that Euglena is sometimes an animal, sometimes not? The answer is that the law of the excluded middle *presupposes that a term has been precisely defined.* No matter how the biologist states his definition of "animal," Euglena will either have the characteristics enumerated or it will not have them. And if Euglena has certain characteristics at one time and lacks them at another then the law tells us "Either it has these characteristics at a given time or it does not." It may be that "animal" should be defined as "an organism that sometimes digests carbohydrates." Then Euglena is an animal. But it is for the biologist, not the logician, to give us an adequate definition of animal.

Some further objections similar to the last one should also be considered. Suppose I say, "Either Whittaker Chambers was a Communist or he wasn't." The law of the excluded middle tells us that one or the other must be true. But not both. Objection: But both *can* be true, for Chambers was a Communist until 1938, and then he wasn't one. So he was and he wasn't, depending on the time. Aristotle, in his formulation of the law, carefully qualified it by saying, "It is impossible to affirm and deny *simultaneously* the same predicate of the same subject." In other words, either Chambers was or wasn't a Communist *at a given time*, and not both.

"It either rained on Sunday or it didn't." Objection: it may have rained in one place but not in another. Answer: We must precisely specify the place as well as the time, when we apply this principle. An example of the required precision is found in the rain-insurance policy taken out some years ago by a Golf Club in Chicago for its "World's Championship" Tournament. For a $750-premium the club was insured for $10,000 if it rained in Chicago on the Sunday of the tournament. "Rain" was defined as "1/10 of an inch." "Chicago" was defined as "the meteorological station at the Chicago airport." "Sunday" was defined as "between the hours of 8 and 11 A.M. on Sunday." (These hours were chosen because most people will not leave their homes if it rains during those hours.) For protection against one twentieth of an inch, we may also note, the premium would have been doubled.

Another type of objection: "The early Christians were communists or they weren't—" but may not "communist" mean different things to different people? This is simply a reminder that words may be ambiguous. Let us deal with this point in terms of the third of our laws of logic: the law of contradiction. When we say, "Nothing can be a book and not be a book," the word "book" must have a single sense, such as "a literary composition of a certain kind." "Book," of course, may also mean a list of race-horse odds, and so the book you are reading is a book in one sense of the term and not a book in another sense of the term. Thus it is a book and it is not a book, but this does not violate the law of contradiction. Aristotle covers this point in a formulation of the law of contradiction, as follows: "An attribute cannot at the same time belong and not belong to the same subject *in the same respect*," i.e., in the same sense.

A quotation from an English critic of the law of contradiction will sum up much of this discussion. Mr. F. C. S. Schiller writes:

> A thing can both be and not be with the utmost ease. It is at one time and not at another. Or in one respect and not in another. Or in one place and not in another. Or for one purpose, and not for another. Or in one context, and not in another.

Mr. Schiller thinks that these possibilities disprove the law. But they merely indicate the careful qualifications that are required in order to apply a principle that requires precision in our thinking.

Before we leave our discussion of the laws of logic, we must consider one more misunderstanding. These laws are often spoken of as "laws of thought." This is misleading because it suggests that the laws are like "scientific laws." A psychological law, for example, is a description of the way our minds actually work. But by "law of logic" we mean only an assumption or presupposition of rational thinking, not a description of actual behavior, or of an invariant pattern of human thinking. The logician does not say that people never contradict themselves, much less that they never change their minds. Some people contradict themselves almost as often as they open their mouths, and they may even admit, without embarrassment, that they do. Walt Whitman, in response to a criticism of this nature, asked "Do I contradict myself? Very well, then, I contradict myself." But when Emerson said, "A foolish consistency is the hobgoblin of little minds," he meant that there are times when we ought to change our minds. The logician agrees.

What the logician insists on, however, is this: Two contradictory statements describing one and the same fact cannot both be true. This principle, it is interesting to note, was recognized by the lawmakers in the State of Illinois. A law concerning perjury passed in 1953 provides for conviction when it is simply proved that a witness has made conflicting statements under oath in two different proceedings. Under an old law, the State had to show which statement was true and which false, a very difficult task in most instances, and convictions were nearly impossible. The new law recognizes that a contradiction is *ipso facto* proof of perjury.

The mistaken assumption that logical laws are psychological descriptions may perhaps underlie the psychological doctrine that the "unconscious" has a logic different from that of the conscious mind. Thus Freud writes, concerning the "id":

> The laws of logic—above all, the law of contradiction—do not hold for processes in the id. Contradictory impulses exist side by side without neutralizing each other or drawing apart; at most they combine in compromise formations under the overpowering economic pressure towards discharging their energy. There is nothing in the id which can be compared to negation. . . . (*New Introductory Lectures on Psycho-Analysis,* p. 104.)

The logician does not presume to question Freud's description of what goes on in the id. Nor does the logician question the fact of ambivalence, the experiencing of opposing emotions, such as love and hate toward the same object or person. These impulses may lie "side by side" in the id. This means, however, that positive impulses in opposite directions lie in the id, not that the id both has and does not have a given impulse at a given time and in the same respect. The id has no logic at all, for logic is a rational science concerned with the conditions of proof. Our description of psychological processes may be adequate or inadequate, but the processes themselves are neither logical nor illogical.

The logician also agrees with another of Freud's insights; that the rational mind finds a contradiction intolerable, but that in an irrational state we may accept contradictions without discomfort. But this does not mean that the laws of logic are abrogated. Even logicians like to indulge their fancies and "irrational" impulses on occasion, as did that noted logician Lewis Carroll, whose flowers carried on sprightly conversations with playing cards.

Though the laws of logic do not describe the way we actually think, they are presuppositions of all rational thinking. Our final answer to the critics of the laws is a dialectical one, which might go like this: "You tell us not to accept the law of the excluded middle. Is that different from accepting it? If it is, can we both accept it and reject it? You say that we can't do both? Well, then, you have said that we must either accept it or not accept it—which is an illustration of the law. You have used it in telling us to reject it. So it seems that we can't think except in terms of the law."[1]

This long discussion of the nature of the laws of logic will help to clarify our next problem, as to whether there is more than one type of logic, and in particular what can be meant by the expression "non-Aristotelian" logic. And what is the relationship of the "Aristotelian logic" to modern symbolic logic?

Aristotle is regarded as the founder of the science of logic. His basic insight was that the validity of reasoning depends on the formal structure of an argument, and he was the first thinker to systematize the principles of validity. He saw that reasoning is discourse in which "certain things being laid down, something other than these necessarily comes about through them" (*Topica*, 100a). He saw too that the syllogism is the basic type of argument used in everyday reasoning.

Aristotle's principle of the syllogism tells us that "If A is in B, and if C is in A, then C must be in B." (If a steel box is in a vault, and if stock certificates are in the steel box, then the certificates are in the vault.) No one who understands this statement can quarrel with it. Aristotle's mistake, or preferably, the limitation of his logic, lies in this, that he thought that all reasoning could be put into syllogisms of the subject-predicate form, in which we say, "A is B, C is A, etc." The "Aristotelian" type of syllogism does not cover every form of reasoning, but what he said of syllogisms of this form is as sound today as it was when he wrote.

For two thousand years there were almost no important changes in the science of logic. Aristotle's prestige was so great that it was thought that he had spoken almost "the last word." Then a new development began with the Englishman George Boole's *Mathematical Analysis of Logic*, and *Laws of Thought* in the middle of the nineteenth century. This development led to

[1] I owe this dialectical formulation to my friend, Professor Warner A. Wick.

modern symbolic logic. What has happened is well described by the late American philosopher, Morris R. Cohen:

> In the history of ideas the past century is one marked by an extraordinary development of logic. A discipline which had remained for more than twenty centuries in approximately the state to which the mind of Aristotle had reduced it, suddenly entered upon a period of rapid growth and systematic development. While the essential elements of the Aristotelian logic have not been overthrown or shaken, the labors of Boole, Peirce, Schröder, Frege, Russell, Whitehead, and a host of fellow workers have produced a calculus of propositions in which the Aristotelian theory of the syllogism is seen to occupy only a tiny corner. The potentialities of the new logic as a scientific instrument have already been indicated in the illumination which the application of modern logic has brought to the foundations of mathematics. There is reason to hope that parallel results may soon be achieved in other fields. (*A Preface to Logic*, ix.)

The Aristotelian logic, then, occupies only a "tiny corner" of the vast domain of modern logic. But Aristotle's work has not been rejected; it has simply been incorporated into the new logic. Thus modern logic is not really non-Aristotelian.

The question is sometimes raised: Can there be a non-Aristotelian logic? There is a non-Euclidean geometry, founded by the mathematicians, Lobachevski and Riemann. Einstein and other physicists have developed a non-Newtonian physics. But a *non*-Aristotelian logic, in the sense of a logic which would *deny* the principle of contradiction, for example, would seem to make no sense, and so such a logic appears impossible. A denial of the principle of contradiction would not only rule out Aristotelian and symbolic logic, but it would also eliminate all of mathematics, and it would make any kind of rational thinking impossible.

XIII.

THE LOGIC OF GAMBLING

THAT EMINENT STATESMAN, Winston Churchill, on one of his last visits to the United States, was interviewed by a reporter who had a touch of philosophy in him. "If you had it all to do over, would you change anything, Mr. Churchill?" The newspaper report continued: "A nostalgic look flitted over the great man's face. 'Yes,' he said, 'I wish I had played the black instead of the red at Cannes and Monte Carlo.' "

In this chapter we shall be concerned with the logic of probabilities as applied to the calculation of one's chances of winning and losing in gambling. We shall also note some of the logical fallacies which afflict the thinking of many gamblers—in particular, an error which has been christened "the gambler's fallacy." Our illustrations will be drawn from some popular games of chance: bingo, lotteries, roulette, slot machines, dice, cards, and horse racing. We shall not be concerned with the moral aspects of gambling, nor with the many deplorable consequences that often flow from the human desire to get something for nothing. And we shall not tell the reader that he should not gamble, even though, as we shall see, those who engage in public gambling such as horse racing are almost sure to be taken for a ride—and not on one of the horses!

We begin with the logic of probabilities. The modern study of probability theory began about three hundred years ago, during the seventeenth century, when the Chevalier de Méré, a famous gambler of the time, called on his friend Blaise Pascal. Pascal was a distinguished moral philosopher, and a brilliant mathematician. The Chevalier asked Pascal to work out the probabilities in games of dice for him, so that he would know how to place his bets in the most advantageous manner. Pascal became interested in the problem, and his study of the odds in gambling led to the development of an important branch of logic and mathematics known today as the "theory of permutations and combinations." We shall examine some of the simpler aspects of probability theory as they appear in games of chance.

We can illustrate the general principle with a penny. I toss it in the air. It may fall heads, or it may fall tails. There are just two possibilities, and if I desire heads then I have one chance in two to win. My chance of getting heads is thus 50-50, or one half. If I cast a die (plural: dice) my chance of getting a given number, say 5, is 1 in 6 ($1/6$), since there are six faces on the die.

The simple principle illustrated in the coin and the die applies in the most complicated computations. But before we go on from here, let us note that when we speak of the probabilities of getting "heads" or a "5" on the coin or die, we make at least four assumptions:

1. We assume, first of all, that the coins or the dice are evenly balanced in weighting, so that they do not have a tendency to fall one way rather than another. This includes the assumption that the dice are not loaded. But crooked gamblers, as we know, use loaded dice. The logic of probabilities assumes that there are no influences of this nature.

2. We assume that the coin and the die are not manipulated or controlled by the thrower. The hand is quicker than the eye in gambling as well as in legerdemain, and we rule out such influences. Where such influences *are* present, the laws of chance are irrelevant. Slot machines, for example, have three wheels, each with twenty slots. If there are three jackpot symbols on one wheel and one each on the others, then the mathematical chances

of hitting the jackpot would be 3 in 8,000 spins—provided that the machine is not fixed. But all slot machines are reputed to be regulated or fixed, and if they are, then the mathematical probabilities are inapplicable. The fixer, like the fates, controls the destinies of the wheels.[1]

3. We make the assumption that the desires or thoughts of the thrower have no influence on the result. No matter how hard you may concentrate on winning, no matter how much you may need to win, no matter how many pairs of shoes your baby needs, and no matter how you may importune those familiar characters known as "Little Joe" and "Big Dick," these considerations have no influence whatsoever on the probabilities, Professor J. B. Rhine of Duke University and his "psychokinesis" experiments to the contrary notwithstanding. In any event, we *assume* that no such influences are at work when we estimate probabilities.

4. And finally, we make one further assumption when we say that the coin will fall heads or tails. This assumption may be illustrated by a little story about the man who always found it very hard to decide whether to have just one more drink before going home. He would debate the matter at great length with himself, and finally toss a coin to decide the issue. The coin would settle the matter in the following way: If it fell heads, our friend would have another whiskey, straight; if it fell tails he would have another whiskey with soda; but if the coin landed on its edge, then he would go home. We, too, assume that the coin won't land on its edge. So much for our assumptions.

Let us now go on to some more complicated examples of mathematical probabilities. Expert mathematicians can figure out the probabilities of any event, or combinations of events in games of chance. Probabilities are stated in arithmetical fractions. Thus, our chance of picking a spade from a deck of 52 cards is 13 in 52, or ¼, since there are 13 spades in a deck. The principle is the same as in the cases of the coin and the die, and the same principle applies in the most complex computations. The chance of

[1] Lord Hertford was asked: "What would you do if you saw someone cheating at cards?" "What would I do?" the lord answered. "Bet on him, to be sure."

a coin falling heads twice in a row is ¼ (½ times ½); the chance of getting heads 10 times in a row is 1 in 1,024.[1] In a crap game it is more likely that the thrower will lose than that he will win. In 495 games the thrower will probably win 244 times and lose 251 times, the fraction 244/495 representing the probability that he will win. A mathematician with some idle time on his hands once figured out the probability of dealing four perfect hands in a bridge game, that is, each of the four hands having all of the cards in a single suit. The probability against this sort of thing happening is represented by a staggeringly large number, consisting of twenty-eight digits: 2,235,197,-406,895,366,368,301,560,000 to 1. This is 2 octillions, 235 septillions, 197 sextillions, 406 quintillions, 895 quadrillions, 366 trillions, 368 billions, 301 millions, 560 thousand to 1! Another way of stating this number is that if a million bridge hands are

[1] The principles for figuring the probabilities in *combinations* of events can be illustrated very simply. When a coin is tossed once, there are two possibilities: H (head) and T (tail). If a coin is tossed twice "in a row," there are four possible combinations:

	1st toss	*2nd toss*
Combination 1.	H	H
" 2.	H	T
" 3.	T	H
" 4.	T	T

These are the four combinations that can occur on two tosses. Combination 1 (two heads) represents *one* of *four* possibilities, each of which is equally probable. So the chance of getting two heads in a row is 1/4. If a coin is tossed three times, there are eight possible combinations (1. H-H-H, 2. H-H-T, etc.) only one of which shows three heads, so the chance of getting three heads in a row is 1/8.

With two dice there are 36 possible combinations. In the following table the left number of each pair stands for the number on one die; the number on the right stands for a number on the other:

6-6	5-6	4-6	3-6	2-6	1-6
6-5	5-5	4-5	3-5	2-5	1-5
6-4	5-4	4-4	3-4	2-4	1-4
6-3	5-3	4-3	3-3	2-3	1-3
6-2	5-2	4-2	3-2	2-2	1-2
6-1	5-1	4-1	3-1	2-1	1-1

We note from this table that the chance of getting 6-6 is 1 in 36; the chances of getting a total of 7 are 6 in 36 (6-1, 5-2, 4-3, 3-4, 2-5, 1-6). The chance of making the number 4 (or 10) is 3 in 36. Thus it is twice as easy to make the number 7 as it is to make a 4 (or 10).

played every day, this combination will occur once in every 3 quintillions of years, that is, once in every billion times 3 billion years. It is most unlikely that anyone now alive will ever see such a combination of cards, but it is not impossible. It may even occur tonight.

Let us now examine an extension of our basic principle. Let us suppose that we toss a coin a thousand times. How many heads and tails should we expect after completing our tosses? Obviously, we should expect five hundred heads and five hundred tails, since there is just as much chance to get tails as heads. We usually don't get an exact division even in a much larger series of tosses, but we expect a close approximation to an equal number of each.

Now, keeping in mind this point concerning the evenness of the chances, let us examine a widespread error concerning probabilities, an error to which logicians have given the name: "the gambler's fallacy." Let us assume that we toss a coin twenty times, and that it falls tails each time. There are some people who will say, "There is now more than an even chance that heads will fall on the twenty-first toss. If tails fall twenty times in a row, heads become 'overdue.'" This is the gambler's fallacy. It is sheer superstition to speak of heads being "overdue," if by this we mean that there is more than a 50-50 chance for heads to occur on the next toss.

We noted earlier that the chance that a coin will fall heads on a *single toss* is 1 chance in 2. It is *always* 1 over 2, or ½. The coin, moreover, is totally unaware of what happened during the first twenty tosses. A coin is not alive. It has no mind, no memory, and what is perhaps of crucial significance, it does not even have a conscience. A coin is nothing but a piece of copper or silver which has two sides, and how it fell in the past has absolutely no influence on its future behavior. If the coin is properly balanced, and not manipulated, then the probability that it will fall heads on *any toss*, regardless of what has gone before, is 1 over 2; no more, and no less.

But the gambler is not yet convinced. He will ask: "Suppose that we throw a coin a thousand times. Is it not likely that we will get approximately five hundred heads and five hundred tails?" Our answer is Yes. "Well, then," he goes on, "suppose that the first twenty tosses are tails. Won't the heads now have to make up their due proportion, in order to come out even in the end?" To this the answer is No. When we say that in a thousand tosses we will probably get five hundred heads and five hundred tails, these are the probabilities *in advance* of tossing the coin. Probabilities refer to the future only, in the sense that we calculate the chances of as yet unrealized, or unknown events. But if, in our project of tossing a coin a thousand times, we get twenty tails "right off the bat," it *now* becomes foolish to expect that there will be five hundred heads and five hundred tails when we complete our one thousand tosses. For there are now 980 tosses to go. The probability is that the remaining 980 tosses will divide evenly into 490 heads and 490 tails, and the most probable outcome *now* is: 510 tails and 490 heads for the full one thousand tosses. This is the logical expectation after getting twenty tails in the first twenty tosses.

Perhaps an even simpler example will be helpful here. The chance of getting two heads in a row is ¼, *in advance of either toss.* But suppose I throw the coin and get heads on the first toss. What are my chances now of making two in a row, *including* the first head? Obviously the chance is now ½, since I need merely get a head on the next toss.

In other words, coins never "make up" for past performances. On any toss, the probability is the same. But the gambler is still unconvinced. He has a new argument. Is there not a "law of averages," he asks, which makes things come out even in the end? The answer, once more, is No. There is no law of averages which makes things come out one way or another. The law of averages, if it means anything, simply means the logical probabilities concerning *future or unknown events*, and in the field of mathematical probabilities these are determined without considering past performances, if we can make the assumptions noted earlier.

This misconception of the significance of the law of averages is a very common one. It underlies the popular notion that "lightning never strikes twice in the same place," as if, once lightning has struck spot "x," it will avoid that spot in the future. The point is that no one knows exactly where lightning will strike. The chance that it will hit a given spot may be 1/1000 in any one year. Now, if lightning strikes spot "x," the chances remain 1 in 1,000 that it will hit this spot again within the next year, and the chances are 999 out of 1000 that it will not hit spot "x" next time it strikes. The same probability holds for any other *specific* spot. The reason lightning seems to hit few spots twice is that the probability that any particular spot will be hit is only once in every thousand strokes, or some such figure.

Exactly the same error was made by the midshipman in Captain Marryat's *Peter Simple*, when he stuck his head through the first hole made in the side of his ship by an enemy cannon ball. "By a calculation made by Professor Inman," he announced, "the odds are 32,647 and some decimals to boot, that another ball will not come in at the same hole."

We cannot leave this topic without quoting John O'Hara's *Pal Joey*. When the night club in which Joey was employed as a singer burned to the ground he felt unjustly treated: "Ten thousand night clubs in this country but I guess they repealed the law of averages because they had to pick the one I was in to have a fire. I notice I never get that kind of odds when I go to the track." But there is no need for a Great Power to repeal the law of averages in order for Joey's club to burn. We take out fire insurance to protect ourselves against such possibilities, and the Insurance Companies prosper because the odds favor them. Similarly the law of averages is not repealed when a lottery ticket holder who has one chance in a million wins, though the odds were a million to one against him.

Let us now go back to the gambler's fallacy in games of chance. In a dice game, when a player has thrown several passes in a row, some players will bet more heavily than usual against him, believing that a loss is "overdue." This is the typical fallacy. But, curiously enough, gamblers also believe in another fallacy which is the exact opposite of the first one! When a player throws several winning passes in a row, the thought arises that "luck is with him," and that it will stay with him, because the dice are now "hot," and gamblers who believe this will now bet more heavily *with* the player. Now, it is undoubtedly the case that the dice have some degree of warmth during a game, due to the transmission of the hand's heat to the ivories. But the dice are never "hot" in any mystical sense. The expression "hot" here can apply only to the past, that is, the dice *were* "hot," meaning that the player has won several times in succession. The same considerations apply to the notion that some people are luckier than others. All we can say is that some *were* luckier in the past; that is, they won; but for the future all of us are on an equal basis. Regardless of what has gone before, the thrower will always have the same chances of winning and losing in a dice game.

The two fallacies, then, are: (1) If a man wins several times in a row, bet against him, for a loss is "overdue"; (2) if he wins several times in a row, he is "hot" and you should bet with him. But neither notion is sensible, and amusingly enough, they cancel each other out.

The belief in a mystical kind of luck, of course, will not down, even though it is sheer superstition. When people gamble on the faith that this mystical kind of luck is in operation, and are fortunate enough to win, they are accounted as "shrewd." Visitors to Las Vegas go to a "club" and see players wager heavy sums and win. If the same people are seen to win several times it is hard to believe that they do not "know what they are doing." But they don't know more than anyone else in a pure game of chance. No one can ever know anything except what the probabilities are. (Some are, of course, better informed concerning the mathematical probabilities against the bettor.) The following newspaper story typifies this confusion between luck and shrewdness. On July 22, 1953, the *Chicago Daily News* ran one of a series of articles on "The Business," of Las Vegas, Nevada. In the Desert Inn's "deep-carpeted lobby," we are informed, there appears an interesting exhibit:

> Locked in a glass case and resplendent on a red velvet cushion, sits the visible symbol of the Vegas gods. It's a pair of ordinary dice. Except that this pair, handled by a young-

> ster in 1950, made 28 straight passes at the Inn's dice table. . . . But this youth was luckier than he was brave. He parlayed only $750 . . . though the Inn dropped $150,000 to shrewd onlookers making side bets.

Now, were these "onlookers" *shrewd* to go along with this youngster? They won, but their shrewdness is determined by hindsight; they won $150,000. Is one shrewd if he wins $1,000 on the toss of a coin? In dice games, the odds on any pass are always the same: 251 to 244 against the thrower. The same probabilities hold on the first pass as on the twenty-seventh or nineteenth or seventh. After the event, the non-bettor bemoans the fact that he "didn't see it coming," that he lacked courage, or shrewdness. But this is just the superstition of gamblers who believe in the mystical Lady Luck.

There simply are no ways of "knowing" how to bet in games of pure chance. There are no gambling "systems" that will guarantee more than your mathematical chances. There are no ways of beating the probabilities. There are no magic numbers, nor any magic combinations of numbers. Gambling when the moon is full won't help, nor will it do you any good to touch a "lucky" person. Walking around a chair will not help, nor standing on your head, nor changing the deck in a poker game. Nor does one refute these principles by pointing out that someone did one of these things, and then won.

There is one "exception" to the rule that there are no systems, or rather, there is a system that would be unbeatable *if* it could be applied. This is known as the "Martingale." It operates as follows: Let us say that I bet $1 on the toss of a coin, or on red or black in roulette. If I win, I put aside the dollar I won and bet $1 again. If I lose, I bet $2 on the next toss. If I win on the second toss, I am $1 ahead on my two bets. If I lose twice in a row, I now bet $4. I have now invested $7: $1 on the first toss, $2 on the second and $4 on the third. If I win now, I collect $8 and am again $1 ahead. If I continue to double up in this way, I will always be $1 ahead when I win after any series of losses. But if a long series runs against me then I am in real trouble. For if a series of twenty-seven passes, or tosses, or reds or blacks comes up against me, that is, if I lose twenty-seven times in a row in craps, or flipping a coin, or roulette, then I must be prepared to back the twenty-eighth toss with $134,217,727. If I can cover the next bet then I must have had an initial capital of $268,435,-455, and twice this if I lose on the thirtieth toss! If I lose three more times I will require a capital outlay of four billion dollars! All this to win that elusive single dollar! Anyone with this amount of money available would probably do better to invest it in tax-exempt bonds.

But, of course, one cannot use this system in any actual gambling house, for each house sets a maximum limit on bets. If the limit is $10,000 one will not be permitted to double up after 13 straight losses. So much for the Martingale.

There is, however, a more promising method for outwitting the house. This method is based, not on a mystical belief in magic, but on quite ordinary physical facts. Several years ago the newspapers reported that two college students were "breaking the bank" in Reno, Nevada. They had no gambling system, so-called: they simply kept tab on the numbers that fell on a roulette wheel. They found that a certain number, let us say 19, was being hit more regularly than it should have been according to the mathematical probabilities. They inferred from this that the machine was imperfectly constructed. The laws of chance, you will recall, assume a perfectly balanced machine. These students then bet exclusively on number 19, and were apparently correct about the imperfection of the machine, for they were very successful. They were successful until the management found out what they were doing and the machines were then replaced at regular intervals.

These students, be it noted, acted on a principle quite different from the theory underlying the gambler's fallacy. The fallacy tells us to *avoid* number 19 on the ground that it has already had more than its "share" of hits. The students acted on the basis of experience with machines. Since no machine is perfectly constructed they suspected that they would find a bias which would cause the ball to fall more frequently in some slots than others, though perhaps not always to a significant degree. Their reasoning which led them to bet on the number that fell most frequently was thus sound. The gambler in the fallacy says: "Bet on the numbers that have fallen *less* frequently than they should have in accordance with the laws of probability, for these numbers are 'overdue.'" The students, who were good reasoners, said, "It is a legitimate scientific principle that a pattern in the form of an apparent bias exhibited in a long series of runs on a particular machine is likely to repeat itself." The fallacy is based on the unscientific principle that what has *not* happened is more likely to happen than what *has* happened.

Let us now turn to a consideration of one's chances of winning in gambling enterprises open to the public. The most important factor here is what is known as the "percentages." At a race track, for example, a percentage of the money wagered is retained by the track for itself and the State, so that the return to the players is the total amount bet minus this percentage. The overall odds are thus against the player by a certain percentage. Gambling houses also operate on percentages. A gambling house arranges the odds in its favor, and in the long run the percentage by which the odds favor it, establishes the minimum "return" for the gambling house on the total amount wagered. The percentages are the basic source of the fabulous profits of organized gambling. (There are a number of other factors–such as the house's larger capital–which also make it likely that it will win.) Thus, for the individual player, gambling is not only a form of risk-taking, but it is also a battle against the percentages. And the higher the percentage in favor of the house, the higher is the average rate of loss by the individual player.

The principle may be illustrated by a simple example. If you toss a coin and agree to pay $2 every time it falls heads, and you receive $1 whenever it falls tails, you would soon lose all of your money. You might win, in the sense that this is theoretically possible, but it is very unlikely.

Now, it is obviously foolish to play games of skill for money when you play with players who are more skillful than you are, for you are almost certain to lose your money. You don't have an even chance. You may be temporarily lucky, and win, but in the long run your lack of skill, like the percentages, counts against you. Gambling houses do not rely on luck. And there are many forms of gambling in which the percentages against the player are so high that it is practically impossible for the player to win in the long run. I refer to bingo games, lotteries, the Irish Sweepstakes, and horse racing in general. In a bingo game, for example, the house may collect $100 on each set of cards, and pay out $50 in prizes. This means that on the average each player will lose one-half of his total bets during an evening of play. Some players will come out ahead, but this means that others will lose *more* than half of their play. The odds against winning are formidably high.

This principle may also be illustrated in its application to a form of gambling established in the United States in the year 1664 by Richard Nicolls, first Governor of New York. Nicolls said that he wished to stage horse races, "not so much for the divertissement of youth as for encouraging the betterment of the breed of horses, which, through neglect, has been impaired." Horse racing also offers other inducements besides the opportunity to improve the breed. When a man visits a race track, he enjoys an outing in a pleasant country-like atmosphere; he can admiringly contemplate those things of beauty, the sleek thoroughbreds; he sees the graceful jockeys perched high on their mounts; and the silken colors of the stables make lovely patterns. And there is always the greatest of all inducements, an opportunity to lose one's money.

The percentages against winning in horse racing are very high. The percentage (or "take") today is about fifteen per cent. Of every dollar bet, the State government takes a fraction, the track owners take a fraction, and there is also what is called "breakage": in making payments, all pennies down to the nearest dime are kept by the track. A total take of fifteen per cent means that of every dollar collected by the track, only eighty-five cents is paid back to the customers. As a consequence each player will lose, on the average, fifteen per cent of whatever he bets.

Let us apply these figures to a situation that is fairly typical. On a holiday, a race track draws, let us say, forty thousand fans, and they bet $4,000,000. A fifteen per cent take means that the track deducts $600,000 from the total amount bet. The customers, in other words, go home $600,000 poorer than they came, if they are taken as a group, and they *are* taken! Divided among the forty thousand fans, we find that, on the average, each individual loses $15. Now, some individuals will break even, and some will win, and this means that there are others who must lose a great deal more than $15. If one man breaks even, another must lose $30—if one wins $15 another must lose $45 to make up for the average loss of $15 each and the $15 that was won. On this basis, the average bettor, over a season of 150 days, will lose $2,250 a year on the take alone. Remember that on a single day all of us together are $600,000 poorer than when we came.

If you are fifteen per cent better than the average in your skill in picking horses, or fifteen per cent luckier than the average on a given day, then you will break even. Fifteen per cent is a very sizable percentage, so this is really a rather remarkable accomplishment. Its unusual character gives point to the story about the very worried-looking gambler who was on his way to the race track. He met a friend who asked why he looked so worried. "I simply have to break even today," he answered, "I sure need that money."

Now, there is a certain amount of judgment involved in betting on horses, for a horse race is not a matter of pure chance in the mathematical sense. One may appraise the horses and the skill and experience of the jockeys. There are other factors not subject to our judgment which we cannot appraise, such as the possibility that a horse may deliberately be held back in order to insure better odds in a later race. And then there are the notorious deviations from rectitude which may be hidden from us in a particular race. And then, of course, there are the handicappers, who seek to eliminate the element of judgment: the best horses carry the heaviest weights. The best horses also carry the shortest odds, so that the chances of winning are equalized, and the value of good judgment greatly discounted. The experience of some California race-news reporters at the Santa Anita track some years ago illustrates how hard it is to profit from even the best judgment. These reporters made their bets at special windows, and a record was kept of their total bets. They won three per cent on their total "investment." Now, these men were experts and the results prove it, for their ability to judge horses and odds was eighteen per cent better than the average. They were three per cent ahead; the average bettor loses fifteen per cent. A reporter whose bets totalled $1000 would have won $30, on the average.

But the ordinary bettor, whose luck is average or not at all bad, should expect to lose $15 on every $100 he wagers. These percentages are likely to prevail in the long run.

Such are some of the gloomy prospects confronting the person who indulges in public gambling. The odds are against us. But it would not be sensible to expect anyone to be influenced by anything that has been said about the foolishness of certain forms of gambling. Fond hopes are too ineradicably fixed in the human heart for us to be influenced by anything so inconsequential as a logical argument. I am reminded of an old story about a gambler who met a friend on the street of a small town. His friend asked him where he was going. "To Joe's gambling parlors," he answered, "to try my luck at the roulette wheel." "What!" cried his friend, "are you crazy? Don't you know that the wheel at Joe's place is fixed, so that you can't win?" "Yes," sighed the gambler, "I know all that, but it's the only wheel in town."

XIV.

TRUTH—OR PROBABILITY?

The truth is something that all of us would like to know, except, of course, when it displeases us. But what is it?

We have been told that the question, "What is truth?" was asked by jesting Pilate, but that he "stayed not for an answer." His hasty departure implied that the question was an unanswerable one. We have been told that the truth is something which, when crushed to earth, is sure to rise again; that it is something which can never lose out when engaged in a grapple with falsehood; that it is something which, when told, shames the devil; that it is folly to tell women the truth; that there is nothing so powerful as truth, and nothing so strange; and that the truth will make us free. But what is the truth? Shall we say, with the Spaniard, "*Quien sabe?*": Who knows?

Mankind has been struggling to know the truth for some years now, and at last accounts the final results are not yet in. There are some who insist that the truth is absolute; others say it is relative. Some believe that mankind can achieve the truth; others, the skeptics, deny this possibility. Empiricists believe that science can give us reliable knowledge, but they are skeptical with respect to metaphysical truths, i.e., the "ultimate" truths concerning man's origin and destiny. These are the matters concerning which Omar Khayyám was so skeptical, as expressed in Fitz-Gerald's quatrain:

> Myself when young did eagerly frequent
> Doctor and Saint, and heard great argument
> About it and about; but evermore
> Came out by the same Door where in I went.

Others are skeptical even concerning the evidence of their senses.

Our primary concern is with a more prosaic kind of truth, the kind we shall call "factual." By "factual truth" we mean only this: a truth relating to the facts of human experience. And, prosaically, let us define truth. What do we mean when we say that a statement is true? We mean that a statement agrees with, or corresponds with, the facts. For example: The statement, "Roosevelt was President of the U.S. from 1933 to 1945" is true, for it agrees with the facts. A true statement describes the facts correctly, something like the way in which a map pictures a territory. When a map shows the relations of towns, rivers, mountains, and valleys just as they exist in reality, then the map is a true map. A true statement is like a true map.

Let us now consider some of the implications of this definition of truth. These implications may be best brought out by considering the theory of "logical relativism." A relativist, in the logical sense, denies the possibility of universal truths. He holds that what is true for one man may be false for another, what is true at one time may be false at another time, and what is true in one place may be false in another. Truth, he holds, is relative to the circumstances of the viewer, to his "frame of reference."

The theory of logical relativism is sometimes associated with the theory of relativity in physics—a familiar theory since Einstein. But they have little in common, though both emphasize the "frame of reference." In physics relativity refers to the importance of establishing a "frame of reference" whenever we describe motion. For example: If we ask, "Is the furniture in your home moving at the present moment?" the answer should be "Yes and No, depending on your frame of reference." Since the earth is moving around the sun at a speed of eighteen miles a second, your furniture is moving at the same speed relative to the sun. But, relative to the earth, your furniture is at rest. In other words, the furniture is moving in one frame of reference, but it is at rest in another. A seated passenger in a moving car is at rest but also in motion.

But the physicist does not say that *truth* is relative. He believes that it is really or "absolutely" the case that motion is relative to a frame of reference. He does not say that the relativity theory is true for some scientists and false for others. And this is precisely what the logical relativist declares. He says that what is true for anyone will depend on his past experience, his training, his education, and the ideas accepted by his time and environment. Another man, with different experiences, will find a different truth. One man's food, in other words, is another man's poison in matters of truth as well as diet.

But when the physicist says that motion is relative he does not think of the principle or law of relativity as relative. He believes that it must be *true for everyone* that motion is relative to the frame of reference.

In support of his position the logical relativist points to the differences of opinion that divide the human race in time and place. People once believed that the sun moved around the earth; today we believe otherwise. But was not the former belief true for the people of the middle ages? The relativist notes the different points of view in the Orient and Occident, and in the countries on different sides of the Iron Curtain. He quotes Pascal's aphorism: "Truth on one side of the Pyrenees, error on the other side."

Now, there is a good deal to say in behalf of this relativistic position, for human beliefs do differ. The candid observer will in fact be deeply impressed by the actual variety of opinions that men hold on all matters of real importance, on politics, religion, and so on. Consider the different versions of events that lead to the breaking up of friendships! Each person seems to be right from his point of view. But none of these considerations requires the conclusion that truth is relative, if we accept our definition of truth: a true statement is one that agrees with the facts.

The issue between the relativist and the non-relativist may be a terminological one. The dispute will then be verbal, depending on how we define the word "truth." By "true" the relativist may mean "believed to be true." Let us try to clear up this semantical confusion. In this discussion we shall assume that it is possible to know whether some factual statements do or do not correspond to the facts. We assume that the statement "Water boils at 212° F. at sea level" does correspond with the facts, and that this is not "just an opinion," or mere "belief." It is statements of this kind that we shall refer to as factual truth, or truth in the strict sense of the term.

There are also looser usages. Thus we sometimes speak of religious or moral truth. "What is right for one person must be right for all similar persons in similar circumstances" is a principle that may appeal to us as a "true" moral principle. What we usually mean is that this moral belief is one that every rational person ought to subscribe to, though we admit that it cannot be verified by the eye, or other senses. It is also difficult to speak of literal truth in assessing the "causes" of great social events, such as the origin of "capitalism," or the causes of a great war. Different theories will appeal to us partly because of our prior sympathies and interests, and national origins. Historical facts, as Dwight Macdonald has put it, are not "solid, concrete (and discrete) objects like marbles. Rather are they subtle essences, full of mystery and metaphysics, that change their color and shape, their meanings, according to the context in which they are presented."

When people argue the respective merits of unrestricted free enterprise vs. government controls in producing higher living standards, value judgments will influence opinion. Some people prefer freedom, others prefer security, just as some enjoy a touch of danger, while others abhor danger. Our reception of theories may also depend on whether we stand to gain or lose by change. It is difficult to attain literal truth in such discussion, even when "factual" predictions are made. Prophecies of ultimate disaster cannot be verified. It is always safe to make a prediction if one does not set a time limit.

These considerations would seem to support the relativistic position. But even in the complex issues and predictions just discussed some views will seem to be more reasonable than others, some will seem plausible or probable, and others preposterous. Our primary interest, however, is in clarifying the meaning of truth in the literal sense. Let us return to our example of a map which purports to delineate an area. A true map will correctly describe; a false map will describe incorrectly. In a largely uncharted area, on the other hand, it may be impossible to determine whether a tentative map is correct or not. Its truth or falsity will then be uncertain.

Now consider a map of the world printed in the year 1492 which did not show the continents of North and South America. The people of that time believed that their map was a true map of the world. Shall we say that their map *was* true in 1492 but false today? Or should we not say, rather, that in 1492 men were ignorant of the true nature of the globe, for some of its continents were as yet undiscovered, and so, since this map corresponded with their ignorance, this map was false? Though believed true, the map was never true, though it corresponded with the known facts. But it did not correspond with the actual facts. Instead of saying that what was true at one time became false at another time, let us say rather that what was *believed* to be true was actually false, or at least that what was believed to be true at one time is believed to be false at a different time.

It is quite inappropriate, then, to say that anything can be true here and false elsewhere, if by true we mean that it correctly describes the facts. We would never think of saying that a map of the United States is true for Americans but false for Russians.

But the relativist has another type of argument. Take the statement: "It is warm today." Is this statement true at all times and all places? Obviously, the answer is No. The statement, "It is warm today," may be true in July but not in January; it may be true in Chicago but not in the northern woods of Wisconsin.

But this does not prove that truth is relative. The plausibility of the relativist's point is based on the fact that "It is warm today" is phrased in the vague language of everyday speech. In order to test the truth of a statement, however, we must first give it the precision of a scientific sentence. A scientific statement is *dated* and *located.* A properly formulated scientific statement concerning the weather would read something like this: "The temperature was 89° Fahrenheit on September 26, 1953, at 3:00 P.M., Central Daylight Saving Time, at the meteorological station in Chicago, Illinois." Now, stated in this form, we have a statement that may or may not correspond to the facts. That it was 89° F. in Chicago at 3:00 P.M. on September 26, however—*if true*—must be true for the Chinese as well as for the Australians, and it must be true forever, for our statement was dated and located for a specific time and place.

Similarly, when we look at a map in a contemporary history book showing "Europe in 1800," it would be incorrect to say that that map was true in 1800 but false today. It is the case, of course, that the map corresponds to the political boundaries of Europe in 1800, but not to those of today. But when a map is drawn it carries with it the qualification of a specific time: this is the way the boundaries looked in 1800. And if the map was true in 1800, then, it will be true forever, for the year 1800.

Let us examine another type of case that seems to support the relativist's argument: the relativity of perceptions. I look at a book and say that it has a blue cover. A color-blind man says that it has a gray cover. Are not both of us correct, though we state contrary ideas? Is not one man's truth, error for another, then? But if we analyze this situation properly we shall find that it does not support the relativist's position. We should distinguish between two types of statements. When I said, "The cover is blue" I may have meant that the cover will appear blue to a person with normal vision, i.e., its pigment reflects light rays measuring about 485 millionths of a millimeter. If the color-blind man denies that it is "blue" in this sense, then at least one of us must be wrong. Whether or not such rays are being reflected cannot be true at a certain time and place, and also be false. It cannot both be true for one physicist and false for another, regardless of whether one is color-blind. But I may have meant something else by "It is blue." Perhaps I meant, "*I* have the experience of seeing a blue cover." And if the color-blind man meant that *he* has the experience of seeing a gray cover, then both of us would be right. There is no inconsistency in saying that two persons have different experiences. It is common, even proverbial knowledge that people feel differently when an ox is gored, depending on the ownership of the ox.[1]

There is a relativity of feeling and of experience, then, but this is not a relativity of *truth*. People have different experiences, depending upon the physical conditions of their bodies, their past experiences, their conditioning and re-conditioning, so that one's perceptions and responses will be relative to one's "frame of reference." A man cannot be wrong if he correctly reports what he has himself experienced. But when we talk about the speed of light, or the light waves reflected from the cover of a book, we are talking about something other than our own experiences, and if our physical frames of reference are the same, then conflicting descriptions cannot both be true.

We do not wish to minimize the great importance of the subjective element in perception. This element is often overlooked, and we frequently objectify subjective experiences. There are many parables and stories that illustrate this point. There is the parable about the blind men and the elephant. The blind men encountered an elephant along the highway and compared notes after examining him. The elephant, said one, is something like a stone, cool and smooth, and shaped like a curved cylinder. No, said another, the elephant is like a hairy rope. A third said, No, the elephant is something very massive and solid, full of little hills and valleys. Now, obviously, each of the blind men

[1] A farmer once approached a lawyer and told him that the farmer's bull had gored one of his oxen to death. What would the lawyer consider a fair compensation? The lawyer replied that he should be given his choice of the farmer's oxen. "I have misstated the case," the farmer replied. "Actually, it was your bull that gored my ox, but I will settle on the terms you suggested." "Ah," answered the lawyer, "I am afraid that we will now have to reconsider the case."

was right in saying that the elephant had the characteristics he mentioned, though no one had the whole picture. Each had a different conception of the elephant and each idea was consistent with the other ideas when put together, for one man had come into contact with the tusks, another with the tail, and the third with the side wall of the body. But each was wrong in thinking that the elephant was nothing but what he had experienced it to be.

So much for the doctrine of "logical relativity." We have argued that *if* a statement is true, then it is always true, and true for everybody. But a new kind of problem now arises: How can we be sure that a statement *does* correspond to the facts? For example: The statement, "There is buried treasure beneath the house in which I am writing," is either true or false, but no one knows which, for certain. It is one thing to define truth as correspondence with the facts, but another to determine whether or not a statement does so correspond. It is true or false that some world leaders intend to start a third World War, but we do not know whether this statement actually corresponds to the facts. Let us examine the new problem: Can we be certain about the truth of any statement?

Are we ever justified in saying, "This belief of mine is absolutely true"? Are there any beliefs of which we can be absolutely certain? Can we ever assert with complete confidence that we are completely right and the other fellow completely wrong? We may deceive ourselves. It is a common experience, in a law court, to find several honest and sincere witnesses giving different reports of how an accident occurred. A person is sometimes quite positive that he saw something he did not see. And then there are the distortions, conscious or unconscious, based on personal interest. In the Japanese film *Rashomon*, a murder occurs, and three different versions of the incident are presented by those involved in it as participants. One naturally expects that each of these will give a biased version in order to justify his own behavior. But there is also a fourth witness, a supposedly impartial observer, and he too presents a version that is distorted and subject to doubt.

The question, then, is whether we can ever be *certain* that any statement is true. Even if a statement is verifiable by observation, and we make the claim of truth in the strict sense, can we be positive that we are not mistaken?

The French philosopher René Descartes raised the question: Can we ever be certain that we really *know?* Descartes had been brought up with a traditionalist education, and he later came to believe that many of the ancient beliefs he had been taught were really false. If some of these beliefs are proved false, he asked himself, "How can I be sure that any of them is true?" On what basis can I say, "This or that belief is certainly true"? He then initiated a new method of philosophical study, the method of doubt, and thereby gave a new direction to the course of modern philosophy. He said that he would doubt everything without exception, and then see whether there was anything that could successfully withstand critical scrutiny.

Descartes even doubted the evidence of his senses. Perhaps, he said, they deceive me. The traveler on the desert sees a mirage in the distance, but the wooded oasis he thinks he sees is only an optical illusion. (The reader may recall the film *Lost Weekend*, in which the hero, if that is the appropriate designation for the central character, saw bats flying around in his room after he had saturated himself with alcohol.) Descartes said that he could even doubt whether he was actually awake at a given moment, for he might merely be dreaming that he was awake. Now, do *you* think that you can be absolutely certain that you are not dreaming at this moment? Is it conceivable to you—I do not mean, is it likely, but is it even conceivable—that your alarm clock will ring shortly, that you will awake, and say: "What a vivid dream that was—I dreamt that I was reading a book—though I forget what it was about"? And perhaps you have heard about the college professor who dreamed that he was lecturing to his college class—and when he awoke he found that that was exactly what he was doing!

In the end, of course, Descartes found that there was one belief he could not doubt, and this was the belief that he himself existed. For, he said, if I doubt my own experience, my doubt implies that there must be a doubter. If I did not exist then I could not even doubt that I existed.

In its philosophical form, skepticism is a doctrine which denies that the human mind is capable of attaining genuine knowledge about anything. In the history of mankind there have been many skeptics who carried doubt very far. In ancient Greece, in the fourth century B.C., there was a sect of skeptics who maintained that they could not be certain of anything whatsoever. The senses are deceivers, they said; they affect us according to the way we feel, and their reports are always uncertain. We see differently in sickness or health, and in joy or sorrow. Nothing seems to be so true, their leader Pyrrho said, but that it has not somewhere been thought false, and nothing seems so false but that it has not somewhere been thought true. The Greeks liked to tell amusing anecdotes about Pyrrho, but they undoubtedly embroidered on his behavior and beliefs, for, if the following story were true, it is hardly likely that he could have lived until the ripe old age of ninety. Pyrrho, one story goes, was crossing a road, when he saw a chariot approaching. "That looks like a chariot," he said, "but how can I be sure that my senses are not deceiving me?" As he considered the matter, the chariot came by, knocking him down. His loyal disciples picked him up and dusted him off. They were always around for just such emergencies. It was also said that when Pyrrho died, his disciples did not mourn him, for they could not be positive that he was dead.

Perhaps we should note here that Pyrrho was really certain about at least one thing, namely, that his senses sometimes deceived him. And this inconsistency confronts all skeptics, for when they say that they know nothing, surely they must *know* that they know nothing, and this is a self-contradiction. A person who says that he knows nothing, in other words, is thereby saying that he does know something. A consistent skeptic will keep his mouth shut and say nothing at all.

Bertrand Russell, in *A History of Western Philosophy*, neatly disposes of this thoroughgoing type of skepticism. "It should be observed," he writes, "that Skepticism as a philosophy is not merely doubt, but what may be called dogmatic doubt. The man of science says 'I think it is so-and-so, but I am not sure.' The man of intellectual curiosity says 'I don't know how it is, but I hope to find out.' The philosophical Skeptic says 'nobody knows, and nobody ever can know.' It is this element of dogmatism that makes the system vulnerable."

Let us sum up for a moment. We began by defining a true statement as one that corresponds with the facts, and this means that if a statement is true, then, when stated with proper precision, it must be true for all. When we say, "The truth changes," or "The truth of one age is the falsehood of another" what we mean is that *beliefs* concerning the truth change. We then discussed the difficulties in determining whether a statement really does or does not correspond with the facts. Relativism and skepticism properly emphasize the formidable obstacles to the doctrine that it is possible for us to know the truth. For what one age considers absolutely true, another age often rejects. And are not the ideas of today just as much subject to error as those of the past? How then can we ever claim to know the truth about anything?

The best answer to this question is found in the theory of probability, which harmonizes the doctrines of relativism and skepticism with the search for truth. The scientist, for example, seeks the truth, but he is also very much aware of the difficulties attendant on this search. He thinks of the actual attainment of truth—the *actual* correspondence of a statement with the facts, where this correspondence is established once and for all—as an ideal which we can never attain, for it is always possible to question any belief whatsoever. We can never be certain that no error has occurred or that some factor has not been overlooked. And to say that a belief may be questioned means that it is not absolutely certain. No scientific statement, then, is exempt from the requirement of proof, and no proof can be final.

But though the scientist believes that the truth can never be completely attained—he believes that we can never be sure that we actually have arrived at a final answer in the sense of a real correspondence of statement and reality—nevertheless he believes that we can come closer and closer to the true answers. By "closer and closer" he means that our answers may acquire higher and higher degrees of probability.

Before we continue it is important to note that we are concerned here with *empirical* probability, and not with the *a priori* probabilities of mathematical calculation. Past experience is of the essence here. We have also seen that we can have *certainty* in *mathematical* probability provided we make certain assumptions. We can be certain that an ideal coin will fall heads or tails with equal probabilities.

There are also other instances of logical certainty, where we deal not with the world of experience, but with the analysis of concepts. Thus we can be certain that no one will ever see a square with 5 sides, for a 5-sided figure is not a square. I also know for certain that $2 + 2 = 4$, by the meaning of the concepts. But this is pure mathematics, and we cannot have the same certainty when we apply mathematics to real things in the world of experience. For 2 gallons of alcohol mixed with 2 gallons of water will add up to less than 4 gallons of liquid, because of the chemical changes resulting from the mixing.

The scientist, then, thinks in terms of empirical probabilities. He says that we can know the probabilities, and that probability is the guide of life. Some beliefs are warranted, and some are not, depending on the evidence, which establishes probabilities. And he thinks of probability in terms of degrees. The notion of degrees of probability may be clarified by a diagram showing the "line" of probabilities:

0 .01 .25 .50 .75 .99 1

On this line "1" stands for Unity, or certainty that something is the case, as when we can say flatly: "This is so." "0" means certainty that something is *not* the case: "This is not so," or "The belief is false." ".50" is the middle state, when we say: "It may or may not be the case, and I don't know which." ".75" means something like "It is very likely," and as we move toward Unity the probability increases. ".99" stands for an overwhelmingly high probability. As we go from ".50" to "0" we use statements like "It is improbable," or "It is highly unlikely," and when we reach ".01" we mean "There is just a theoretical possibility." These are not to be taken as technically exact descriptions of these numbers, but the general idea should be clear.

If we could be sure that we have reached Unity or Zero we could be sure that we have discovered what is really true or false, without any question. Now, in common-sense terms, there are many statements about which such certainty seems justified. I know that I am not sitting in a jet bomber as I write these lines, and I know that at least some motion pictures are not exhibited at the bottom of the ocean. I know that there is at least one grandfather who cannot run around the circumference of the earth in less than ten seconds. But in what follows we shall ignore such simple certainties. For when the scientist says that "probability is all: we never can be certain" he usually refers to statements that go beyond our immediate experience; he refers to judgments in which error really is possible. I can be certain that the water I am now drinking is cold—this is an immediate experience—but did I have water with my lunch on Monday of last week? A judgment that I did goes beyond immediate experience; it relies on memory, and memory is notoriously tricky. Not many of us, of course, are like the fabled university professor who was walking near the campus one day around the noon hour. He stopped a student: "Would you please tell me whether I am walking north or south?" "You are walking north, sir," the student replied. "Ah," said the professor, "then I've had my lunch." And waiters, as Jacques Barzun has observed, are often even more absent-minded than professors.

Memory goes beyond immediate experience, but so does every inference from things observed to things unobserved. And scientific generalizations and predictions not only go beyond immediate experience, but beyond all past experience of any kind whatsoever. And so, whenever we deal with a scientific law or prediction, we can have no more than probabilities. It is not certain, for example, that the sun will rise tomorrow: some sort of cosmic cataclysm may occur five minutes from now. That "all men are mortal" is also only highly probable. When we carefully state what we mean by this generalization, which says that all human beings must someday die, we find that we are making a prediction that all human beings now alive will die before reaching a certain age, say 200. To be testable, a determinate time limit must be placed on a prediction. And this prediction, of course, is not absolutely certain.

Similarly we cannot be absolutely certain that some things are impossible. There is a certain probability that plant life exists on the planet Mars, for photographs indicate a likelihood of the presence of lichen. But it is unlikely that men exist there, and still less likely that Mars has "big beat" bands. But even the last fantasy cannot be ruled out as completely impossible. Strange things do occur, and also strange coincidences. There is just enough possibility in the following story to make it amusing: The story is told of two friends who were patients of the same psychoanalyst. One day they decided to play a practical joke on him. Each would tell the analyst the details of a fantastic dream they invented, every phase of which would be narrated in exactly the same way. One patient told his story, and then, two hours later his friend repeated exactly the same story. Toward the end of the second recital the analyst could no longer contain his amazement, and blurted out his astonishment: "What a coincidence! In the last twenty-four hours I have heard exactly the same dream told to me three times!"

There is an important difference between the meaning of truth and the meaning of probability. This difference can be brought out very simply by showing the possible relations of truth and probability: A statement can be true and probable, both false and improbable; but it can also be true and improbable, or false and probable. By truth, in other words, we mean the actual correspondence of a statement with the facts, but probability is *relative* to the evidence available to us. The statement, "The earth is motionless" once appeared highly probable, in the light of the evidence then available, but today we say it is false; "The earth moves" once seemed improbable in the light of the evidence of the senses, but today we think it is true.

The statement, "There is buried treasure beneath the house

in which I write" is either true or false at this moment. Either the facts correspond, in which case the statement is true, or they don't, in which case the statement is false. The truth of a statement is not relative to the evidence—the statement either corresponds with the facts or it doesn't—even though we do not know which. This follows from our definition of truth. But when I say, "There probably is treasure," or "There probably is no treasure" I mean relative to a certain body of evidence.

A statement cannot be true for one man and false for another, but it can be probable for one and improbable for another, depending upon the available evidence. On the basis of the evidence available to me, it may be reasonable for me to suppose that Jones is guilty of cheating at cards; on the basis of the evidence available to you, it may appear highly unlikely. He is or he is not, but neither of us may really know for certain which. The truth of a statement cannot change, but *probability judgments* vary with every change in the evidence. In May it may appear likely that there will soon be an end to the state of international tensions; in July this may appear highly improbable. At any given moment we make our estimate of probabilities on the basis of the evidence available to us at that time. And, the scientist adds, we can never reach more than a highly probable conclusion, for *all* the facts can never be known.

What practical applications can we make of these matters? We can try to assess the probabilities of the facts upon which we rely whenever we make decisions. We should be exceedingly careful before we claim that we know something for certain. We should *be* certain when we have the right to be, of course. A reliable observer can give an accurate report of what he actually witnessed. In general, however, we ought to abandon the use of the expression "absolutely true," except for matters within our immediate experience. And where there is controversy, let us use more modest expressions, such as, "The evidence indicates that this or that is probably the case." And let us also remember Jefferson's distinctions between truths, probabilities, possibilities, and lies. There is no golden touchstone to guide us in each case. We can simply try to avoid two extremes. One is a too uncritical attitude, whereby we jump to conclusions whenever we hear an idle rumor; the other is a too skeptical attitude which refuses to believe despite good evidence.

A final point. Though it happens that different opinions are sometimes reasonably held by different observers, this does not mean that "everything is just a matter of opinion." This is a form of skepticism which denies both the possibility of knowledge, on the one hand, and of ignorance, on the other. Nor is it the case that everyone is "entitled" to his own opinions, except in a legal sense. When we say "not entitled," we mean from a rational or logical point of view. For consider: A man says that every professor at a certain university is a Communist and an atheist, and then adds the words, "in my opinion." If you disagree with him, he says that simply means that his opinion is not your opinion, but that everyone is "entitled" to his own opinion on the matter. But the facts may make it overwhelmingly probable that his opinion is a false opinion. Unless one is intellectually irresponsible, he will inquire into the truth or probability of his opinions. One is not forgiven for making a dangerously irresponsible statement merely because he tells us that such is his opinion. We ought to examine the evidence before we talk. The question the careful thinker will always ask himself is: "What is the evidence?"—the title of the next chapter.

XV.

WHAT IS THE EVIDENCE?

IN THE YEAR 1932 a spectacular kidnapping stunned the nation. In the evening, on the first day of March, the infant son of Charles Lindbergh was kidnapped from his nursery at the Lindbergh home near Hopewell, New Jersey. A broken ladder and a chisel were found near the house, and a note, signed with a symbolic device, was left in the nursery. The note asked for $50,000 in ransom money. Lindbergh announced that he desired to deal directly with the kidnappers rather than through the police since this approach might better insure the safety of his child. A week later, Dr. John F. Condon, a retired schoolteacher living in the Bronx, in an interview with a reporter for the *Bronx Home News*, offered his services as a go-between. On March 9, eight days after the kidnapping, Condon received a note asking him to communicate with Lindbergh and to arrange for the payment of the ransom. This note contained the symbolic device of interlocking blue circles with a red disk and three punched holes, the same as the one on the original ransom letter.

Condon communicated with Lindbergh, and they agreed that Condon should meet with the writer of the note. On March 12 Condon met the writer in the Woodlawn Cemetery and was convinced that this man, who called himself "John," had been in the Lindbergh nursery; but Condon asked for further evidence that John was the kidnapper. Four days later the baby's sleeping garment was delivered by mail to Condon's home. Then, on April 2, after an extended series of negotiations, Condon and Lindbergh met the man John at St. Raymond's Cemetery, where Condon gave him $50,000 in five-, ten-, and twenty-dollar bills. In return Condon received a note stating that the child was on a boat called the *Nelly*, which could be found "between Horsenecks Beach and Gay Head near Elisabeth Island," an area in Buzzards Bay, which separates Martha's Vineyard from the Massachusetts Coast. There was no such boat. About five weeks later, on May 12, the dead child was accidentally found in the woods near the Lindbergh home. The child's skull was fractured. He had evidently been killed when the kidnapper's ladder broke: the skull had been smashed against the wall when the kidnapper fell.

For the next two years the search for the kidnapper was fruitless. Many ransom bills turned up but none could be traced. It was really the great depression of 1932 which indirectly led to the capture of Bruno Richard Hauptmann. The United States went off the gold standard in 1933, and President Roosevelt ordered all gold coins and all gold certificates returned to the Treasury. The yellow-backed certificates then passed out of circulation, and anyone who possessed them was regarded as a gold hoarder. This was an important matter because the ransom money was chiefly in gold certificates, and a record had been made of the serial number of each bill. In September of 1934 a man purchased gas from a filling station in Manhattan and paid for the gas with a $10 gold certificate. When the attendant remarked that such bills were rare, the man answered casually that this was so, and added, "I only got a hundred more left." Thinking that the man was a gold hoarder, the attendant wrote the license number of the man's car on the bill. When the bill was returned to the bank, its number was checked against the list of the ransom payment money and found to be one of the listed bills. The license number was traced to Bruno Richard Hauptmann. He was arrested on September 19.

The evidence presented to the jury by the prosecution when the case came to trial may be summed up as follows:

When arrested, Hauptmann had another twenty-dollar ransom bill in his pocket, and in his garage the police found an additional $14,600 of the ransom money. This incriminating evidence required explanation, as did also his financial operations during the thirty months since the payment of the ransom. On April 2, 1932, when Condon gave the man called "John" $50,000, Hauptmann had $203.90 in a savings bank and owned fifty shares of Warner Brothers stock worth about $100. A day or two after April 2, he quit his job as a carpenter and never worked thereafter. His wife quit her job in a bakery. From April 2, 1932, until September 19, 1934, when arrested, he was shown to have come into the possession of funds in the amount of $44,486, the procurance of which was unaccounted for. He opened brokerage accounts in April and May, depositing about $17,000 for the purchase of stocks. He made a loan of $3,750 secured by a mortgage. He bought a $400 radio; his wife made a trip to Europe and he made several trips, including a hunting trip to Maine and a motor trip to Florida. His total assets when arrested were about $40,000. He could not have earned this money in the stock market, as he claimed, for his total stock transactions showed a net loss of about $5,700.

Hauptmann explained his possession of the ransom (and other moneys) by saying that it had been left with him for safekeeping by a friend named Fisch whom he had met in July or August of 1932. But this claim could not be proved. Fisch was no longer available for questioning. He had returned to Europe and had died there of tuberculosis. The evidence also indicated that he had always been a poor man. Hauptmann was then confronted with the fact that he had opened his brokerage accounts in April and May, before he had met Fisch. Hauptmann now said that he must have met Fisch in February, but other witnesses testified that he had not met Fisch until July.

The kidnapper's notes (there were fourteen in all) were evidently written by a man who was of German origin, and Hauptmann was a German immigrant, albeit an illegal one, since he smuggled himself into the U.S. after breaking out of a German jail. His notes contained errors in spelling, such as "ouer" for "our," "anyding," "someding," "gut health," and he made the same errors when asked to write a note dictated to him. Eight nationally recognized handwriting experts, each working separately, testified that the ransom notes were in Hauptmann's handwriting, when compared with acknowledged instances of his handwriting.

Within twenty-four hours after the kidnapping, two men testified that they had seen a man driving a car containing a ladder, near Hopewell. One of these men testified that the driver had a pointed face; the other testified that the car was a 1930 Dodge. Hauptmann's face was somewhat pointed, and he owned a 1930 Dodge when he was arrested. Condon identified Hauptmann as the man called "John," with whom he spoke at the Woodlawn and St. Raymond's cemeteries, and Lindbergh identified his voice. A taxi driver testified that Hauptmann paid him a dollar to deliver a note to Dr. Condon on March 12.

The ladder found near the scene of the crime was made up of three sections which could be held together by dowel pins. It could fit into an automobile. Though the ladder was roughly finished, it was made by an expert carpenter. Carpentering was Hauptmann's trade. By microscopic examination of the marks made by the planing machine on the wood, the wood in the ladder was traced to a lumberyard where Hauptmann was a customer. One rail on a ladder section was made of wood identical with the wood in Hauptmann's attic, from which part of a floor board had been ripped out. The rail matched the attic wood in grain, annual rings, and texture. Four nail holes in the rail matched exactly four nail holes in the attic joist from which the wood had presumably been ripped. The chisel marks on the ladder were made with the chisel that was found near the Lindbergh home. This chisel was a three-quarter-inch Stanley. In his home Hauptmann had a set of Stanley chisels from which the three-quarter-inch size was missing.

The ladder had been broken, probably when the kidnapper was descending with the child. It had not been strong enough to support both. The police had constructed an identical ladder shortly after the kidnapping, and they had then tested this ladder in order to determine the weight of the kidnapper. They found that it would break if it carried a weight of as much as 180 pounds. The police then predicted that the kidnapper weighed between 150 and 180 pounds. Had he weighed more than 180 pounds the ladder would have broken before he reached the second-story window; if less than 150 pounds it would not have broken even with the added weight of the child. The child weighed 26 pounds; Hauptmann, 170 pounds.

When the ladder broke, the kidnapper fell. Witnesses testified that Hauptmann had limped at about the time of the kidnapping, and used a cane for several weeks.

Penciled on a shelf in Hauptmann's closet was Condon's address and telephone number. This was a 1932 number; it had since been changed. When asked why he had written these items on the shelf, Hauptmann answered: "I must have read it in the paper about the story." But the telephone number had never been published.

His reluctance to answer questions was also considered an indication of guilt. He had a criminal record in Germany (burglaries and highway robbery) before coming to the United States.

There is very little to say concerning Hauptmann's defense. He said very little to anyone, not excepting his own attorneys. He spent most of his time in trying to explain his financial transactions. His claim of an "alibi"—that he was in New York on the day and evening of March 1—was not satisfactorily substantiated. His chief defense was the simple statement: "I did not do it; others committed the crime and received the money."

The trial began on January 2, 1935. The jury found Hauptmann guilty of murder under a New Jersey law which provided that "where death occurs as a result of the commission of a burglary" a verdict of murder in the first degree could be sustained. He was sentenced to the electric chair, and was electrocuted April 3, 1936. He died proclaiming that he was completely innocent of any connection with the kidnapping, or with the death of the child, or that Condon had paid him the ransom money.

Now, our concern with this case is due, not so much to its intrinsic interest, as to the fact that it presents such a wealth of evidence. It should be noted, further, that the evidence in this case is almost exclusively of the type called "circumstantial." There were no witnesses who testified to having seen Hauptmann commit the crime. But each bit of circumstantial evidence was like a mute witness, pointing to Hauptmann with the unspoken words, "Thou art the man." There were of course the two men who saw a Dodge car carrying a ladder, and there were the identifications by Condon, Lindbergh and the taxi driver, but no witness identified Hauptmann as having been near the Lindbergh home at the time the crime was committed. The eyewitness testimony was directed chiefly to the fact of extortion.

There are some who think that circumstantial evidence is not altogether trustworthy as a basis for determining guilt. They prefer testimonial evidence, such as that of eyewitnesses, who testify that they themselves have seen the accused commit the crime. We shall discuss a case involving testimonial evidence in a moment. But most lawyers regard the evidence in the Hauptmann case as overwhelming in its total mass and effect, and the jury found that the evidence was sufficient to prove the accused guilty beyond a reasonable doubt.

Now, there have been many who have urged that it was possible that Hauptmann was not guilty.[1] It may be argued that it is not inconceivable that he was innocent; that all of the listed bits of evidence may simply constitute a series of remarkable or strange coincidences, and that Fisch may really have given Hauptmann the ransom money. We may grant that all these things are possible. But these are possibilities only, and they do not furnish the kinds of probabilities on which human beings must

[1] Mr. Dooley, Finley Peter Dunne's sharp observer of the American scene, once contrasted English and American attitudes toward procedural justice: "In England," he said, "a man is presumed to be innocent until he's proved guilty, and they take it for granted he's guilty. In this country a man is presumed to be guilty until he's proved guilty, and after that he's presumed to be innocent!"

act. We may grant that there was no absolute proof of guilt. But the law does not require absolute proof of guilt, for absolute proof is unattainable.

In a civil case, a decision will be rendered in accordance with the preponderance of the evidence, as in a lawsuit over a contract. But in a criminal case, the law requires more than a mere preponderance of the evidence. In order to eliminate the danger of punishing the innocent, the law requires that the State must prove its case beyond any *reasonable* doubt. This does not mean "beyond any *conceivable* doubt." If such a requirement were in effect then no one could ever be convicted of anything.

Absolute certainty is an unattainable ideal in a court of law. A jury can never be absolutely sure that the accused man is guilty, even if a score of witnesses testify that they saw him commit the crime. It is *conceivable* that these witnesses are engaged in a frame-up, or conspiracy. Nor does a confession give absolute certainty, for innocent men have been known to confess to "any and all" kinds of crimes. In a famous murder case in Chicago, a number of fake confessions were made to the police. The police do not take all such confessions seriously, but one man told the police a convincing story and claimed that he had hidden his murder weapons among the rocks along the lake front. An investigation was ordered, but the tools were not found. Then a telegram arrived from the man's wife in Arizona. She wanted to know whether her husband was in Chicago confessing to the murders, for, she said, every time her husband heard of a spectacular murder he boarded the earliest train and rushed off to confess.

And people have been known to confess to crimes in order to shield others. But, in any case, absolute certainty is unattainable in a courtroom. There is always a possibility of error in cases involving circumstantial evidence, but this is also true of cases involving the testimony of eyewitnesses.

Let us now examine another famous murder trial, this one involving eyewitnesses. In the Sacco-Vanzetti case, a cause célèbre of the '20's, two Italian anarchists, Sacco and Vanzetti, were sentenced to death for a payroll robbery and murder. They claimed that they were innocent, and the case aroused international interest because of a widespread belief that their unpopular political philosophy was one of the reasons for the finding of guilt. The trial was conducted in an overcharged atmosphere of emotional excitement and hatred during the aftermath of the so-called "Red scares" of the early 1920's. Vanzetti's final statement, the reader may recall, is one of the central items in Thurber and Nugent's play *The Male Animal.*

I shall discuss only one of the items in the testimony against Sacco, the eyewitness testimony given by one of the witnesses for the prosecution. Mary Splaine worked in a factory with windows giving a view of a railroad crossing close to the place where the robbery and murder occurred. She heard a shot and ran to the window. She saw an automobile crossing the tracks. She was sixty to eighty feet from the car, and it was in her line of vision for two or three seconds. She was called as a witness immediately after Sacco was arrested, but was unable to identify him. At a preliminary hearing in Quincy, Sacco and Vanzetti were brought into her presence, and she was asked whether she could identify Sacco as the man she saw in the car. She testified: "I will not swear positively he is the man, and I don't think my opportunity afforded me the right to say he is the man."

Mary Splaine also appeared as a witness at the trial, held fourteen months later. When called upon to testify she now said, "From the observation I had of him in the Quincy court and the comparison of the man I saw in the machine, on reflection I was sure he was the same man." She then described the man she saw in the car: "The man that appeared between the back of the front seat and the back seat [of the car] was a man slightly taller than the witness. He weighed possibly from 140 to 145 pounds. He was muscular, an active-looking man. His left hand was a good-sized hand, a hand that denoted strength. . . . He had a gray, what I thought was a shirt—had a grayish, like navy color, and the face was what we would call clear-cut, clean-cut face. Though here [indicating] was a little narrow, just a little narrow. The forehead was high. The hair was brushed back and it was between, I should think, two inches and two and one-half inches in length and had dark eyebrows, but the complexion was a white, peculiar white that look greenish."

The prosecutor then pointed to Sacco, and questioned her: "Is that the same man you saw at Brockton?" She answered, "It is." "Are you sure?" the prosecutor now asked her. She answered, "Positive."[1]

Now, in this item we find testimonial evidence, but it is of very low quality. Mary Splaine's acuity of vision, as exhibited in this testimony, appeared to have been acquired during the interval between her first testimony, immediately after the murder, and her appearance at the trial more than a year later. When we contrast eyewitness testimony such as hers with the circumstantial evidence in the Hauptmann case we see at once that the significant question is not, "Was the evidence testimonial or circumstantial?" but, "How much evidence was there, and how good was it?" The quantity and the quality of the evidence are the important things, when we ask, "What is the evidence?"

In his book *Convicting the Innocent,* Edwin Borchard describes a number of cases in which innocent men were convicted on the basis of circumstantial evidence. But there are also numerous cases in which witnesses falsely testified against innocent men. The common suspicion of circumstantial evidence appears to be unwarranted. It may be that such evidence is weak in some cases, but it may also give an overwhelming probability. And lawyers (and logicians) are very conscious of the fallibilities of witnesses. There are dishonest witnesses who perjure themselves, and what is more important, honest witnesses are often mistaken. Many of us are imperfect observers, and even when we observe well, our memories may play tricks on us.

It is because witnesses are fallible or dishonest that the courts permit searching cross-examinations concerning the matters to which they have testified. Cross-examination is for the purpose of exposing inconsistencies and contradictions in the testimony of hostile witnesses. If mistakes or falsehoods are uncovered this will impair the credibility of damaging testimony. The exposure

[1] From transcript as found in Felix Frankfurter's *The Case of Sacco and Vanzetti,* pp. 11–12.

of a dishonest or mistaken witness, however, is not always an easy task, and great astuteness on the part of the cross-examiner is often required to trap such witnesses. In his *Art of Cross-Examination,* Francis L. Wellman describes the methods and techniques used by successful cross-examiners and cites many examples of masterpieces in this art. The technique of "interruption," for example. If the examiner suspects that the witness has memorized his testimony, he may deliberately interrupt the witness in order to expose this fact. Perhaps you yourself recall your childhood days when, after memorizing a poem or a musical composition, you were interrupted in the middle of your recitation. You may have found it impossible to resume where you had left off in the recitation—you had to start all over again, from the beginning. In the same way, the witness who has memorized his testimony may have to start over again from the beginning after an interruption by the cross-examiner, and this will be fairly convincing evidence that the testimony is not his own. Wellman also describes one of his own tricks of cross-examination, one that has since become a classic. A man sued a transit company for damages suffered when a car started just as he was about to board it. He claimed that the fall had resulted in the loss of the use of his right arm. In his cross-examination Wellman was sympathetic, and asked the plaintiff to show the jury just how high he was able to raise his arm since the accident. The man showed that he was just barely able to move his arm. "Now," the cross-examiner continued, "will you kindly show the jury how high you were able to raise your arm *before* the accident?" "Oh," said the witness, "before the accident I could raise it *this* high," and he raised his arm above his head.

On the other hand, a witness may be telling the truth, and yet be confused by the cross-examiner. Above all, the witness should guard himself against being susceptible to suggestion, thus being led into admissions of things that he isn't sure of. We recall how easy it is to be trapped into making concealed admissions via the "complex question," the question that contains a concealed assumption. A typical form of suggestibility is illustrated in the following experiment performed in a psychology class. A group of college students were shown a picture of the interior of a farmhouse for about thirty seconds, and were then asked questions concerning what they had seen. One of the questions was, "On which side of the picture was the cat?" Some students said, "To the left," others "To the right." But there was no cat in the picture. The question contained a false assumption, and the suggestible students accepted the bait.

So much for some of the problems of evidence in a law court. Probability is all that can be expected, and the probability will be high or low depending upon the quantity and quality of the evidence. If we turn now from the problems confronting courts and juries to those confronting historians who seek to reconstruct the events of the past, we shall find that the basic questions are exactly the same. When we read Carl Sandburg's *Abraham Lincoln*, or a recent history of the Civil War, we assume that the historian has received a substantial part of his information from other historians. But somewhere along the line we find the "first histories" of an event, and these are based upon the testimony of witnesses, and circumstantial evidence.

Histories of World War II are based on the reports of observers and participants, such as newspaper and radio reporters, Winston Churchill's memoirs, etc. Official documents will also be consulted. The first-hand accounts of events are written by witnesses, and the historian's problem of evaluating the accuracy and reliability of these accounts is the same as the problem of the judge and jury in evaluating the evidence in a law court.

When a historian deals with the past, he cannot inspect it directly. He finds monuments and other remains, and he finds documents containing reports concerning events of the time. Some of these documents are accounts written by eyewitnesses. There are two important questions concerning such documents. The first question concerns the genuineness of the document. Is it genuine or a forgery? If genuine we raise the second question: Who is the "witness," i.e., the writer? Was he competent and reliable, so that we can count on him to know and to tell the truth? What was his reputation for veracity? And even if we grant that he was honest and sincere, was he suggestible? Was he biased or prejudiced? An ardent major-league baseball fan, for example, is a wholly unreliable witness in a close decision involving his team. And the historian carries his caution further. He hesitates to rely on the uncorroborated testimony of a single witness and seeks for other independent witnesses who give substantially similar accounts.

The first history of an event may have been based on examination of the original documents, but since the first historian was also human, hence fallible, his history may contain errors. Later historians may accept his account and his errors will be perpetuated. Hence a really careful historian today will trust no second-hand account of an event, but will want to see for himself the original documents on which the first account was based.

In closing our discussion of the problems of logic in history, let us consider some remarks made by Katherine Mayo, in her *Mother India*, published in 1927. According to Mrs. Mayo, it is quite the usual thing for Indian girls to get married and to have children while they are themselves still in a state of childhood. It is common practice, she says, for Indian girls to become mothers nine months after they reach puberty, and puberty, she adds, takes place in India somewhere between the ages of seven and thirteen. The age of seven, she admits, is rather extreme, but she assures her readers that the age of thirteen is "well above the average."

These are rather surprising facts, and very interesting, if true. But are they true? What is the evidence? Let us examine what another investigator has to say about the matter. Dr. M. I. Balfour, of Bombay, reporting in the *Calcutta Times of India* in 1927, says that he studied 6,580 cases of childbirth, and he found that the average age of the mother at the time of the delivery of her first child was almost nineteen years in Bombay, and nineteen and a half years in Madras. He tells us further that of all the women he studied, none were mothers under thirteen, and only forty-two out of the 6,580 cases were mothers under fifteen.

Parenthetically, here, we may note that when *Mother India* was published in 1927 many American readers were shocked by

Mrs. Mayo's revelations, and they condemned child marriage as a sign of barbarism. But these readers obviously forgot, if indeed they ever knew, that in the United States six of our states still allow girls to marry at the age of twelve, one state sets the limit at thirteen, and ten others at fourteen. If indignation toward Indian customs was in order, it would have been more appropriate for the Turks to wax indignant, for they place the minimum age for girls to marry at fifteen.

But let us return to the problem of proof. Dr. Balfour's facts do not bear out Mrs. Mayo's conclusions. Whom shall we believe? You must be the judge. As between accepting an unsupported conclusion and a detailed study such as Dr. Balfour's, I should be inclined to go along with the doctor. At this point, however, let me confess that I am no authority on this subject, nor have I investigated these facts for myself. I found the items concerning Mrs. Mayo's book in a book by Bergen Evans called *The Natural History of Nonsense*. Mr. Evans shows us how little evidence there is for many of the things we take for granted. The point of all this is that we ought to exercise a little caution in believing what we read until we learn something about the evidence that supports it, especially when the facts are remarkable or startling.

We have discussed some of the problems of evidence in this chapter. We seek the truth, but must be content with high probability and not demand absolute certainty. The probabilities depend upon the evidence that is available. Above all, we must be critical- minded, and never forget to ask the question: "What is the evidence?" When the evidence is confused, we ought to suspend judgment and wait for further evidence. When people say, "This must be so; I saw it in a book," let us remember that an author may be mistaken. To quote Mr. Evans: "The civilized man has a moral obligation to be skeptical, to demand the credentials of all statements that claim to be facts, for a refusal to come to an unjustified conclusion is an element in an honest man's religion."

XVI.

HOW THE SCIENTIST THINKS

Scientific thinking is not something quite different from ordinary thinking. It is simply reflective thinking at its best: careful, methodical, and systematic. It is the kind of thinking all of us will find useful whenever we are confronted with difficult problems. As an illustration of scientific thinking in action we shall adapt an incident from A. J. Cronin's novel *The Citadel.* Though our illustration is fictional it vividly describes the essentials of scientific method.

Andrew Matson, a young physician, has been employed as assistant to Dr. Bramwell. One morning Andrew receives a message from Bramwell, asking him to help certify one Emrys as a dangerous lunatic. Emrys, who had always been regarded as a well-adjusted individual, has been ill and unlike himself for about three weeks, and during the previous night had turned violent and set upon his wife with a knife.

Andrew arrives at the sickroom, and at first hardly recognizes Emrys. His face is swollen; his skin waxy. Andrew speaks to Emrys, who first mutters an unintelligible reply, and then, clenching his hands, breaks forth with a tirade of aggressive nonsense.

Dr. Bramwell is positive that this is a case of "acute homicidal mania" and asks Andrew to sign the certification. Andrew feels that he ought to be convinced; yet, inexplicably, he is not satisfied. "Why, why, he kept asking himself, *why* should Emrys talk like this? Supposing the man had gone out of his mind, what was the cause of it all? He had always been a happy, contented man —no worries, easygoing, amiable. Why, without apparent reason, had he changed to *this?* There must be a reason, Andrew thought doggedly; symptoms don't just happen by themselves."

Let us pause at this point to note that the narrative thus far gives us the *background* of scientific thinking. Scientific thinking begins with a *problem:* Andrew's problem is one of finding the cause of Emrys' symptoms. In this respect scientific thinking resembles reflective thinking in general, for, as John Dewey insisted over and over again, reflective thinking is a problem-solving activity. We think hard, in other words, only when we have a problem which requires solution, when our thinking is directed toward a definite goal. When our thinking lacks such direction we engage in daydreaming, or reverie, or random thinking.

Problems, of course, do not arise out of nowhere. They have backgrounds: they reflect disturbing or puzzling situations which must be set right. Problems may be of a purely intellectual as well as of a practical nature. A mathematical or logical puzzle requires reflective thinking, as does a problem of medical diagnosis. Our problems may also be of the "everyday" variety: choosing a job, figuring out why a cake did not turn out as expected, and so on.

One more point before we go on with the story. A scientific problem should be formulated in a precise manner. It should be "localized," and admit of a definite answer. "What's wrong with the world?" is not a scientific question, as Will Rogers well knew when he quipped that both he and Bernard Shaw knew that the world was all wrong, but neither of them knew what was the matter with it. Andrew's problem was specific; it is the medical problem of diagnosing a disease: to know the reasons for the symptoms exhibited by Emrys. We return to the narrative.

Andrew now examines the patient. He stares for some time at the swollen features before him, "puzzling for some solution of the conundrum." And then "he instinctively reached out and touched the swollen face, noting subconsciously, as he did so, that the pressure of his finger left no dent in the edematous[1] cheek."

"All at once, electrically, a terminal vibrated in his brain. *Why* didn't the swelling pit on pressure? Because—his heart jumped—because it was no true edema[1] but myxedema.[2] He had it, by God, he *had* it! No, no, he must not rush. Firmly, he caught hold of himself. He must not be a plunger, wildly leaping to conclusions. He must go cautiously, slowly, be sure!"

We interrupt again. The inquiry was initiated by two "steps": the disturbing situation which generated the inquiry, and the precise formulation of the problem. The next step in the method of science is that of observation: observation of the facts in the case. But *what* facts? The world is made up of an infinity of facts, and we cannot observe all of them. There are also an infinity of facts concerning Emrys: the color of his eyes and hair, his schooling, his personal possessions, and so on. We cannot take account of every fact concerning Emrys. The facts to be observed, obviously, are those that are relevant to, that is, those that have a bearing on the problem. How do we know which facts are relevant?

The scientist, in seeking to solve a problem, brings a fund of previous knowledge to his task. His knowledge tells him that he should look for the answers in certain directions and not in others. He knows, in a general way, what is likely to be significant and what is apt to be a "likely lead." His knowledge furnishes him with a set of "preliminary hypotheses," or suggestions toward the solution of the problem. These preliminary, or "working" hypotheses give him a set of alternative possible solutions.

[1] Edema is the medical term for "a morbid accumulation of a water-like fluid in organs or tissues of the body." Strictly, Cronin should have said "apparently edematous cheek," for, as he notes in a moment, the swelling in Emrys' cheek is not really due to edema.

[2] A disease associated with the thyroid gland and characterized by swelling of the face, dryness of the skin, and progressive mental deterioration.

These hypotheses may of course not be clearly formulated in the conscious mind of the scientist, but they are there.

The scientist has a storehouse of general knowledge when he begins his investigation. This knowledge also may not be clearly formulated in his mind, but it is ready to be awakened by some observation that ties in with it.

When the scientist collects facts or data, then, he knows what types of facts are relevant to his problem, and what types he may disregard as being irrelevant. An untrained individual cannot diagnose a disease, because he doesn't know what symptoms to look for, or how to interpret what he sees. Previous knowledge gives the scientist "ideas"—provisionally accepted assumptions as to what *may* be the solution of the problem. In the *Citadel* incident, Andrew "reached out and touched the swollen face," because his knowledge of medicine tells him that a swollen face is a symptom of several different diseases. Its softness or hardness is apt to be significant, and he notes that the pressure of his finger leaves no dent in the cheek. He then re-interprets the apparently edematous condition. Flesh that does not pit on pressure ties in with his knowledge of myxedema.

The trained observer sees more than the untrained. This is as true in a picture gallery as it is in a scientific laboratory. "The artist," said Leonardo da Vinci, "sees what others only catch a glimpse of." The painter not only has a hand more skilled than that of the man who "can't paint a stroke," but he also sees the subtle and infinitesimal gradations of light and shadow, and structures and forms which most of us simply do not see.

"They do not serve science who only stand and stare." The scientist doesn't just "look at" the facts. Nor is he a mere fact-collector. He does not go aimlessly about, picking up scattered information, but seeks facts relevant to a particular problem. All of his observations center around his problem; and his working hypotheses tell him what to look for. Charles Darwin was well aware of the importance of "theory" in observation. "No one can be a good observer," he said, "unless he is a good theorizer." On another occasion he wrote: "How odd it is that anyone should not see that all observation must be for or against some view, if it is to be of any service." There is a famous anecdote concerning this great scientist which illustrates the importance of a "point of view" in making observations. Darwin and a fellow scientist were searching for fossils in the north of England. They were not aware of the glacial theory at the time. Years later Darwin revisited the area, and he was now astonished to discover how clearly marked were the glacial ridges on the rocks. He had not noticed them on his earlier visit because he was not looking for them. In other words, it is quite likely that we shall not see what we are not looking for, even though what we look at is quite obvious.

This aspect of observation, that we don't see what has no significance for us, has resulted in a rule of procedure for many archaeologists. When new excavations are opened up, such as those following upon the discovery of ancient ruins, the archaeologists will not excavate the new "find" completely. They realize that future archaeologists will know more than they know, and that their present state of ignorance may blind them to significant clues for some later theory. They leave part of the find untouched. Later observers may find significance in evidence that had no special significance in our generation, in the manner in which Darwin was able to appreciate the glacial markings only after he became aware of the glacial theory.

Observation, then, is necessarily selective, but it should not be "subjective." The scientist must guard himself against the kind of bias that makes him see only what he wants to see even though it is not there, or to ignore what *is* there because it is inconsistent with the theory he wishes to verify. This very human factor is held to a minimum in science but it cannot be completely eliminated. Even the faking of evidence is not wholly unknown, as in the case of the notorious "Piltdown man," that glorious hoax who was christened *Eoanthropus*, the "dawn man." There is a wicked little anecdote about a young geologist who had worked out a highly original theory concerning the rock formations in a certain valley. The formations he examined confirmed his theory, and he was in a state of exultation over the sensation his paper would make in scientific circles. He walked up a hill to enjoy a final glance at "his" valley, when his eye fell on a large boulder, formed of a type of rock which should not have been there if his theory were true. He thereupon put his shoulder to the boulder and pushed it down the other side of the hill! Fortunately science has safeguards against such hoaxes and aberrations, for science is *self-corrective*. Every scientific statement is open to constant questioning. Science itself finally caught up with the Piltdown man.

So much for observation based on previous knowledge. There is one more essential aspect of scientific method illustrated in our selection from the *Citadel*. This is the *explanatory hypothesis*, or *theory*. An explanatory hypothesis is the formulation of a *suggested solution of the problem*. Andrew's explanatory hypothesis to explain Emrys' condition is this: Emrys is suffering from myxedema. This hypothesis ties together Emrys' behavior and his apparently edematous cheek.

There are two kinds of hypotheses: the preliminary, provisional guesses which tell us what to look for in the beginning of an investigation (the "working hypotheses" which delimit the relevant facts); and the major explanatory hypothesis or theory which is put forth as a solution of the problem. A good explanatory hypothesis should have two main characteristics: It must fit all the known facts, and it must be capable of being tested. Andrew's hypothesis fits the known facts, and it is capable of being tested. We shall deal more thoroughly with "the capability of being tested" in a moment.

But first, the question may be raised: Where did the explanatory hypothesis come from? Cronin describes the origin of Andrew's hypothesis as a situation in which "a terminal vibrated in Andrew's brain." Scientists often speak of the "flash of insight" which penetrates into the heart of a difficult problem. Albert Einstein once said that "the really valuable factor is intuition." This "flash of insight," or "intuition," requires imagination, and in this respect the scientist is like the poet or artist. A great explanatory hypothesis involves the ability to see new connections, and new abstract relationships. Thoroughness of research may often be a satisfactory substitute for imagination, as in industrial research, but in the higher levels of science it is never a complete substitute. Previous knowledge, however, is always of great importance for genius and non-genius alike. Previous knowledge may even give us our explanatory hypotheses, when we suddenly see the connection between an observed fact and a known principle.

We can now see how Andrew got his hypothesis. His knowledge of medicine tells him that myxedema is a disease characterized, among other things, by swelling of the flesh and progressive mental deterioration. He has observed these characteristics in Emrys. He draws the syllogistic conclusion from these premises: Emrys has myxedema. Though this is not a valid syllogism, since the sharing of characteristics does not guarantee "identity," his conclusion has a modicum of probability. He is well aware of the tentative nature of this explanation: He must not leap to conclusions—"he must go cautiously, slowly, be sure!" Let us return to the narrative and complete our discussion of the episode.

Andrew proceeds with his examination. He lifts Emrys' hand. He finds the skin dry and rough, the fingers thickened at the ends. Emrys' temperature is subnormal. "Methodically he finished the examination, fighting back each successive wave of elation. Every sign and every symptom—they fitted as superbly as a complex jigsaw puzzle. The clumsy speech, dry skin, spatulate fingers, the swollen inelastic face, the defective memory, slow mentation, the attacks of irritability culminating in an outburst of homicidal violence. Oh! the triumph of the completed picture was sublime!"

Andrew concludes this investigation by saying that "Emrys is sick in mind because he's sick in body"; that he is suffering from thyroid deficiency—"a straight case of myxedema." Andrew then treats Emrys with thyroid extract, to which he responds successfully.

Let us now examine the logical elements in the conclusion of the episode. Andrew has formulated a hypothesis, a hypothesis which fits the known facts. So far, so good. But an adequate explanatory hypothesis, we noted above, must also be capable of being tested.

Let us note the implications of the scientific requirement that a hypothesis must be "capable of being tested." Suppose that Andrew had said that Emrys was possessed by devils; that the presence of devils in Emrys' body was the explanation of his condition. During the middle ages, we may recall, this was a widely used hypothesis to explain insanity. But we cannot verify the presence of entities such as devils. The devil hypothesis *may be true*, but there is no evidence in its favor, and, in any case, it is not a *scientific hypothesis*. By definition, a scientific hypothesis is one capable of being tested. This requirement is indispensable if we are to have reliable and verified knowledge. Unverifiable entities are not allowable in scientific hypotheses, for they cannot be tested. The inconsequentiality of appealing to the unverifiable is amusingly illustrated in an old controversy carried on by Galileo and one of his contemporaries, a scientist in the Aristotelian tradition. The traditionalist refused to believe that there were mountains on the moon, despite what could be clearly seen through Galileo's telescopes. "It is impossible," said the traditionalist, "for Aristotle says that the heavenly bodies are perfect spheres. The moon may *appear* to have mountains, but this can only be because the valleys are filled with an invisible substance, so that it is really a perfect sphere." Galileo's retort, a classic, went something like this: "If we are permitted to postulate invisible substances," he said, "then I assert that there are enormous mountains on the moon, extending far beyond the outside of the perfect sphere, and made of this very same invisible substance!"

An explanatory hypothesis must be *capable* of being tested, and it must also *be* tested. A hypothesis may fit the known facts, but other hypotheses may fit the known facts equally well. A test is required to determine which of them is true. When two confirmed hypotheses are capable of explaining the known facts equally well, then the scientist will generally prefer the simpler one.

In order to test his hypothesis, the scientist must first deduce its implications. By "deduce" we mean a process something like this: On the basis of our observations, we formulated the hypothesis that Emrys has myxedema. Myxedema is a disease characterized by swelling of the flesh and mental deterioration, which have already been observed in Emrys, and also by dry, rough skin, spatulate fingers, etc. *Assuming* that Emrys has myxedema we now *deduce* that he will have these further symptoms, for anyone having myxedema must also have these other symptoms, and anyone who does not have these other symptoms cannot have myxedema.

The next step is to make further observations or experiments to determine whether Emrys does in fact have these further symptoms. If he does, then we may regard the hypothesis as confirmed or proved. If he does not have these symptoms, then the hypothesis is not confirmed.

This is the pattern of Andrew's reasoning when he seeks to verify his hypothesis. He has really made a prediction that he will find certain symptoms if he looks further. He finds the anticipated symptoms (by further observations), and his hypothesis is confirmed.

Before we go on to discuss some further general features of scientific thinking and methods, it may be helpful to sum up our long discussion of the *Citadel* case. On analysis we find eight distinct steps in scientific method, and we shall list these eight steps in tabular form, showing the application of each to the *Citadel* illustration:

The 8 Steps of Scientific Method	*Application to the* Citadel *case*
1. The situation which generates the inquiry.	1. There is a disturbing situation which must be set right: Emrys, a hitherto well-adjusted individual, is acting strangely.
2. The precise formulation of the problem.	2. What is the cause of Emrys' symptoms and behavior?

3. Observation of the *relevant* facts[1] based on	3. Andrew notes that Emrys' swelled flesh does not pit on pressure. (His flesh is non-edematous.)
4. The use of previous knowledge.	4. Myxedema is characterized by mental deterioration and swelled, but non-edematous flesh.
5. The formulation of the explanatory hypothesis.	5. Andrew puts Steps 3 and 4 together: Myxedema fits the observed facts.
6. Deductions from the hypothesis: If the hypothesis is true, certain consequences can be predicted. The working out of the implications of the hypothesis tells us what facts will verify or confirm the hypothesis.	6. If Emrys has myxedema, then he should have *all* of the symptoms that characterize this disease, including symptoms that have not as yet been observed: dry, rough skin, spatulate fingers, etc.
7. Testing the hypothesis, by further observation or experiment.	7. Andrew observes that Emrys has all of the characteristics of myxedema: dry, rough skin; spatulate fingers, etc.
8. Conclusion: the hypothesis is confirmed or not confirmed.	8. Andrew's hypothesis is confirmed. If it were not, he would have to go back to Step 3, and start over again.

With Step 8 we have solved the problem of *diagnosis*. Andrew then tries a *cure*. He performs the experiment of treating Emrys with thyroid extract, predicting that this will cure his disorders. It does. This gives added weight to the correctness of the diagnosis.

These, then, are the essential steps in scientific thinking. We see that the scientist combines careful observation with rigorous reasoning. "Armchair" reasoning is characteristic of mathematics, which says nothing about the facts of the "real" world; but it is not sufficient in the "empirical" sciences, which investigate the

[1] There are also certain "given" facts in any situation, accepted before the inquiry is begun. Andrew, for example, has observed Emrys' general appearance and behavior. Observations of this kind occur before we go on to Step 3.

facts of nature. But, as we have seen, it is also inadequate to think of the scientist as one who is exclusively concerned with observing facts through his sense organs. Science tells us that the earth rotates on its axis and revolves around the sun. We do not *observe* the movement of the earth. Seeing is *not* believing, then, for we see the sun rise and set. Science combines rational and empirical procedures: without reasoning there is no science. And without theories, and deductions from theories (done in an armchair, perhaps), there could be no developed science. As Morris R. Cohen has put it, "Theories are points of view or perspectives for seeing things in their connections. They are, as Chauncey Wright pointed out, the true eyes of the scientist, wherewith to anticipate and discover things hitherto invisible." To paraphrase what Immanuel Kant said of concepts and percepts: theories without facts are empty; facts without theories are blind. Both are necessary.

But, in the last analysis, theory has as its purpose the discovery and understanding of the facts. An explanatory hypothesis must be in accord with the known facts, and if predicted facts do not turn up as expected, the theory must be discarded. Many beautiful hypotheses, as T. H. Huxley once observed, have been slain by ugly facts. In practice, however, things are not always so simple as these remarks may seem to imply. For scientists are not gods, or rational machines, and sometimes they will stubbornly hold fast to their theories despite contrary evidence. And sometimes they are right in doing so!

A notable example of justified stubbornness in the face of contrary evidence is found in the work of Mendeleyev, the great Russian chemist who discovered the law of the "periodicity" of the chemical elements. Mendeleyev believed that the elements could be arranged in a "periodic chart," a kind of calendar-like table. He arranged the elements on his calendar one below another in seven groups as if each group stood for a day of the week, Sunday through Saturday. In the first "day of the month" he put the element having the lightest atomic weight, and followed this one with elements having increasingly heavier weights. Mendeleyev said that the elements in each group have chemical properties resembling others in its group. His hypothesis was that the chemical properties of the elements were "periodic functions of their atomic weights," that is, their properties repeated themselves periodically after each series of seven elements.

Mendeleyev's table was incomplete in that there were gaps: some of his "dates" were not filled by elements. He predicted that new elements would be discovered having certain specific properties and that these new elements would fit into the gaps in the table.

But there was one serious flaw in his hypothesis. It did not fit all of the facts as they were known in 1869, the year in which Mendeleyev presented his discovery in a paper read before the Russian Chemical Society. Two elements, tellurium and gold, had characteristics which required positions in Mendeleyev's table other than those to which their known atomic weights would have assigned them.

Now, what was Mendeleyev's attitude toward these discrepancies in his theory? Did he say, "I must abandon my hypothesis, for it is not in accord with the facts"? No, his attitude was rather this: "If my hypothesis does not accord with the facts, why, then, so much the worse for the facts"! What he really meant, of course, was that since his hypothesis explained so much, so neatly, then it *must* be true, and so, if certain "facts" are not in accord with the hypothesis, then let us re-examine these "facts." Perhaps these so-called facts are not facts at all; perhaps we are mistaken in what we consider to be the facts.

Mendeleyev's hypothesis had a remarkable confirmation. Not only did his predictions come true with respect to the discovery of new elements with specific characteristics, but it was also found that the weights of tellurium and gold had been miscalculated. When they were properly measured, they fitted neatly into the positions Mendeleyev had originally assigned to them. Obstinacy is justified when one happens to be right.

Science, as a method, is loyal not to persons or institutions, but to the process of attaining truth. And the scientist, insofar as he is true to the ideal requirements of his methods, is a modest man. He tells us about what he has tested, and whether his tests have confirmed or disproved his hypotheses. He claims only probabilities for his conclusions, though these probabilities may be very high. The scientist is always aware of the possibility that some important fact may have been neglected, or that we have simply been fortunate—or unfortunate!—in having found no exceptions to date. The scientist is conscious of the possibilities of error, but he is no skeptic, for he accepts what is most probable as the best guide for thought and action.

Our discussion of the nature of scientific method in this chapter may be summed up in a colorful definition by Percy Bridgman, the physicist-philosopher:

> The scientific method, so far as it is a method, is nothing more than doing one's damnedest with one's mind, with no holds barred. This means in particular that no special privileges are accorded to authority or tradition, that personal prejudices and predilections are carefully guarded against, that one makes continued check to assure one's self that one is not making mistakes, and that any line of inquiry will be followed that appears at all promising.

XVII.

THE LOGIC OF SHERLOCK HOLMES

SHERLOCK HOLMES was a great detective and a master of the art of deduction. He was not a completely new type, however, for he had precursors, literary as well as living. One of these was Zadig, the hero of Voltaire's tale of that name. In the chapter "The Dog and the Horse" in *Zadig* we read:

> One day, while Zadig was walking in the wood, the finest horse in the king's stables had broken away from the hands of a groom in the plains of Babylon. The grand huntsman and all the other officers ran after him in great anxiety. The grand huntsman accosted Zadig and asked him if he had seen the king's horse pass that way.
>
> "It is the horse," said Zadig, "than which none runs better; he is five feet high, and has small hoofs; his tail is three and a half feet long; the studs on his bit are of gold twenty-three carats fine; his shoes are silver of eleven pennyweights."
>
> "Which road did he take? Where is he?" asked the grand huntsman.
>
> "I have not seen him," answered Zadig, "and I have never even heard anyone speak of him."
>
> Zadig is condemned to the knout for stealing the king's

> horse, and he is sentenced to pass the rest of his life in Siberia. Scarcely had the sentence been pronounced when the horse was found.
>
> The judges were now under the disagreeable necessity of amending their judgment; but they condemned Zadig to pay four hundred ounces of gold for having said that he had not seen what he had seen. He was forced to pay his fine first, and afterwards he was allowed to plead his cause:
>
> "Stars of justice," he said to his judges, "I swear to you by Ormuzd that I have never seen the sacred horse of the king of kings. Hear all that happened: As I was walking along the road in the little wood, I perceived the marks of a horse's shoes, all at equal distances. There, I said to myself, went a horse with a faultless gallop. The dust upon the trees, where the width of the road was not more than seven feet, was here and there rubbed off on both sides, three feet and a half away from the middle of the road. This horse, said I, has a tail three feet and a half long, which, by its movements to right and left, has whisked away the dust. I saw, where the trees formed a canopy five feet above the ground, leaves lately fallen from the boughs, and I concluded that the horse had touched them, and was therefore five feet high. As to his bit, it must be of gold twenty-three carats fine, for he had rubbed its studs against a touchstone, the properties of which I had ascertained. Lastly, I inferred from the marks that his shoes left upon the other stones that he was shod with silver of eleven pennyweights in quality." (Translation by R. B. Boswell, slightly modified.)

And Sherlock also had a living precursor. Conan Doyle has told us that the actual model for his detective was a Dr. Joseph Bell, surgeon at the Edinburgh Infirmary, where Doyle had been Bell's assistant. Dr. Bell, however, always insisted that Sherlock went far beyond the original. Here is an example of Bell's method: He would look at a patient, and say, "A cobbler, I see." Turning to his students, he would point out that the inside of the knee of the man's trousers was worn; that was where the man rested a lapstone, an instrument used only by cobblers. Doyle remembered many such instances, but the one that impressed him most went as follows:

"Well, my man, you've served in the army?" "Aye, sir."
"Not long discharged?" "No, sir."
"A Highland regiment?" "Aye, sir."
"Non-com officer?" "Aye, sir."
"Stationed at Barbados?" "Aye, sir."
"You see, gentlemen," explained Bell to his students, "the man was a respectful man, but did not remove his hat. They do not in the army, but he would have learned civilian ways had he been long discharged. He had an air of authority, and he is obviously Scottish. As to Barbados, his complaint is elephantiasis, which is West Indian, and not British." (*Conan Doyle, His Life and Art,* by Hesketh Pearson, pp. 88-89.)

And here, finally, is Sherlock Holmes in action. Dr. Watson, of course, is describing the incident:

The portly client puffed out his chest with an appearance of some little pride, and pulled a dirty and wrinkled newspaper from the inside pocket of his greatcoat. As he glanced down at the advertisement column, with his head thrust forward, and the paper flattened down upon his knee, I took a good look at the man, and endeavored, after the fashion of my companion, to read the indications which might be presented by his dress or appearance.

I did not gain very much, however, by my inspection. Our visitor bore every mark of being an average, commonplace British tradesman, obese, pompous, and slow. He wore rather baggy gray shepherd's check trousers, a not over-clean black frock-coat, unbuttoned in the front, and a drab waistcoat with a heavy brassy Albert chain, and a square pierced bit of metal dangling down as an ornament. A frayed top hat and a faded brown overcoat with a wrinkled velvet collar lay upon a chair beside him. Altogether, look as I would, there was nothing remarkable about the man save his blazing red head and the expression of extreme chagrin and discontent upon his features.

Sherlock Holmes' quick eye took in my occupation, and he shook his head with a smile as he noticed my questioning glances. "Beyond the obvious fact that he has at some time done manual labor, that he takes snuff, that he is a Freemason, that he has been in China, and that he has done a considerable amount of writing lately, I can deduce nothing else."

Mr. Jabez Wilson started up in his chair, with his forefinger upon his paper, but his eyes upon my companion.

"How in the name of good fortune, did you know all that, Mr. Holmes?" he asked. "How did you know, for example, that I did manual labor? It's as true as gospel, for I began as a ship's carpenter."

"Your hands, my dear sir. Your right hand is quite a size larger than your left. You have worked with it and the muscles are more developed."

"Well, the snuff, then, and the Freemasonry?"

"I won't insult your intelligence by telling you how I read that, especially as, rather against the strict rules of your order, you use an arc and compass breast pin."

"Ah, of course, I forgot that. But the writing?"

"What else can be indicated by that right cuff so very shiny for five inches, and the left one with the smooth patch near the elbow, where you rest it upon the desk."

"Well, but China?"

"The fish which you have tattooed immediately above your wrist could only have been done in China. I have made a small study of tattoo marks, and have even contributed to the literature of the subject. That trick of staining the fishes' scales of a delicate pink is quite peculiar to China. When, in addition, I see a Chinese coin hanging from your watch-chain, the matter becomes even more simple."

Mr. Jabez Wilson laughed heartily. "Well, I never," said he. "I thought at first that you had done something clever, but I see that there was nothing in it after all."

"I begin to think, Watson," said Holmes, "that I make a mistake in explaining. . . . My poor little reputation, such as it is, will suffer shipwreck if I am so candid." ("The Red-Headed League.")

We turn now to an analysis of the logical method used by Zadig, Dr. Bell, and Holmes. Holmes refers to the method as deductive, which it is. These deductions involve the syllogistic pattern of reasoning. But the process is not an automatic one. Anyone can perform deductions from sufficiently obvious principles and facts—Johnny's face is smeared with blackberry jam—but it requires imagination and insight to relate less obvious facts to the right principles. Dr. Bell described the prerequisites of good medical diagnosis as follows:

> "The precise and intelligent recognition and appreciation of minor differences is the real essential factor in all successful medical diagnosis. . . . Eyes and ears which can see and hear, memory to record at once and to recall at pleasure the impressions of the senses, and an imagination capable of evolving a theory or piecing together a broken chain or unravelling a tangled clue, such are the implements of his trade to a successful diagnostician." (Hesketh Pearson, *op. cit.*)

We shall add some comments, shortly, on "an imagination capable of evolving a theory," but let us first note the relation of observation to Holmes's deductive method. This is nicely stated in "The Sign of Four":

> "You spoke just now [Watson says to Holmes] of observation and deduction. Surely the one to some extent implies the other."
>
> "Why hardly," he answered, leaning back luxuriously in his armchair, and sending up thick blue wreaths from his pipe. "For example, observation shows me that you have been to the Wigmore Street Post Office this morning, but deduction lets me know that when there you dispatched a telegram."
>
> "Right!" said I. "Right on both points! But I confess that I don't see how you arrive at it. It was a sudden impulse upon my part, and I have mentioned it to no one."
>
> "It is simplicity itself," he remarked, chuckling at my surprise—"so absurdly simple that an explanation is superfluous; and yet it may serve to define the limits of observation and deduction. Observation tells me that you have a little reddish mould adhering to your instep. Just opposite the Wigmore Street Office they have taken up the pavement and thrown up some earth, which lies in such a way that it is difficult to avoid treading in it in entering. The earth is of this peculiar reddish tint which is found, as far as I know, nowhere else

> in the neighborhood. So much is observation. The rest is deduction."
>
> "How, then, did you deduce the telegram?"
>
> "Why, of course I knew that you had not written a letter, since I sat opposite to you all morning. I see also in your open desk there that you have a sheet of stamps and a thick bundle of postcards. What could you go into the post-office for, then, but to send a wire? Eliminate all other factors and the one which remains must be the truth."

This selection calls for a number of comments. First, we note that Holmes makes a slight error here, for deduction is involved in both cases. There are really two problems. The first is: Where did Watson go? Holmes notes the reddish earth on his instep, and he observed reddish earth at the post-office. But these are disconnected observations. He connects them by assuming that this earth is found *only* at the post-office—he saw it nowhere else—and he then draws the deductive inference: Watson was at the post-office. Holmes's inference is so obvious that no reasoning seems to be involved. He *assumes,* as a fact, the general rule: "If anyone has this reddish earth on his shoes, he must have been at the post-office," and he observes the reddish earth on Watson's shoes. Similar considerations apply to the item in "The Red-Headed League," when Holmes concludes that Jabez Wilson has done a considerable amount of writing. This is a deduction from the assumed general rule that a shiny cuff implies that its owner has been writing, plus the observation that here is a shiny cuff.

The second problem: Why did Watson go to the post-office? Holmes assumes a general rule here also: There are only three reasons why people go to a British post-office, namely, to post a letter, to buy stamps, or to send a telegram. The first two reasons are ruled out in this case, so only the third remains. The process of deduction is more apparent here, for the reasoning is more complex.

Another matter calling for remark is one concerning the *validity* of these arguments. All are valid; that is, the conclusions must be true if the premises are. But Holmes cannot be certain that his conclusions are true for he cannot be certain that the premises are true. The premises consist of facts—that is, statements about facts, based on observations—and general rules which are assumed to be true. But Holmes cannot be certain that his assumed general rules *are* true. Is the reddish earth found *only* at the post-office? Can't a shiny cuff be caused in other ways? Do people go to a British post-office for these three reasons alone? Can one be certain that there are just three and only three reasons? Can't one walk in just to look around, or to meet a friend, etc.? And can Holmes be certain that two of the three alternatives are impossible? May not Watson have bought more stamps, or posted a letter he wrote on the preceding day? But insofar as these assumptions are probable; that is, insofar as one is apt to be right in making these assumptions much more frequently than one is likely to be wrong, one's conclusions will be right more frequently than wrong.

The logical "method of exclusion" is one of Holmes' favorite methods: "Eliminate all other factors and the one which remains must be the truth." "The Sign of Four" contains another version of this principle: "When you have eliminated the impossible, whatever remains, *however improbable*, must be the truth." Referring to the suspect in this case, Holmes applies this principle as follows: "We know that he did not come through the door, the window, or the chimney. We also know that he could not have been concealed in the room, as there is no concealment possible—so he came through a hole in the roof."

The logical principle is this: If either "p" or "q" or "r" are the only possibilities, and "p" and "r" are impossible, then "q" must be true. The logic is impeccable; *if* we are certain that our alternatives actually do exhaust the possibilities, and *if* we are certain that all alternatives except one are ruled out, then we can conclude with certainty that we have the right answer.

Holmes sometimes speaks as if it were possible to reach inferences that are certain rather than probable. In "The Five Orange Pips," Watson remarks on "that absolute logical proof which was so dear to him," as contrasted with "explanation founded on conjecture and surmise." But we can never completely eliminate conjecture and surmise with respect to *the facts*, as distinguished from the logical *form* of the *argument*. When we observe a man with one hand much larger than the other, we cannot be sure that he has done manual labor. He may have been a baseball catcher. And there are times, also, when we find Holmes somewhat more modest. In "The Sign of Four" he examines Watson's watch and deduces that it once belonged to Watson's elder brother, who inherited it from his father; that the brother was an untidy and careless man who had been left with good prospects but threw away his chances; that he had lived for some time in poverty with occasional intervals of prosperity; and that he had finally died after taking to drink. Watson denounces him for pretending that he has read all this from the watch alone; surely Holmes must have made previous inquiries into the history of his unhappy brother. Holmes assures Watson that he never even knew that he had a brother until he examined the watch.

> "Then how in the name of all that is wonderful did you get these facts? They are absolutely correct in every particular."
>
> "Ah, that is good luck. I could only say what was the balance of probability. I did not at all expect to be so accurate."

Holmes then goes on to explain how he did it. The initials "H. W." on the back of the watch suggested "Watson." "The date of the watch is nearly fifty years back, and the initials are as old as the watch: so it was made for the last generation. Jewelry usually descends to the eldest son. Your father has, if I remember right, been dead many years. It has, therefore, been in the hands of your eldest brother. I then stated that your brother was careless. When you observe the lower part of that watch-case you notice that it is not only dented in two places but it is cut and marked all over from the habit of keeping other hard objects, such as coins or keys, in the same pocket. Surely it is no great feat to assume that a man who treats a fifty-guinea watch so cavalierly must be a careless man. Neither is it a very far-fetched inference that a man who inherits one article of such value is pretty well-provided for in other respects."

Watson nods to show that he follows Holmes's reasoning.

> "It is very customary for pawnbrokers in England, when they take a watch, to scratch the numbers of the ticket with a pinpoint upon the inside of the case. It is more handy than a label as there is no risk of the number being lost or transposed. There are no less than four such numbers visible to my lens on the inside of the case. Inference—that your brother was often at low water. Secondary inference—that he had occasional bursts of prosperity, or he could not have redeemed the pledge. Finally, I ask you to look at the inner plate, which contains the key-hole. Look at the thousands of scratches all around the hole—marks where the key has slipped. What sober man's key would have scored all those groves? But you will never see a drunkard's watch without them. He winds it at night, and he leaves these traces of his unsteady hand. Where is the mystery in all this?"

In the remainder of this chapter we shall consider Holmes' works as an illustration of scientific method (as outlined in Chapter XVI) and we shall note some of his reflections on various aspects of this method.

Thinking, we have noted, always begins with a problem. Holmes's mind was no exception. As is well-known, he was addicted to drugs in a moderate sort of way, but this was only when he lacked fascinating problems:

> "My mind," he said, "rebels at stagnation. Give me problems, give me work, give me the most abstruse cryptogram, or the most intricate analysis, and I am in my own proper atmosphere. I can dispense then with artificial stimulants. But I abhor the dull routine of existence. I crave for mental exaltation." ("The Sign of Four")

His active mind, of course, could see problems where most people saw none. He once wrote a paper in which he advised his readers to look for such problems in everyday life:

> Let him, on meeting a fellow-mortal, learn at a glance to distinguish the history of the man, and the trade or profession to which he belongs. Puerile as such an exercise may seem, it sharpens the faculties of observation, and teaches one where to look and what to look for. By a man's finger-nails,

> by his coat-sleeve, by his boots, by his trouser-knees, by the callosities of his forefinger and thumb, by his expression, by his shirt-cuffs—by each of these things a man's calling is plainly revealed. ("A Study in Scarlet")

But he is most in his element when the police call on him for help in a baffling crime. This is what happened in the first of the Sherlock Holmes stories, "A Study in Scarlet," in which an American named Enoch J. Drebber was found murdered in a house at 3, Lauriston Gardens, off the Brixton Road. There had been no robbery, and though there was blood in the room, there was no wound on the body of the deceased. Tobias Gregson, of Scotland Yard, wrote that he "would esteem it a great kindness if Holmes would favor him with his opinions." Shortly after this note was received, Watson writes, "we were both in a hansom, driving furiously for the Brixton Road."

The investigation has been initiated. Next comes Step 3, the observation of the relevant facts. Let us watch Holmes making his observations: Holmes insists on alighting from the hansom about a hundred yards from Lauriston Gardens. He examines the clayey soil for carriage marks and footprints. He then enters the house, and examines the body:

> His nimble fingers were flying here, there, and everywhere, feeling, pressing, unbuttoning, examining. . . . So swiftly was the examination made, that one would hardly have guessed the minuteness with which it was conducted. Finally, he sniffed the dead man's lips, and then glanced at the soles of his patent leather boots.

Holmes then turns his attention to the room:

> He whipped a tape measure and a large round magnifying glass from his pocket. With these two implements he trotted noiselessly about the room, sometimes stopping, occasionally kneeling, and once lying flat upon his face. . . . For twenty minutes or more he continued his researches, measuring with the most exact care the distance between marks which were entirely invisible to me, and occasionally applying his tape to the walls in an equally incomprehensible manner. In one

> place he gathered up very carefully a little pile of gray dust from the floor, and packed it away in an envelope. . . .
> "They say that genius is an infinite capacity for taking pains," he remarked with a smile. "It's a very bad definition, but it does apply to detective work."

Holmes is now ready to announce his theory or hypothesis concerning the presence of the dead man in the house off the Brixton Road:

> "There has been murder done, and the murderer was a man. He was more than six feet high, was in the prime of life, had small feet for his height, wore coarse, square-toed boots and smoked a Trichinopoly cigar. He came here with his victim in a four-wheeled cab, which was drawn by a horse with three old shoes and the new one on his off foreleg. In all probability the murderer had a florid face, and the fingernails of his right hand were remarkably long.
> "These are only a few indications," he says to Lestrade and Gregson, the Scotland Yard operatives, "but they may assist you."
> Lestrade and Gregson glanced at each other with incredulous smiles.
> "If this man was murdered, how was it done?" asked the former.
> "Poison," said Sherlock Holmes curtly, and strode off.

Now, how did Holmes get his hypothesis? By observation and deduction. Step 4 in our outline of scientific thinking is "the use of previous knowledge." This knowledge serves two purposes: It furnishes us with preliminary hypotheses concerning relevant factors; that is, it tells us what to look for; and it also tells us how to account for significant facts which turn up unexpectedly. Thus, in our present story, Holmes finds a dead man who shows no signs of external violence. The hypothesis of poison occurs to him (previous knowledge) and he then tests this preliminary hypothesis by sniffing the man's lips. His suspicions are confirmed and he announces "poison" as an explanatory hypothesis. We already know his methods in reconstructing the picture of the murderer.

Let us now consider some of Holmes's ideas concerning the role of the hypothesis in scientific method. While he and Watson were in the hansom on their way to the scene of the crime, he "prattled away about Cremona fiddles and the difference between a Stradivarius and an Amati." Watson finally interrupted his musical disquisition by remarking that he didn't seem to give much thought to the matter at hand. "No data yet," Holmes answered. "It is a capital mistake to theorize before you have all the evidence. It biases the judgment."

Holmes is partly right and partly wrong here. We should not formulate a *major* explanatory hypothesis or theory before all of the available evidence is in, but *preliminary* hypotheses are indispensable if one is to *observe* properly. As Darwin put it, "No one can be a good observer unless he is a good theorizer." Darwin's point is illustrated by Holmes himself in the story "Silver Blaze." In that story Holmes suspects that the murdered man had burned a wax taper in a hollow. Holmes descended into the hollow.

> Then stretching himself upon his face and leaning his chin upon his hands, he made a careful study of the trampled mud in front of him. "Hullo!" said he suddenly. "What's this?" It was a wax vesta, half burned, which was so coated with mud that it looked at first like a little chip of wood.
>
> "I cannot think how I came to overlook it," said the inspector with an expression of annoyance.
>
> "It was invisible, buried in the mud. I only saw it because I was looking for it."
>
> "What! You expected to find it?"
>
> "I thought it not unlikely."

On the other hand, Holmes is right in warning us against allowing preliminary theories to blind us against seeing the facts as they really are. We find what we look for, but we must see what is there, and not merely what we want to see. In "A Scandal in Bohemia" he warns us again that "it is a capital mistake to theorize before one has data." The reason is: "Insensibly one begins to twist facts to suit theories, instead of theories to suit facts." And in "Silver Blaze" he says that that case is one

> where the art of the reasoner should be used rather for the sifting of details than for the acquisition of fresh evidence . . . we are suffering from a plethora of surmise, conjecture, and hypothesis. The difficulty is to detach the framework of fact —of absolute undeniable fact—from the embellishments of theorists and reporters. Then, having established ourselves upon this sound basis, it is our duty to see what inferences may be drawn and what are the special points upon which the whole mystery turns.

The process of theorizing, in its relation to facts, then, is one that works both ways: Theories lead us to facts, and theories must be based upon the facts. But it is the preliminary theories that lead us to the facts on which our major, or explanatory hypothesis is based, and this explanatory hypothesis will then lead us to still more facts.

One more word concerning the explanatory hypothesis. This is the point at which insight and imagination are most important. A complete picture of the situation must be drawn up, in which all of the facts are seen to fit together. Imagination is needed to formulate such "pictures." Holmes neglects to mention the element of imagination when he says of a French detective . . . "he possesses two out of the three qualities necessary for the ideal detective. He has the power of observation and that of deduction. He is only wanting in knowledge, and that may come in time." But knowledge is not a substitute for imagination, and Holmes sees this clearly when he says of Inspector Gregory, in "Silver Blaze": "See the value of imagination. It is the one quality which Gregory lacks. We imagined what might have happened, acted upon the supposition, and find ourselves justified."

Let us return now to "A Study in Scarlet." Holmes has formulated a hypothesis. Though he is certain in his own mind—perhaps too certain—that he has solved the case with his hypothesis that the cause of Drebber's death was poison, the evidence is not yet complete. He must now test his hypothesis (Steps 6, 7, and 8). The deceased man's secretary is later found dead, with a box of pills near the body. Holmes predicts that they contain poison, and feeds them to his landlady's "poor little devil of a terrier," which has been sick so long that it is ready to be put out of its misery. On taking the poisonous pill the dog dies instantly. The hypothesis of poison has been verified. Predictions of this kind are found in many of the stories. He predicts, for example, that the members of the "Red-Headed League" will appear in the vaults of the bank adjoining Mr. Jabez Wilson's shop. They do.

We shall comment on one further aspect of Holmes' scientific method, as narrated in "A Study in Scarlet." When Holmes feeds the pills to the ailing terrier, the first pill proves harmless. Holmes had confidently expected the dog to die, and "an expression of the utmost chagrin and disappointment appeared upon his features. The two detectives smiled derisively, by no mean displeased at this check which he had met":

> "It can't be a coincidence," he cried, at last springing from his chair and pacing wildly up and down the room; "it is impossible that it should be a mere coincidence. The very pills which I suspected in the case of Drebber are found after the death of his secretary. And yet they are inert. What can it mean? Surely my whole chain of reasoning cannot have been false. It is impossible! And yet this wretched dog is none the worse. Ah, I have it! I have it!"

Holmes has decided that the box contains both harmless and poisoned pills. A second pill proves fatal.

> Sherlock Holmes drew a long breath, and wiped the perspiration from his forehead. "I should have more faith," he said; "I ought to know by this time that when a fact appears to be opposed to a long train of deductions, it invariably proves to be capable of bearing some other interpretation."

Holmes once again shows an over-reliance on the conclusiveness of his deductions as applied to the facts. But this fault, we have seen, sometimes leads to important discoveries. The spirit of Holmes's last remark reminds us irresistibly of Mendeleyev's attitude toward the supposed flaws in his theory of the periodicity of the elements.

XVIII.

KNOWING THE CAUSES OF THINGS

On May 12, 1951, the following item appeared in the *Chicago Daily News:* "The Kingsbury Ordnance plant, 9 miles southeast of La Porte, Indiana, had been troubled for weeks by little firecracker poppings of powder on the shell loading lines. The officials figured that static electricity was to blame, and they checked everything, including the shoe buckles and shoe strings of the 2000 employees, more than half of whom are women. The cause: the swishing of nylon bras, slips, and panties on the women. The women have all switched to cotton."

This item illustrates the "cause and effect" relation. Something goes wrong; we ask "Why?"—what caused things to go wrong? We then search for the cause. This is exactly what happens when a housewife finds that a cake did not turn out as expected: after being baked, it caved in. Her problem also is one of finding the cause, and her thinking resembles that of the officials at the Kingsbury plant, or the thinking of a biologist when he searches for the cause of a disease. The chief difference between the scientist and the housewife is that the former is a specialist who has vast stores of knowledge to aid him in solving such problems.

When Francis Bacon said: "Knowledge is power," he meant that science could give man mastery over the forces of nature by discoveries and inventions. Bacon's aphorism is a modern echo of the ancient poet Virgil's saying: "Happy is he who knows the causes of things." For, in large measure, man's power and control over nature have their origins in his understanding of the causal connections among events. Our understanding of causal connections enables us to improve the fertility of the soil; it is because we know the causes of diseases and other unpleasant occurrences that we can eliminate them. Perhaps some day we will know, more precisely, the causes of business depressions, and then the fear of widespread unemployment will disappear forever in the free world.

Before we proceed further, let us note the assumption which is taken for granted by the Kingsbury plant officials, the housewife, and the biologist, in our examples. This assumption is that everything has a cause. We believe that "things don't just happen by themselves," but that something is responsible for every single thing that happens. This assumption is sometimes called the "principle of determinism," and it is a postulate of rational thinking about the events of human experience. It is called an "assumption" or "postulate" because it is obviously impossible to prove that *everything* has a cause, including *all future* events. We don't even know the causes of all sorts of contemporary events, cancer, for example, but we are sure that there is a cause. Why are we sure? Because, we say, there *must* be a cause! The point of the principle is this: We have made up our minds not to regard any events as being beyond explanation. No events in human experience are inherently unexplainable.

Let us look at the semantical aspects of our problem: Exactly what do we mean by "cause"? In popular speech a cause means "that which is responsible for a thing's happening," or "the power that produces an event." These are question-begging definitions, however, for we immediately ask: What is meant by "responsible" and "produces"? The notion of *cause* is involved in the meaning of these words. Nevertheless we shall begin with the common-sense meanings of the term, and try to refine them as best we can.

Let us also examine the way in which the scientist uses the words "cause and effect." When a biologist tells us that yellow fever is caused by a filterable virus transmitted by the bite of a certain kind of mosquito, he means that when this virus enters a host body the host will suffer from yellow fever, and if an individual suffers from yellow fever then we know that this virus has entered his body. By "cause" the scientist means the *necessary* and the *sufficient* conditions for the occurrence of an event. These terms require definition.

A catarrhal affection of the respiratory tract, commonly called "a cold," is probably due to a virus. But this virus is presumably present in many persons all of the time, without their having "colds." The cold occurs when body resistance is lowered, owing to fatigue, or exposure to low temperatures, dampness, or drafts. If we can assume that this is the correct theory concerning some types of colds—there is no universal agreement on the matter—then the virus is not strictly the cause of the cold, but only an indispensable prerequisite. A necessary condition is defined as a condition *without which* an effect *cannot occur*. We have assumed that colds cannot occur unless the virus is present, so the virus is a *necessary condition* of the cold's occurrence.

A sufficient condition, on the other hand, is illustrated by the following: A murderer administers cyanide of potassium to his victim, and the victim dies. We say that the poison was the cause of death. But the relation of poison to death is quite different from the relation of the virus to the cold. Death may occur in other ways than by poisoning: old age, to give just one example. Poison (of a certain amount under certain conditions) is sufficient in itself to cause death, but it is not a necessary condition of death. In the former example, the virus is not sufficient to cause a cold, but there can be no cold without the virus.

In other words, some conditions are *necessary but not sufficient* for a given effect: the virus and colds. Some conditions are *sufficient but not necessary* for a given effect: poison and death. If a person has the virus in his body, he may or may not have a cold, but if he has a cold then we know he has the virus. If a certain amount of poison has been administered to man, then we know that he will die, but if all we know is that a person is dead, we do not know whether or not he was poisoned.[1]

Though scientists often speak of a sufficient condition as "the cause"—poison is a cause of death—and though they may even speak of a necessary condition as the cause, the scientist seeks for something more than *either* a necessary or a sufficient condition. He has an ideal conception of a cause as that set of conditions which are both *necessary* and *sufficient* to bring about a certain effect. The scientist seeks to know the entire constellation of conditions which will *always result* in the effect and *without which* the effect will *never occur.* C is the cause of E (in the ideal sense) when E always occurs following on C's occurrence, and E never occurs unless C has occurred.

This ideal notion of "cause" may be illustrated by considering a forest fire. A lighted cigarette is thrown into the brush by a camper. A forest fire results. Can we say that the cigarette was the cause of the fire? Common sense tells us that it is quite proper to speak in this way, but the scientist seeks a more accurate type of statement. He notes that no fire would have resulted if the leaves had been damp from a recent rain. Dry leaves, then, are a necessary condition for a forest fire. Dry leaves, plus an igniting element, plus sufficient wind, make up "the cause," for these are the necessary and sufficient conditions of a forest fire. Without any one of these conditions the forest fire would not occur; when all occur together a forest fire will always occur.

In law, and in the ordinary affairs of life, of course, the smoker would be held responsible. For in law and ordinary affairs we seek the causes of *individual events* in order to ascribe responsibility—the lawyer thinks of the cause as some identifiable act or event without which the result would not have occurred. The scientist, on the other hand, does not seek to ascribe "responsibility." He seeks for *general* causal connections, i.e., repeatable

[1] There is a certain vagueness in the notion of a condition that is "sufficient but not necessary." We speak rather loosely when we say that "death" may be caused by poison, drowning, etc., as if the end result were the same in each case. A coroner finds a different "biological picture" in each case, and there is only one kind of cause for each specific type of biological condition.

patterns in nature, and so he looks for the conditions that are both necessary and sufficient.

In practice, however, even scientists are often satisfied with less than the "ideal" statement of the cause. Nor is it always necessary to know the cause in the strict sense. It may be enough to learn either the necessary *or* the sufficient condition in order to achieve the purpose in mind. Practical considerations are involved here. It all depends on what one is after: to *produce* or to *prevent*. If scientists wish to *produce* something, such as a specific to cure a disease, or synthetic leather, or a stimulus to business activity, they need only know the sufficient conditions of these effects. If they wish to *prevent* or eliminate an effect, such as a disease, it is very helpful if they know the necessary conditions without which the disease cannot occur.

We shall now examine a famous example of the search for the cause of a disease. In the year 1910 the disease known as pellagra was widespread in many of our Southern states. Pellagra is characterized by skin eruptions, gastric disturbances, and nervous derangement. The problem became so serious that the U.S. Public Health Service sent its Dr. Goldberger to the State of Mississippi to search for the cause of the disease.[1]

In the early years of the twentieth century it was the prevailing doctrine among biologists that there was only one possible cause of disease, namely, germs or microbes. This is the "germ theory" of disease. It was therefore assumed, at that time, that pellagra must also be caused by a microbe. The *Webster International Unabridged Dictionary*, published in 1900, defined pellagra as "a disease caused by a microbic parasite," and added that it was probably carried by a fly. Now, one of the implications of the germ theory is that the disease will be "catching," i.e., infectious, and that it will be transmitted from one person to another through contact. Goldberger began with the hypothesis that the disease of pellagra was caused by microbes, and he first investigated to see whether there was personal contact among the victims. There was.

[1] The facts concerning Dr. Goldberger's investigations are taken, for the most part, from the story as told by Paul de Kruif in *Hunger Fighters* (Harcourt, Brace and Company).

Goldberger began with a preliminary hypothesis which told him what to look for. His first observations seemed to confirm his hypothesis. But he was a man who refused to take anything for granted, and he decided that it would be wise to test the microbe theory further before undertaking a full-scale search for the particular microbe which might be the cause of the disease. And so he reasoned as follows: If pellagra is catching, then whenever we find healthy people coming into contact with victims, under normal circumstances, the hitherto healthy persons will acquire the disease. He decided to test this implication by investigation. He visited a hospital, and he observed that the nurses, orderlies, and doctors were in close contact with the patients, and that they made no efforts to avoid such contacts. But none of the nurses, orderlies, or doctors had ever caught the disease from the patients. Goldberger thereupon decided that he was on the wrong track, and he rejected the hypothesis that microbes were the cause of pellagra.

Goldberger had predicted, on the basis of the then prevailing theory, that contact would cause the acquisition of the disease. The facts were against this theory, and so he abandoned it. For the scientist there is no such thing as "a good theory which does not work." If "the stubborn and irreducible facts" are against a theory, so much the worse for the theory. If a theory does not work, then it is a bad theory and must be discarded. The *apparent* exception to this rule is the case where the facts are misinterpreted, as in the Mendeleyev case.

Goldberger now had to make a completely fresh start. He was sure now that pellagra was not caused by microbes. He had to look elsewhere for the cause. He investigated further, and noted that only poor people seemed to suffer from the disease. He carefully observed their habits of living, especially their diets. He noted that the pellagra victims lived on a rather uniform diet, consisting of corn-meal mush, hominy grits, and similar foods. On one occasion, while visiting an orphanage, he found that some children suffered from pellagra, and others not. The pellagra victims, further, were all in the six to twelve age group. This was a surprising situation, and he made further inquiries. He was told that the children who were over twelve were required to work on the farm, and they were fed meat to provide them with the necessary energy. The children under six were given milk, since they were regarded as being in the "baby" stage. The orphanage's funds were very limited, and so the six to twelve group received no milk or fresh meat. They were too young to get meat and too old to get milk.

Goldberger now developed a new hypothesis: that a dietary deficiency, specifically, the absence of milk and fresh meat, is the cause of pellagra. He predicted that if the children in the six to twelve age group were supplied with milk or meat, their pellagra would disappear. The Public Health Service supplemented the children's diet with the missing ingredients, and all cases of pellagra in the orphanage were cured. His hypothesis was confirmed.

But science is a never-ending search for truth, and no proof is ever final. Even confirmed hypotheses will be subjected to retesting, again and again, for confirmation in previous experiments may have been due to the presence of special factors. Unknown factors may produce exceptional results in a specific case. So Goldberger did not stop at this point. And there was another reason why further tests were called for: Many scientists were still unconvinced that his investigations had actually disproved the germ theory. After all, they said, the *sufferers* from pellagra were *in contact* with each other, even though the attendants did not catch the disease. They may have been blessed with immunity. The critics wanted further proof. And we have seen, in the Mendeleyev case, that a stubborn refusal to give up a theory in the face of contrary evidence may in the end be justified.

Goldberger proceeded with new tests. He was given permission to try out a dietary experiment at one of the State's prison farms. He proposed to feed a group of convicts a special diet for six months, to test his hypothesis that a deficiency in diet is the cause of pellagra. Volunteers were asked for; the reward for participation was to be freedom after the experiment was finished. One or two lifers accepted, then several others, and he finally had twelve subjects, all of them in good health. The twelve convicts were isolated from the others, and fed almost nothing but white bread, corn pone, grits, sweet potatoes, salt pork, cane syrup, and cooked cabbage for six months. They received no milk or fresh meat. After several months of this diet, beginning in April of 1915, the twelve convicts became listless, they began to develop severe abdominal pains, and finally developed skin eruptions of the pellagra type. But the rest of the convicts at the prison farm suffered no such disorders.

Goldberger had now established a solid confirmation of his hypothesis that nutritional deficiencies alone are sufficient to cause pellagra. The convicts were now fed a proper diet and, as expected, all of them recovered and were given their freedom. No further proof of his hypothesis seemed to be necessary, but there were still some skeptics among the microbe theorists, and so Goldberger and his assistants decided to do one further experiment to convince the doubters. The experimenters performed this last test on themselves. They injected blood from pellagra victims into their own blood streams, and no ill effects followed. This was a crucial experiment, for if pellagra was caused by microbes, then they should have become infected. After this test it was an accepted fact among all biologists that pellagra was caused by nutritional deficiencies. Later research has confirmed Goldberger's findings; our knowledge today is simply more precise than his. It is not the absence of milk and fresh meat *as such* that causes pellagra, but rather the absence from the diet of certain factors in the vitamin B complex. These factors are found in muscle meats, milk, liver, kidney, fish, and green vegetables.

Goldberger's experiment with the convicts illustrates one of the most reliable scientific techniques for discovering causes. A careful analysis of the method employed in this case will enlighten us concerning the nature of a scientific proof that one kind of thing is the cause of another. This method requires the setting up of two situations which are identical except for the presence or absence of the factor which is being investigated. There were two sets of convicts at the prison farm: those who received a special diet and those who did not. The living conditions of both groups were identical except for the diet, and only those who were on the restricted diet got pellagra.

Goldberger's method may be made clearer by a somewhat more detailed example. Let us assume that a young woman, call her Susan, suffers from skin irritation and inflammation of the face. She seeks for the cause. The hypothesis occurs to her that it may be due to her use of face powder. She stops using the powder for a period of time, and the irritation disappears. She then uses the powder again, and the irritation reappears. She has solved her problem: She knows the cause of the irritation and how to avoid it. Face powder seems to be a necessary and sufficient condition for the occurrence of the irritation.

But this new-found knowledge does not make Susan completely happy. She hates to give up the use of face powder, for she isn't quite so attractive when she doesn't use it. The thought occurs to her that it may not be the powder as such that is the culprit but rather one of the ingredients contained in face powder. So she consults a chemist friend and asks him for a solution to her problem. The chemist makes an analysis of the powder, and finds that it contains six ingredients: talc, kaolin, magnesium carbonate, zinc oxide, ochre (for coloring), and perfume. The chemist now formulates the hypothesis that the perfume may be the cause of the irritation. To test this hypothesis he prepares a batch of face powder containing all the ingredients except the perfume, and he then divides this batch into two parts, to one of which he adds perfume. Susan now uses the powder without perfume and suffers no ill effects. Then she tries the part with the perfume added, and irritation appears. This is sufficient proof that she is allergic to the perfume in the face powder, and not to the powder itself. (Or to some ingredient in the perfume.)

The method we have been illustrating is sometimes called the laboratory or "controlled experiment" method for determining cause and effect. The English philosopher, John Stuart Mill, who pioneered in the field of scientific logic, called it the "Method of Difference." The basic idea is to use two cases, identical in all respects except one. In the face-powder example this method was used twice, first to determine that the original powder was the cause of the irritation and then to determine that it was a specific element in the powder and not the powder as such that was the cause. Goldberger also used this method, for he kept all living conditions for his two groups of convicts identical except for one factor: the diet. "Identical," of course, means "the same in all respects that are considered relevant to the experiment." This kind of identity is achieved most perfectly in the sciences of physics and chemistry, where we can be fairly certain that there are no relevant factors outside the conditions of the experiment. This method can also be applied with a large degree of precision in the biological sciences.

The most important point to remember in applying this method is to keep the two groups of things identical (or substantially the same) *except for one element*. If the "addition" of this element results in the effect, and if the effect never occurs when it is absent, then we have found the probable cause. But it is not always possible to apply this method, for it may be impossible to isolate one factor and keep all others the same. This is especially true in the social sciences. The variables involved in human actions are exceedingly large in number, and human behavior is vastly more complex than is the career of a germ. Since we cannot be sure that we have accounted for all the relevant factors in a situation, we cannot be sure that we have an identity of all factors except one. An illustration or two may be helpful here. Suppose we try to isolate a single factor to explain why X defeated Y in an election. Let us assume that X favored the extension of civil rights and Y did not. If it is claimed that this was the reason for his victory, we must look to see whether all other factors were substantially the same. Were the men equally able, and did they agree pretty much on all other issues? Did they have the same number of influential friends and enemies, did they have equal campaign funds, etc? The attitude toward civil rights may have been a factor in X's victory, but not necessarily the cause, or even the most important factor.

Let us now examine a sociological problem. Consider the difficulties in applying the differential method to the problem of juvenile delinquency. Can we find two individuals, one a delinquent, and one a good junior citizen, in whom all characteristics except one are alike? It is unlikely that their antecedents and experience will differ in one respect and one respect only. No two individuals are identical except for a single difference. Similar considerations apply to such problems as finding the causes of divorce, or war, or dope-addiction. But many people apply the Method of Difference carelessly, forgetting that other conditions are not the same. The next time someone tells you that he knows "the cause" of war, or juvenile delinquency, or some other social evil, check to see whether he has isolated a single causal factor, all others remaining the same. If not, has he used one of the other causal methods to be described shortly?

These difficulties have led some social scientists to abandon the search for the "causes" of social behavior and to limit themselves to a search for "tendencies" stated in statistical form. Children from broken homes, for example, may show a greater tendency toward delinquency than those from stable families. If so, that would be useful knowledge. A tendency, however, is simply a modest way of indicating a possible causal connection.

When appropriate, and when properly applied, the Method of Difference, or the differential method, is the most convincing possible kind of proof that we have found the cause. But sometimes it is impossible to apply this method.

We turn now to a second method for determining the causes of events. This method is called the "Method of Variations," known in statistics as the "Method of Correlations." Examples: A manufacturer of cosmetics uses newspaper advertising to sell his product. Each ad contains a coupon offering the reader a free sample. The advertiser finds that an increase in the lineage of the ad brings in a larger number of coupons; a decrease brings a smaller number. An increase in the crop of oranges (other things "being equal") is followed by lower prices; a smaller crop by higher prices. In other words, if two kinds of factors vary "directly," so that an increase in one factor is always followed by an increase in a second, and a decrease by a decrease (the cosmetics example), or if they vary "inversely," so that an increase is always followed by a decrease, and a decrease by an increase (the orange crop), then there is a good reason to suspect a causal relation between the two factors. They vary together, or concomitantly.

There are of course possibilities of error in applying this method. It has been pointed out that there is a tendency for women's dresses to be shortened during periods of "prosperity" (the 1920's, the period of the second World War, and, as we know, they reached new heights in the unparalleled boom of the 60's), and lengthened in periods of depression (1932). But the correlation may be an "accidental" one. It was once discovered that over a period of time the number of storks in Sweden varied in precise proportion to the number of human births in the United States, but this does not prove a causal relation between the two factors. We should also seek other kinds of evidence which make it reasonable to believe that a causal relation does in fact exist.

A third method, called the "Method of Agreement," seeks a common factor in the conditions which precede the effect that interests us. If a single common factor is discovered, this often gives us some probability that we have found the cause. For example, the public health authorities in a small town were confronted with an outbreak of typhoid fever. The authorities investigated the food and beverages consumed by the victims just prior to the outbreak of the fever, and found that all of the victims had just one thing in common: they had all attended a picnic and had drunk from the water in a well at the picnic grounds. Since this was the only common factor, it was a reasonable inference that the well was contaminated. Laboratory tests showed that the water contained the typhoid bacillus.

The Method of Agreement, or "common factor method," is not so convincing as the differential method, but it is useful when the more precise method cannot be applied. The Method of Agreement also is subject to careless applications. As an example of the dangers involved in the use of this method, consider the anecdote concerning the man who wished to find the cause of his becoming intoxicated every time he attended a cocktail party. This man had heard of the success of the public health authorities in using the "common factor method," and he decided to emulate them. He looked for the single common factor in the beverages he had imbibed on each occasion when he became intoxicated. After making an exhaustive study of the matter, he found that intoxication followed after drinking bourbon and soda, Scotch and soda, rye and soda, rum and soda, brandy and soda, and vodka and soda. Since soda was the only common factor in every instance, he concluded that soda was the cause, and at the next party he attended he insisted on drinking his whiskey straight!

Thus far we have examined methods which tell us how to search for causes, and how to discover them. It is also well to remember two *negative* tests which must be "passed" by hypotheses which assert a causal connection. The tests are these: (1) Nothing can be the cause if the effect fails to occur in its presence, and (2) Nothing can be the cause if the effect occurs in its absence. Let us illustrate.

Dr. Goldberger eliminated microbes as a possible cause of pellagra, for, although microbes are always carried in the blood stream, pellagra failed to occur when the blood of victims was injected into the blood streams of the investigators. Microbes are *not* the cause of pellagra, then, for the effect (pellagra) failed to occur in their presence. An ancient Roman, Pliny the Elder (A.D. 23–79) once disproved the claims of the astrologers by using the same test. "If a man's destiny is caused by the star under which he is born," Pliny wrote, "then all men born under the same star should have the same fortune. But masters and slaves, kings and beggars are born under the same star at the same time." In other words, the star cannot be the cause of a particular kind of destiny, for in its presence that particular kind of destiny fails to occur. One more example: the belief that a "broken home" is the cause of juvenile delinquency. But not all children from broken homes become delinquents. There may be some connection, of course, but we cannot yet speak in terms of "cause and effect."

The second negative test may also be illustrated by the delinquency case. Children from stable homes sometimes become delinquents. The effect has occurred in the absence of the factor "broken home," so this cannot be the "cause" of delinquency. All too often we forget to apply the negative test. We often jump to the conclusion that one thing is the cause of another because we forget that there may be negative evidence. This happens most frequently when our emotions cause us to try to prove what our hearts desire. Sir Francis Bacon called this tendency to ignore evidence that does not suit our purposes, an "Idol of the Tribe," by which he meant a faulty habit of thinking, common to the human race.[1] In Aphorism 45 of his *Novum Organum* he gave a striking example of this error:

> And therefore it was a good answer that was made by one who, when they showed him hanging in a temple a picture of those who had paid their vows and then escaped shipwreck, and would have him say whether he did not now acknowledge the power of the gods—"Aye," asked he, "but where are they painted that were drowned after their vows?" And such is the way of all superstition, whether in astrology, dreams, omens, divine judgments, or the like; wherein men, having a delight in such vanities mark the events where they are fulfilled, but where they fail, though this happens much oftener, neglect and pass them by.

The search for causes, as we have seen, is beset with numerous forms of fallacious reasoning. Perhaps the most important of the general fallacies in causal reasoning is the "post hoc," an abbreviation for the Latin expression "*post hoc, ergo propter hoc*": "after this, therefore because of this." This means: The fact that one thing follows upon another is no proof that the first is the cause of the second. For example, I have a pain in my shoulder and take a pink pill. A little later the pain disappears. I say that the pill was the cause of the disappearance of the pain. Why? Because I took the pill and then the pain disappeared. But the mere

[1] This is one of Bacon's "Four Idols," his famous classification of the basic types of errors in thinking. The "Idol of the Tribe" refers to faulty habits of thinking common to all of us; "Idol of the Cave" refers to errors peculiar to individuals, each of whom has his own personal slant or bias (the individual mind is like a dark cave); "Idol of the Theater" refers to our unthinking acceptance of authority and traditional ideas: we accept these ideas passively, like spectators at the theater. "Idol of the Market Place," finally, refers to errors that are based on a faulty understanding of the nature of language, the instrument of human communication. "Market place" refers to the arenas of discussion. One of Bacon's illustrations of the last Idol is our tendency to take words as guarantees of facts. We discussed this as an item in "Semantics."

fact that one thing follows another is no proof that the first is the cause of the second. To prove a causal connection we must use one of the procedures discussed earlier. It may be that the pain would have disappeared even if I had not taken the pill. An effect, of course, always follows the cause. When one thing follows another the first *may* be the cause, but more proof must be forthcoming before we can say "proved." Mere succession in time is not proof.

I have finished my lunch in a restaurant, and light a cigarette. The moment I do so a waitress drops a tray of dishes. Event "x" was followed by event "y" but it would appear unlikely that there is any connection whatsoever between them. Mr. Hoover became President in March of 1929. About seven months later the stock market crashed, ushering in the great depression. Isn't that *proof*, we ask, that Mr. Hoover was the cause of the depression? During the election campaign of 1940 Wendell Willkie noted that the birth rate had fallen off sharply about the time that Roosevelt became President (1933). Did he imply that Roosevelt was responsible for the decrease in procreation? A succession of events *may* involve a causal connection, as in the sharp increase in births in New York City following upon the Great Blackout of October, 1965. The fact that the increase came nine months later indicates the likelihood of some connection. In this case the inference is based on more than mere succession in time.

And here are some more post hocs: Old man Jones celebrates his one hundredth birthday and the newspaper reporters, as usual, are on hand, curious to know just how he did it. "Well," says old man Jones, "I drink a pint of beer every day." He drank a pint of beer and he lived another day, and he did this again and again. But there are teetotalers who live until one hundred, and some beer drinkers have been known to die young. Post hoc reasoning is common also at baseball parks. A fan yells, "Hit a home run!" and the batter hits one over the fence. It will be difficult indeed to convince this fan that his yell was not the cause of the home run. Baseball players are notoriously superstitious, and their superstitions are based on post hoc reasoning. Their managers are superstitious too. If a manager fails to shave on the day when his team ends a losing streak, he will probably assume that his failure to shave was the cause of the victory, and allow his beard to grow until his team loses again. A recent example of post hoc reasoning: In the early months of 1953 the United States was plagued with a succession of tornadoes. Prior to the occurrence of these tornadoes several atomic bombs had been tested in Nevada. This was quite sufficient evidence for many people. They were absolutely certain that the bombs were the cause of the tornadoes.

Another error in causal reasoning is that of reversing the connection between the cause and the effect. An English writer once argued that since those among the English poor who had cows were the most industrious, the way to make the others industrious was to give them cows. Though the writer's reasoning was fallacious, he may, nevertheless, have a point. Is it not possible that, with cows to care for, many people would become more industrious, and more concerned with their own welfare? The next example is a clearer example of the fallacy of reversing cause and effect: We find that students who major in mathematics generally rank high scholastically. This is considered proof that the study of mathematics makes students bright. But perhaps only bright students major in mathematics.

The error of reversing cause and effect puts the cart before the horse. An interesting application of this reasoning occurs in the frequent controversies concerning the "low cultural level" of TV programming. We accuse the television industry of debasing the taste of the public by a "vast wasteland" of low-quality shows. The industry retorts that it gives the public what it wants; if it aims higher it will lose money. The industry claims that it is the low taste of the public that is responsible for a situation that they too deplore. This situation is one of *reciprocal* causation. The low taste affects the industry, and the industry may further debase an already low taste. This is the familiar "vicious" circle. But there is also a "beneficial" circle. If the programs improve, taste will improve, and then the spiral will be reversed.

One final point. Suppose we find that students who smoke heavily are less successful in their studies than students who don't smoke. It would be a mistake to conclude from this that smoking is the cause of low grades. It may be so, but the facts cited are not proof that it is. For it may be that both the heavy smoking and the low grades are due to other factors, such as personality traits, lack of academic interests, extracurricular activities, or other factors.

A summary of this chapter may not be unwelcome. We defined a "cause" as the set of necessary and sufficient conditions of an event. When we say that X is the cause of Y we mean: (1) if X occurs, Y will always occur; that is, that X is the *sufficient* condition of Y, and (2) if X does not occur, Y will not occur; that is, that X is the *necessary* condition of Y. This is the meaning of "cause" in the ideal sense of the term; in practice scientists are often satisfied when they know either the sufficient or the necessary conditions.

We then noted three methods used by scientists in discovering causes: the methods of Difference, Variations, and Agreement. The first is the most rigorous of these methods, but it demands complete control over all of the factors in a situation, and so is difficult to apply outside of the physical and biological sciences. Two situations must be exactly alike except for the presence or absence of a single factor, the effect occurring when this single factor is present.

These three methods tell us what the cause *is;* but there are also methods for eliminating "false causes," which tell us what the cause *is not:* "Nothing can be the cause in whose absence the effect occurs," "Nothing can be the cause in whose presence the effect fails to occur."

We noted some of the errors or fallacies which result from the careless use or application of the methods, and we concluded with a discussion of some of the fallacies with which the search for causes is beset. The major fallacy is called the "post hoc": the assumption that if Y follows X, this in itself is sufficient proof that X is the cause of Y. We also reverse causes and effects, and we sometimes assume that when two things are associated with each other, one must be the cause of the other, when actually both may have a common cause.

XIX.

ARE ALL GENERALIZATIONS FALSE?

We begin with a generalization: human beings are great generalizers. Every race has its proverbs, and proverbs are generalizations. "It never rains but it pours." "Faint heart never won fair lady." "Familiarity breeds contempt." Sometimes, of course, these proverbs are incompatible with each other, as in "Absence makes the heart grow fonder," and "Out of sight, out of mind."[1]

Listen attentively to those around you, and note the generalizations that float into every conversation: Europeans are lazy and shiftless. European girls make good wives. American girls are selfish. Politicians are crooks. Gentlemen prefer blondes. On a somewhat more "intellectual" level, we find: Liberals never think a matter through. Intellectuals always show a lack of practical judgment. Americans are idealists. Americans are materialists. All American men suffer from "mom-ism." Economics is bunk. Modern art is trash. Psychiatrists never bring up their own children properly. In the middle ages everyone was religious. And so on. After more of the same we may be tempted to agree with Justice Holmes that "the chief end of man is to frame general propositions, and no general proposition is worth a damn."

[1] Once translated by a foreign student as "invisible idiot."

Our awareness of the inadequacy of "sweeping generalizations" may lead us to say that all generalizations are false. But this is truly a sweeping generalization! And worse: if it is true, then the witticism that "all generalizations are false, *including this one*" would appear to be justified. But this will not do either, for this generalization asserts that it itself is false, from which it follows that it is not the case that all generalizations are false. Or perhaps we should say that "all generalizations are half-truths–including this one"? But this is not much better. The fact of the matter is that some generalizations are true, others are false, and still others are uncertain or doubtful. The deadliness of this platitude may be forgiven because of its truth.

By a "generalization" is meant a general law or principle which is inferred from particular facts. As a sample of the way in which we arrive at such generalizations consider the following: Some years ago I visited France, and ate at a number of Parisian restaurants that had been recommended to me. The food was excellent in each. Then one day I was unable to get to any of my customary eating places. I ate in a small restaurant in an outlying district of Paris. The food was excellent. I then tried other restaurants, always with the same results. I ate in large restaurants, small restaurants, on ships and trains, and in railway station restaurants. I generalized: All French restaurants serve excellent meals.

A generalization is a statement that *goes beyond* what is actually observed, to a rule or law covering both the observed cases and those that have not as yet been observed. This going-beyond is called the "inductive leap." An inductive leap is a "leap in the dark," for the *generalization may not be true*, even though the *observations* on which it is based *are* true. Thus, somewhere in France there may be a poor French restaurant–happily I am ignorant of its location–but if so, then I should not say that *all* are good.[1]

A generalization involves an "inductive leap." The word *induction*, from Latin roots meaning "to lead in," means that we ex-

[1] Since writing this, unhappily, I have found several. But let us assume that the generalization is true.

amine particular cases (French restaurants), and "lead in" to a generalization. Induction is the method we use when we learn lessons from our experience: we generalize from particular cases. *Deduction*, on the other hand, refers to the process of "drawing out" the logical consequences of what we already know (or assume) to be true. By induction we learn that French cooking is delectable. If a friend tells us that he had tasteless meals while in Europe, then by deduction we know that he did not eat these meals in French restaurants. Both induction and deduction are essential characteristics of rational thinking.

A generalization is a statement of the form: "All A's are B's." "All" means exactly what it says: *all* without exception. A single exception overthrows a generalization of this kind. Before we proceed further we must first dispose of a popular confusion concerning the expression: "The exception proves the rule." This is a sensible statement when properly interpreted, but it is sometimes understood in a manner that makes it nonsense. If I say that "all A's are B's," a single exception will make my statement false. Now, suppose that someone says: "The fact that there is a poor French restaurant proves that *all* are good because *it* is an exception, and the exception proves the rule!" Does a wicked woman prove that all women are saints? The sensible interpretation of the expression, "The exception proves the rule" is this: When we *say* that a certain case *is* an "exception," we imply that there is a rule which generally holds. When a mother tells her daughter, "Have a good time at the prom, and, for tonight, you have my permission to stay out until 3 A.M.," she implies that this is an exception to the rule which requires earlier reporting. A statement that *creates* an exception implies a rule for all non-exceptional cases; but a generalization that is stated as a rule without exceptions (all A's are B's) would be overthrown by a single exception.

Scientific laws, stated in the form "All A's are B's," or some variation thereof, are never "violated." When an exception to a law is definitely established, the law in its previous form is abandoned, but it may be possible to revise it to exclude the "exception" as a special case because of special circumstances. The revised law: "All A's, under such and such conditions, are B's." Water freezes at 32° F. *at sea level.*

All too often "general propositions are not worth a damn," as Holmes remarked. This is because we generalize too hastily on the basis of insufficient evidence. The fallacy called the "hasty generalization" simply refers to the fact that we jump too quickly to conclusions concerning "all." For example, we see a woman driving carelessly, and generalize: "All women are poor drivers." We see a car weaving in and out of traffic, and note that it has a California license: "Wouldn't you know," we say. "A California driver. That's the way they all drive out there." Anita Loos' gay heroine thought that gentlemen preferred blondes because she was a blonde and men were attracted to her.

We learn that Napoleon got along on five hours of sleep. From this we may conclude that "five hours of sleep is all that anybody really needs." Our assumption is that what Napoleon could do, anybody can do, until we learn that we are not Napoleons. (If we don't learn this eventually, we aren't permitted to circulate freely.) The next example is undoubtedly the worst example of generalizing ever committed: A man declared that all Indians walk single file. When challenged for his evidence, he replied, "How do I know that? I once saw an Indian walk that way."

Hasty generalizing is perhaps the most important of popular vices in thinking. It is interesting to speculate on some of the reasons for this kind of bad thinking. One important factor is prejudice. If we are already prejudiced against unions, or businessmen, or lawyers, or doctors, or Jews, or Negroes, then one or two instances of bad conduct by members of these groups will give us the unshakable conviction that "they're all like that." It is very difficult for a prejudiced person to say, "Some are, and some aren't." A prejudice is a judgment formed *before* examining the evidence.

A psychological reason for asserting "wild" generalizations is exhibitionism: The exhibitionist desires to attract attention to himself. No one pays much attention to such undramatic statements as "Some women are fickle," or that some are liars, or

"Some politicians are no better than they ought to be." But when one says that "all women are liars" this immediately attracts notice. Goethe once said that it is easy to appear brilliant if one respects nothing, not even the truth.

Let us avoid careless and hasty generalizing. The proverb warns us that one swallow does not make a summer. Unfortunately, we usually forget proverbs on the occasions when we ought to remember them. We ought to emulate "the Reverend" in Faulkner's novel, *The Hamlet*. He was discussing the efficacy of a rural remedy. "Do you know it will work, Reverend?" his friend asked. "I know it worked once," the Reverend answered. "Oh, then you have knowed it to fail?" "I never knowed it to be tried but once." The fault of bad generalizing, however, need not make us take refuge in the opposite error: the refusal to generalize. This error is illustrated in the anecdote concerning the student who wrote an essay on labor relations, in which he argued for equal pay for women. Women, he wrote, work hard, they need the money, they are the foundation of the family, and, above all, they are the mothers of most of the human race! There is another old anecdote about the cautious man whose friend pointed to a flock of sheep with the remark, "Those sheep seem to have been sheared recently." "Yes," said the cautious man, "at least on this side."

Generalizations are dangerous, but we must generalize. To quote Justice Holmes once more: he said that he welcomed "anything that will discourage men from believing general propositions." But, he added, he welcomed that "only less than he welcomed anything that would encourage men to make such propositions"! For generalizations are indispensable guides. One of the values of knowledge lies in its predictive power—its power to predict the future. Such knowledge is stated in generalizations. It is of little help to me to know that water froze at 32° F. yesterday unless this information serves as a warning to put anti-freeze in my car radiator before winter comes. History, in the "pure" sense of this term, merely tells us what has happened in the past, but science furnishes us with general laws, and general laws tell us what *always* happens under certain specified conditions.

Science is interested in the general, rather than in the particular or individual. When Newton saw an apple fall from a tree in his orchard—even if this story is a fable, and therefore false in a literal sense, it is true in its insight—he was not interested in the size and shape of the apple. Its fall suggested an abstract law to him, the law of gravity. He framed this law in general terms: Every particle of matter attracts every other particle of matter with a force directly proportional to the product of their masses and inversely proportional to the square of their distances. Chemists seek general laws concerning the behavior of matter. The physician wants to know the general characteristics of the disease called myxedema, so that when he has a case he will recognize it and know exactly how to treat it. The finding of general laws, then, is the aim of all science—including history insofar as it is a science.

The problem of the scientist is one of achieving sound generalizations. The scientist is careful not to make assertions which outrun his evidence, and he refuses to outtalk his information. He generalizes, but recognizes that no generalization can be more than probable, for we can never be certain that *all* the evidence is in, nor can the future be guaranteed absolutely—not even future eclipses of the sun and moon. But the scientist knows that certain laws have a very high degree of probability.

Let us look at the logic involved in forming sound generalizations. The number of cases investigated in the course of formulating a scientific law is a factor in establishing the truth of the law, but it is by no means the most important one. Obviously, if we observed one hundred swans, all of which are white, our generalization that "all swans are white" does not have the same probability it would have if we observed one thousand swans. But no matter how great the number of specimens involved in this type of observation, no more than a moderately high degree of probability is ever established. Countless numbers of white swans were observed throughout the ages (without any exceptions) and then in the nineteenth century black swans were observed in Australia.

The weakness of the method of "induction by simple enumeration of cases" is amusingly illustrated by Bertrand Russell's parable in his *A History of Western Philosophy:*

> There was once upon a time a census officer who had to record the names of all householders in a certain Welsh village. The first that he questioned was called William Williams; so were the second, third, fourth. . . . At last he said to himself: "This is tedious; evidently they are all called William Williams. I shall put them down so and take a holiday." But he was wrong; there was just one whose name was John Jones."

Scientific generalizations based on other types of evidence than simple enumeration often acquire a much higher degree of probability after only a few observations. When a chemist finds that pure sulphur melts at 125° C., in an experiment in which every factor is accurately analyzed and controlled, the law concerning the melting point of sulphur achieves as great a degree of certainty as is humanly attainable. Accurate control of every element of one case, then, is more important in establishing probabilities than is *mere enumeration* of many cases.

A single carefully controlled experiment, such as the sulphur experiment, can give us a much higher degree of probability than the mere observation of thousands of swans. The reason is that we also know that no chemical element thus far observed has a variable melting point under conditions of constant pressure. The chemical law is thus consistent with and is borne out by the rest of chemical knowledge, whereas the "law" holding that all swans are white was based on an "accidental" factor. Or consider the generalization concerning the mortality of mankind. This law is based not merely on the fact that countless numbers of human beings have died in the past, but also on the fact that all living beings must, by reason of physiological limitations, die; and that all matter wears out in time. So the harmony of a particular generalization with the rest of our knowledge is also a factor in giving it a high degree of probability.

So much for the logical analysis of generalizations. Thus far, we have been concerned with "uniform" generalizations, which take the form: "All A's are B's." A generalization, we have seen, is a statement that says something about "all" of a group, the evidence consisting of observations of items in which we always find a single characteristic. The observed cases are taken as a *sample* of the whole group or population with which we are concerned. We observe a number of swans, and take these as a sample of all swans, past, present, and future. We find that all are white, and make the inductive leap: Swans are always white, everywhere.

We shall now examine "statistical" statements. Statistical statements give us information not about characteristics possessed by *all* of a group or population, but by a definite proportion (or most) of the group or population, as when we say, "Most A's are B's," or "Sixty-five per cent of all A's are B's." The first thing to note here is that statistical statements may in fact be *generalizations*, and thus involve the notion of "all." This point involves very important (and common) misunderstandings.

In order to make this point clear, let us re-interpret our "uniform" generalizations. We say: "The sample is so-and-so (all observed swans are uniformly white)—*therefore*, the whole population of swans is uniformly white." Now, we do the same sort of thing in statistical generalizations. We say: "In the sample of red-heads we examined, fifty-three per cent were hot-tempered—therefore, fifty-three per cent of *all* red-heads are hot-tempered." (Or: fifty-three per cent of the whole population of red-heads is hot-tempered.) Logically, both examples, uniform and statistical, are of the same type, for in each we make the inductive leap from the sample to the whole population. The only difference between them is that in the one case we assert a *uniform* character in the whole population; in the other we assert that a characteristic holds in a certain *proportion* in the whole population.

This fundamental point will help us to evaluate the degree of probability of a statistical generalization. We saw earlier that uniform generalizations can never be absolutely certain—though for practical purposes we often consider them so, especially in the physical sciences. The probability of a generalization depends especially on the *quality* and also on the *quantity* of the cases that constitute the sample. The same holds for statistical generalizations, which may have a high probability, depending on the character of the evidence. Though the inductive leap is involved in all generalizations, in some cases the leap is justified. Let us examine the criteria of justification for the leap.

Before we proceed we shall discuss an important distinction: that between the sample and the inference we draw from it. It is one thing to describe a sample accurately; quite another to draw an accurate inference. If I say, "I have observed ten swans (the sample) and all were white," we may assume that the sample is accurately described. But if I now go on to generalize (that is, draw the inference) concerning *all* swans, my inference may not be a good one. A generalization always involves a "leap in the dark," sometimes justified and sometimes not. Similarly, if I say, "I have talked to ten friends concerning their income, and six [sixty per cent] told me that they earned more than $10,000 a year," the description of the sample may be accepted as true. But suppose I now go on to make the following inference: "Therefore, sixty per cent of all Americans earn more than $10,000 a year." This would be a hasty generalization indeed.

We distinguish, then, between the sample and the inference. A statistical statement concerning the sample is purely descriptive. The book *They Went to College* is a statistical study of the incomes, as of 1947, of 9,064 college graduates. The averages that were given may be of historical interest. Fifty-three per cent were in business, sixteen per cent were doctors, lawyers or dentists, sixteen per cent were teachers. The doctors earned the most: over half making more than $7,500 a year. Teachers and preachers earned the least: median income $3,584. Now, these averages involve no inferences. They simply describe the actual facts *in the sample*. We draw an inference, on the other hand, when we assume that the whole population of six million college graduates in 1947 would have shown the same kinds of averages as the sample. In our discussion, henceforth, we shall be concerned only with the logical problems involved in statistical inferences.

Suppose that a public opinion poll was recently taken. The polling organization tells us that fifty-eight per cent of the

American people approve of the record of the present administration in Washington. How do they know this? Let us examine the evidence on which this finding is based. Obviously not everyone was consulted. A sample was taken. There were three thousand interviews. Since there are approximately one hundred and twenty million adults in the United States, each individual in this sample is taken as representative of forty thousand adults. Further, in the sample, one thousand persons said that they had "no opinion." Eleven hundred and sixty said that they "approved," and eight hundred and forty said they did not. Thus fifty-eight per cent of those with opinions approved, and this means, we are told, that nearly seventy million Americans approve. The pollsters assume that the undecided individuals will probably divide in the same proportion as the others when they make up their minds.

Now, we are not raising any questions concerning the truth of the report made of the sample. But is the inductive leap from the sample to the generalization concerning one hundred and twenty million people justified? It may be. It all depends upon the reliability of the sample. What makes a sample reliable? It must be *fair*, *unbiased*, and *representative* of the whole. But the crucial problem is to determine whether or not it has these characteristics.

The size of the sample is obviously important. A sample of one hundred would not be so reliable as one of one thousand, and one thousand would not be so reliable as one of a million. But large numbers in themselves may not be the most important factor in establishing the reliability of generalizations or inferences.

The unimportance of large numbers as such is best illustrated by the ill-fated *Literary Digest* presidential election poll in 1936. The magazine sent pre-election ballots to ten million persons, and received over two million responses. The responses showed Landon running ahead of Roosevelt. In the election in November, however, Roosevelt got about twenty-eight million votes; Landon around eighteen million.

The reason for this colossal failure was the unrepresentative character of the sample. The *Digest* took names "at random" from telephone directories and lists of registered owners of automobiles. These were relatively well-to-do folk. The lower income groups, however, were completely, or almost completely, unrepresented.

An ideal sample is one taken "at random" from the entire population, and not from a selected portion of the population being studied. The Gallup poll, for example, uses a special kind of random sampling, and, barring a spectacular failure in 1948, has been far more successful than the *Literary Digest* poll. Let us see how the Gallup poll operates. A sample of three thousand individuals is taken, but with great care to make the sample representative. The population is classified into sub-groups by geographic regions, by rural or urban residence, economic status, age, education, and declared politics. In 1948, for example, Gallup estimated that twenty-eight per cent of the American people lived in the Middle Atlantic states, ten per cent on the West Coast; that thirty-four per cent lived in cities of over 100,000 population; that twenty-three per cent were of an "average" economic station; that forty-three per cent were between the ages of thirty and forty-nine; that forty-two per cent had gone to high school; and that thirty-eight per cent called themselves Democrats, thirty-six per cent Republicans, and twenty-six per cent independents or members of smaller parties. The three thousand interviews in the sample were distributed so that each geographic area, each economic group, etc., would be represented in its appropriate numerical strength.

Individuals are then chosen "at random," rather than by selection, from within each sub-group, and the resulting sample is highly representative of the whole population. The Gallup poll enjoys a successful record, on the whole, except for 1948. In other words, the method works, and one must respect its findings. But no poll can ever eliminate the possibility of error, or guarantee accuracy except within a margin of error of several percentage points. And in a presidential election forecast the pollster is either completely right or completely wrong in predicting who will win. Odds of 10 to 1 against a candidate of one of the major parties are probably not justified even if all the polls are confidently unanimous as to the final results. These were the odds against Harry Truman in the presidential election of 1948!

An election prediction can be judged by the election results, and a long series of successful predictions gives us confidence in the methods of the pollsters. This check cannot be made on polls which tabulate public opinion on issues of the day, for the whole population is never counted. Similarly for polls which rate television shows, for the whole audience is not counted. Such polls, of course, also generalize on the basis of samples. To illustrate the logical problems in assessing the reliability of a statistical study of the "public opinion poll" type we shall comment on *Sexual Behavior in the Human Female*, by Alfred C. Kinsey and his staff.

Kinsey's study, published in 1950, tabulates and classifies data concerning 5,940 white American females, ages two to ninety. He did not claim that his averages necessarily apply to all human females, despite the title of his book, nor even to all American women, of whom there were approximately seventy millions in 1950. It is inevitable, however, that such inferences will be drawn, and our question is: Are such inferences justified? This depends entirely on the representativeness of Kinsey's sample.

Critics of Kinsey's report have emphasized the unrepresentativeness of his sample. His subjects were not distributed proportionately in geographic areas: most were from Illinois, Florida, and California. They were more highly educated than a representative cross-section of the population: seventy-five per cent of his subjects went to college, as compared with a national average of thirteen per cent. Three per cent of his women did not go beyond grade school as compared with the national average of thirty-seven per cent. A larger than average proportion are from middle and upper economic groups. Very few of the women were Roman Catholics or orthodox Jews.

Critics have also argued that the very nature of the study involves a kind of bias, for many women will refuse to discuss matters of such "delicate privacy" with interviewers, so that his volunteers must be unrepresentative of women in general. And there is also the problem of credibility. Critics have said that people who like to talk about such things tend to understate or overstate, and even to embroider a little.

Kinsey, of course, recognizes the limitations and incompleteness of his sample, and, as noted, did not claim that it was representative of the whole population. But it will be interpreted in this way, and if Kinsey wished to avoid such interpretations, he should have called his study "Sexual Behavior of 5,940 Women." Inferences would probably be drawn, however, even if he had so titled his study.

The elements of distortion in Kinsey's sample detract from its reliability as a basis for generalizing. On the other hand, as a review of the book in *Life* put it, though the statistics are not perfect they are at any rate "the only statistics in town." His study is by no means worthless as an index of sexual behavior. We must not use an "all or nothing" approach here. The reliability of his sample with respect to university women as a single group, for example, is certainly much higher than that for the female population as a whole. But we cannot conclude that the whole female population resembles the sample since the sample is not a representative one.

Generalizations in statistics, then, are judged by the same logical criteria we use in judging any generalizations. Fallacies, however, are more common in statistical than they are in uniform generalizations. For it is easier to check on the reliability of a uniform generalization: one exception overthrows the general rule or "law." In statistics, however, since nothing is said about any specific individual, an "exception" is a meaningless term. An exceptional individual does not disprove an "average." But there is, as we have already noted, a method for checking the reliability of a statistical generalization concerning a population, and that is to count the whole voting population in an election. But even a test of this kind is not conclusive, for many of the voters do not vote on election day, because of laziness, overconfidence, or some other reason.

Errors of inference in statistics are frequently overlooked because of the mathematical language in which statistics are presented. The spell which numbers weave often prevents us from seeing errors in arguments—errors which would be obvious were they not clothed in mathematical garb. And many dishonest reasoners take advantage of this fact and present highly selected data for purposes of propaganda rather than information. Misuses of the science of statistics have resulted in such jibes as, "Figures don't lie, but liars figure," and "There are three kinds of lies: ordinary lies, damnable lies, and statistics." But these cynical remarks should not be taken as criticisms of statistics. The fault never lies with the figures, or with the science, but with their careless use. It is simply not the case that "you can prove anything with figures" (or statistics), just as it is never the case that "you can prove anything by logic." To the uninitiated, it just *seems* that you can.

XX.

OF MATTERS OF TASTE AND OPINION

WE HAVE BEEN ENGAGED in analyzing matters of logic and science. In science, we all agree, statements must be proved by evidence. In physics and chemistry, certainly, scientific laws are not just "matters of opinion." A successful laboratory test is something quite definite and convincing. The law court, too, requires proof. In a criminal trial the evidence must prove a man guilty ' beyond a reasonable doubt." There may be differences of opinion concerning some verdicts–miscarriages of justice occurring in acquittals as well as in convictions–but the rule is that it is the evidence that counts. The "reasonable man's judgment" is the ultimate criterion for questions of fact in a law court, and reasonable men the world over would probably reach the same verdict in a given dispute. In the social sciences, too, we try to get beyond matters of mere opinion. Carefully tabulated statistics tell us what percentage of paroled convicts will probably "go straight" thereafter, within a given "margin of error."

We agree that logic is relevant in questions concerning facts, for these questions involve evidence and proof. There is an important class of statements, however, which we have not yet examined. These are "value judgments," which many people regard as exempt from the requirement of proof or as incapable of proof. Examples: "T. S. Eliot was a great poet." "The wartime bombing of cities is morally wrong." A value judgment, as we shall use the term in this discussion, is an assertion that something is either good or bad in an *aesthetic* or a *moral* sense. This restriction means that we shall exclude the purely technical sense of good (or bad) in this discussion, as when we speak of "a good automobile tire" (one that will run a long distance), or "a good repair job." Value judgments, then, are statements such as "X is beautiful" (possessing aesthetic excellence) or "X is morally right." Value judgments obviously refer also to statements that things are ugly or that actions are morally wrong.

Value judgments are usually contrasted with "factual statements," which make assertions about events that can be observed in the world of space and time. By a factual statement we do not necessarily mean a true statement. A factual statement, in the sense in which we use this term, refers to one that is *about* facts. Factual statements are true or false, for they may describe the facts correctly or incorrectly. "The Tribune Tower in Chicago is higher than the Leaning Tower of Pisa" is a factual type of statement. So also is "The Leaning Tower is higher than the Tribune Tower." "The Tribune Tower is more beautiful than the Leaning Tower," on the other hand, is a value judgment.

"It is illegal to serve liquor to women at bars in the state of Indiana" is a statement of fact, which happens to be true. We can verify this statement by looking up the law. "Women ought not to sit at bars" is a value judgment which asserts that such conduct is morally wrong. Now, there is general agreement that it is possible to specify the kind of evidence which would prove factual statements true or false, but many people think that value judgments are incapable of proof. Value judgments, it is said, are "mere matters of opinion." It is important to note the precise sense in which this ambiguous phrase is meant. An "opinion" sometimes means a judgment that has a certain measure of probability, but not certainty, as when a man expresses the opinion that higher taxes are necessary to stave off inflation. When the evidence is conflicting, as in a case of this kind, we may speak of "legitimate differences of opinion." But the "opinion" which asserts that higher taxes are necessary may be true, and the opposite opinion may be false. When people say that value judgments are *mere* matters of opinion, on the other hand, they usually mean "a matter of personal feeling or preference," or a "matter of taste." When we qualify the word "opinion" by *mere* in this discussion, this is the view to which we refer. According to this view, value judgments are incapable of proof and thus outside the realm of logical or scientific criticism.

If the "mere opinion" point of view is correct, then one value judgment is "as good as another" and proof is not only impossible but irrelevant. If one value judgment is as incapable of justification as another, then reason and intelligence are irrelevant in the discussion of such matters. In this chapter we shall endeavor to show that logic *is* relevant in the discussion of value judgments as well as in the realm of scientific or "factual" statements. We shall first discuss two theories which hold that value judgments are incapable of logical or scientific justification. One of these we shall call the "taste" theory; the other the "approval" theory. We shall then discuss the sense in which logic is relevant in value judgments.

There is an ancient adage which tells us that "of matters of taste there is no disputing." This is sensible advice. If you prefer the light meat of turkey and I prefer the dark, this establishes a basis for harmony such as prevailed in the famous Spratt family, and it would seem fruitless to argue the question as to which *really* tastes better. We may grant that it is impossible to prove that the taste of black caviar is superior to that of red, even though most "epicures" prefer the former. Some people may argue that it is a fact, not a "matter of taste," that French cuisine is superior to English cooking, but mankind has wisely decided that these are matters that *ought* not to be disputed. But how far, and to what kinds of things, can this principle be applied? "Matter of taste" is frequently used for things other than gustatory flavors. It often covers individual preferences and likes or dislikes in the arts as well, and it is sometimes held that ethical judgments are matters of taste. Let us examine the "taste theory" as applied in the fields of aesthetics and ethics.

No logical problem arises when one says that he prefers the sound of a piano to that of a violin, or when he says "*I prefer* Tchaikovsky to Brahms." He is merely describing his personal taste. The interesting problem for logic arises when he says, "Tchaikovsky is a better composer than Brahms," or "Tchaikovsky's symphonies are more beautiful than those of Brahms." Some literary critics regard *Gone with the Wind* as a second-rate novel, despite its phenomenal popularity all over the world, and there are professors of English literature who say that Joyce Kilmer's "Trees" is bad poetry. Are these judgments true, or false, or *neither?* The "taste" theory holds that they are neither. When we assert value judgments of this kind, the taste theory tells us, the judgments merely express the preferences of the speaker, so that "second-rate," "bad," etc. are not words with any objective reference. "X is beautiful," this theory tells us, means nothing more than "I like X," and "X is better than Y" means only "I prefer X to Y." If we grant that the speaker is telling the truth, and not lying about his actual preference, that is the end of the matter.

Is there no disputing "matters of taste" in the arts? In practice, of course, we do dispute such matters. The word "taste" is often used in a sense other than "personal preference": for "keenness of discernment, or insight." Immanuel Kant, in one of his rare flashes of humor, once played on the double meaning of "taste" when he said: "Art is a matter of taste, but there is no point in arguing matters of taste with the tasteless." Even when a person says that he prefers Tchaikovsky to Brahms, a Brahmsian is apt to accuse him of having a perverse taste. The Brahmsian believes that a person of "genuine" taste will prefer Brahms to Tchaikovsky. When some people tell us what they prefer, it thus appears, they regard their preferences as authoritative!

In practice, moreover, most persons will place limits on the taste theory. They may believe that one's preference for Brahms or Tchaikovsky is a matter of taste, but they will hesitate to say that the judgment "Most male opera singers at the Met sing more beautifully than some truck drivers" is simply a matter of opinion, incapable of justification. Most of us do believe that there are shared standards of merit which go beyond merely individual liking and disliking. Semantically, then, it would appear that "I like X" is an inadequate translation of "X is beautiful." We never ask others to justify their feelings, as when they say "I just happen not to like Picasso's "Guernica." But we do think it is reasonable to ask them why they think a painting lacks aesthetic merit.

We have been discussing the taste theory in aesthetics. It may also be applied to ethical judgments. "X is morally right" (or "ought to be done") is held to be translatable into "I like X," and such judgments are also held to be mere matters of opinion, hence unarguable. But here again it seems that no one who understood the meaning of the words could fail to agree with the judgment "A teacher ought not to flunk a student in English 101 on the sole ground that he wears a beard." This sentence means a good deal more than "I dislike teachers who do such things." Consciously or unconsciously we carry in our minds a definition of "wrong," or a standard of justice, and when we say the action of the teacher is wrong, we have classified it under our conception of wrongful or unjust actions. Again, to say that this judgment is a "matter of taste" and to attempt its translation into "I dislike X" is inadequate.

The second theory, which holds that value judgments cannot be logically supported or justified, is the "approval theory." This theory tells us that judgments concerning right and wrong can be translated into, "My group approves or disapproves." This view is usually associated with the doctrine of "ethical relativism."[1] The relativist holds that nothing is always right or wrong, but that these terms are relative to time, place, and circumstance. The relativist is impressed by the great variety of contrary customs in different parts of the world. Monogamy is customary in western countries; polygyny in Arab countries; and in some places polyandry is the custom. The customary, the relativist notes, is considered morally right; the uncustomary morally wrong. And so what one country considers morally right, another considers

[1] "Relativism" is a vague word. We may mean "relative to the individual," "to a social group," or "to the human race as a whole." In this discussion we refer to the most common type of the doctrine: group relativism.

wrong. And their customs of today may not be their customs of tomorrow.

Thus far the relativist merely cites commonplaces known since the beginning of tourism. He now makes his distinctive contribution: What a group of people consider right, he says, *is* right. Thus, monogamy *is* right for Americans, and polygyny *is* right for Saudi Arabians. Right, of course, means right *for them.* When we say that polygyny is wrong in the United States, the relativist says, we mean only that Americans disapprove of this matrimonial system. Right and wrong are relative to group customs and group approvals.

But we noted earlier that the mere fact that people believe something is not sufficient to make it true, and similarly the fact that people practice certain customs doesn't make them right. Let us sum up the relativist position in a quotation from Pascal:

> Three degrees of latitude reverse all jurisprudence; a meridian decides the truth. Fundamental laws change after a few years of possession; right has its epochs. . . . A strange justice that is bounded by a river! Truth on this side of the Pyrenees, error on the other side.

This theory has an appealing plausibility when we consider the variable customs throughout the world. It appears presumptuous for one nation to tell another that its customs are "immoral." It would be too easy to return the compliment. But the group-approval theory also seems quite inadequate as a reflection of what we *mean* by right and wrong. If group approval *makes* an action right then it would be nonsensical, if not meaningless, to say: "I think this action is wrong, but I am in a minority." For "wrong" can have no meaning in this remark if the approval of the majority *makes* the action right. But does anyone seriously believe that the majority can never be mistaken in its judgment about right and wrong?

Let us now consider some of the implications of the two "translations" of aesthetic and moral judgments that we have been discussing. The taste and approval theories deny the possibility of genuine disagreements over values. What appear to be disagreements, they hold, are merely "verbal disputes." Consider a difference over moral values. When one man says that selfishness is morally wrong, and another preaches that it is a virtue, if the first means "I dislike selfishness" and the second "I like it," then they are not really disagreeing with each other. They are merely uttering confessions about their feelings, or making disguised autobiographical statements. It is as if I say I like whipped cream in my coffee and you say you don't. Similarly, when one man says that polygyny is wrong, and another says it is right, if what each means is that his group disapproves on the one hand, and approves on the other, then each is reporting a sociological fact about his society, and one statement does not contradict the other.

The approval theory also makes moral discussion impossible within a given group. If a moral problem arises, say over the denial of civil rights to a minority group, all the approval theory can tell us is: Take a "Gallup poll"; find out who has the votes. If fifty-one per cent vote "right," then it *is* right. But "This has the vote of the majority" seems quite different from saying, "This is morally right." The majority have the power to decide what the civil laws shall be, but legality and morality are not the same; they sometimes diverge from each other. Would the abolition of the freedom of religious worship in the United States be right if fifty-one per cent approved? Is the morality of such a matter determined by making an accurate count of the votes?

We shall now discuss a new approach to the problem of values, the "value standard" theory, which makes logical analysis relevant in matters of values. We shall illustrate the theory by applying it to a problem in social ethics: Ought we to legalize gambling? My first reaction may be, "Yes, I don't see why not. Let people gamble if they wish to," or "No, gambling is wrong." But there is a counterpart of the "law of rationality" in the field of values. The law of rationality tells us that we ought to justify our beliefs by evidence and reasons, instead of asserting them dogmatically. Similarly, if I am a reflective person, I will seek to justify my value judgments. (A value judgment which gives no reasons can scarcely be called a *judgment*). I will think about my reasons for approving or disapproving of gambling, instead of saying, "I like (or dislike) gambling," or "The community approves (or disapproves) of gambling." I ought to consider the logical consequences of my choice. My thinking may proceed along the following lines: "It is impossible to suppress the human desire to gamble. If this desire is denied a legal outlet it will find an illegal one. Illegal gambling funnels vast sums of money into the hands of undesirable elements in the community, and gives these elements great power. They corrupt the police force and may even control the political machines in our great cities." These considerations make me lean toward legalization. Now I consider the other side: "If gambling is legalized it may become respectable to gamble, and many more people may take to this vice. It is also possible that undesirable elements may manage to obtain control of legalized gambling."

Implicit in my thinking about this problem is the notion that the "public good" ought to be served. If I finally decide that, considering all the consequences, we ought to legalize gambling, I may justify my decision in some such fashion as this: "We ought to promote the general welfare. This duty requires us to choose the greater of two possible goods, or the lesser of two evils. The consequences that will follow from the legalization of gambling will, on the whole, diminish the general welfare less than the alternatives. Therefore we ought to legalize gambling." This is a "logical proof" of a value judgment. My major premise is a value standard which I *assume* as a basis for value decisions. My minor premise is a factual assertion to the effect that legalized gambling will diminish the general welfare least. ("General welfare," of course, is a term whose minimal meaning connotes freedom *and* respect for law, and I must define it in any actual discussion.) I then arrive at my conclusion.

Similarly, if I say that "government regulation of newspapers is wrong," I ought to define what I mean by "wrong" in terms of a value standard. I should make my value standard explicit—whatever that value standard may be. I should then show how my standard applies to the matter of government regulation. If by "wrong" I mean "that which diminishes the general welfare," I must show how regulation will have that effect.

The value-standard analysis of value judgments makes logical discussion possible. A discussion of the legalization of gambling is not only a legitimate procedure but very useful when each disputant accepts the same value standard. Public discussion of such questions helps to clarify the consequences that follow from one or another course of action and thus leads to a thoughtful decision. Most value disputes, actually, involve disagreements concerning the appropriate means to mutually accepted ends. This is of course not necessarily the case: Some may have standards other than that of the general good, and not everyone who says that he seeks the general good actually does. Some may pay lip service to this standard, but belie their acceptance by their actual behavior. "Hypocrisy," as La Rochefoucauld said, "is the homage which vice pays to virtue."

A similar type of value standard analysis may be applied to aesthetic judgments. When I say that a novel is "good"—not merely that I like it—I must justify my judgment. I should define what I mean by "good," and I thus presuppose an aesthetic or critical standard of excellence in fiction. Perhaps my standard is that a good novel should have characters who are "real people," a significant human conflict situation properly developed and resolved, and an interesting story. One may quarrel with my standard, or with its application to a particular work, but such questions are not entirely outside the realm of rational discussion, as the taste theory presupposes. The thoughtful application of a standard is quite different from a snap-judgment made on the basis of surface liking or disliking, such as "This is a good novel; I always like to read stories about artists."

We have presented some examples of the way in which the value standard theory is used to justify value judgments. This approach is quite different from that of the taste theory. We shall now contrast the value standard type of analysis and that of the theory of moral relativism.

The "untouchable" taboo in India is probably approved by the majority of the Indian people. According to the approval theory, if the people of a foreign country approve of a custom then that custom must be right *for them.* It is thus not only improper for us to criticize the Indians for their caste system, but it must also be wrong for *Indians* to criticize, for the mere fact of approval makes the system morally right in India. The present government in India, however, seeks to abolish this system. This government obviously does not accept the approval theory. It believes that the system is wrong *in India* because it believes that the outcast system diminishes the general welfare of the Indians, or because it violates the principle that every human being should be treated as an end-in-himself, and never as a mere means to an end.

To many, it would seem outrageous to condemn the Indian government for seeking to abolish untouchability. If we believe that the Indian government is right, then we do not accept the approval theory. And if Indian critics of untouchability are at least logically justified in their criticism of the system, then it is logically permissible for Americans to join in these criticisms, at least on the same grounds as those used by the Indian government. It is of course an extremely complex and difficult problem to decide whether a given custom is right or wrong. In judging untouchability we must consider the history of India, its traditions, religion and customs of life, and we should also consider the adequacy of the standard we employ in making our value judgment. But these are matters open to logical discussion.

Ethical relativism has the insight that different customs may be equally right, depending on the history, traditions, and circumstances of life in different countries, and that we ought not to judge the customs of other countries by a blind application of the customs that happen to prevail in our own. Time, place, and circumstance do alter cases. But the relativist theory fails to distinguish customs and local rules, on the one hand, from standards and principles on the other. The principle that every human being ought to be treated as an end-in-himself is not on the same level as that of a marriage custom. And the relativists also deny that a custom may be *wrong*, as when a practice violates a standard that may be used to judge customs. In the United States, for example, the principle of equality has been violated in the custom of racial segregation.

Approval theorists are of course seldom consistent in applying their theory. This inconsistency indicates that most approval theorists do not themselves really believe that it is approval alone that makes an action right. They, too, assume that there are reasons for value judgments. They may say that polygyny must be right in a particular community "because the people approve of this custom." But if we ask them: "*Why* do the people approve?" we may get an answer something like this: "Large numbers of men were killed off in constant wars, or in dangerous occupations like seal-hunting, and this resulted in a 'surplus' of women." A reason of this kind, however, indicates that this community judged polygyny right because it was thought desirable for the general good, and this is the use of a standard. Anthropologists, indeed, tell us that most customs are based on the necessity (or the presumed necessity) for particular kinds of behavior. If a group is to cope successfully with its environment it must of course adapt its customs to that environment. Obviously approval has its basis in reasons, and the *reasons* are conceived as those which make the action right.

We have been seeking to justify the value standard theory in ethical and aesthetic value judgments. Reflection, we believe, will reveal that most of us do apply standards even though we may not be conscious of doing so. Let us consider an example.

In the following scene from Shaw's *Pygmalion*, on which the musical "My Fair Lady" was based, Alfred Doolittle, the dustman, has asked Higgins for a five-pound note if he is to allow his daughter Liza to remain with Higgins for the linguistic experiment.

PICKERING: I think you ought to know, Doolittle, that Mr. Higgins' intentions are entirely honorable.

DOOLITTLE: Course they are, Governor. If I thought they wasn't I'd ask fifty.

HIGGINS [revolted]: Do you mean to say that you would sell your daughter for fifty pounds?

DOOLITTLE: Not in a general way I wouldn't; but to oblige a gentleman like you I'd do a good deal, I do assure you.

PICKERING: Have you no morals, man?

DOOLITTLE [unabashed]: Can't afford them, Governor. Neither could you if you was as poor as me. Not that I mean any harm, you know. But if Liza is going to have a bit out of this, why not me too?

HIGGINS [troubled]: I don't know what to do, Pickering. There can be no question that as a matter of morals it's a positive crime to give this chap a farthing. And yet I feel a rough sort of justice in his claim.

DOOLITTLE: That's it, Governor. That's all I say. A father's heart, as it were.

The reader may regard this selection as a witty presentation of the relativistic point of view. "Morals" seem to depend on one's situation in life. Circumstances alter cases. But implicit in Shaw's satire is the assumption that Doolittle's "honesty" is somehow praiseworthy, and that hypocrisy is the great sin. Honesty may be the standard we regard as "absolute." And most relativists justify their position by the argument that relativism leads to tolerance of other people's ways. Tolerance, once more, is accepted as an unquestioned good, in other words, as a standard.

Value judgments, then, can be justified in terms of value principles or standards. But we must now deal with a question which may have been in the mind of the reader throughout this discussion: Can value standards themselves be justified by logical reasoning? This is indeed a difficult question, and its difficulty accounts for the continuing popularity of the taste and approval theories.

We have been justifying value judgments by the use of value standards without attempting to prove these standards. Value standards, of course, are neither true nor false in a literal sense, for they tell us what "ought to be," and are not mere descriptions of facts. We have simply been *assuming* these standards in our proofs. At this point a more sophisticated "taste" theorist may say, "That is my real point. I grant that we can use logic in proving that the means are efficacious or not efficacious in achieving a given end, as in the discussion of legalized gambling, or in a marriage custom in relation to human happiness, but the end, as formulated in the standard must simply be assumed. Whether we accept it or not is a matter of taste, unprovable."

This sophisticated version of the taste theory has a wide following among philosophers. But it is a long step beyond the simple form of the theory, for it synthesizes tastes and the use of standards. We may make the following comments on this version of the theory which asserts that the acceptance of standards is in the end an arbitrary matter:

1. Many, if not most differences over values are differences with respect to the ways in which a certain end may be achieved, not differences with respect to the standards, and so discussion may turn disagreement into agreement. This is also true when we disagree over the application of a commonly accepted standard.

2. Some standards are more basic than others. We may say that the compulsory arbitration of labor-management disputes is wrong, because it would violate the principle of free enterprise. This indicates that we have taken free enterprise as our standard for judging social policy. But if someone should challenge our acceptance of this standard we may wish to justify it by a more basic standard, such as "the general welfare," believing that free enterprise is a necessary means to that end.

And further, we ought never to consider even our basic standards exempt from discussion, for no standard can be known to be absolutely final. As we develop in maturity we may see beyond our present "ultimates."

3. The thoughtful person chooses his standards, not by mere "liking" but by a personal commitment after surveying the consequences of his commitment with respect to everything he desires out of life. It is a question of how we really want to live. If this is in the end an arbitrary choice, it is one based on consideration of all relevant factors. It is not arbitrary in the way in which likes and dislikes may be.

Before we close this discussion we shall briefly examine a different kind of philosophical theory of ethics which seeks to prove that some standards *ought* to be accepted, and others not. It seeks to use reason and rational thinking to justify standards.

The philosopher Immanuel Kant believed that there was a

supreme moral principle which could be established by reason itself. Men are rational beings, said Kant, and the essence of rationality is consistency and the avoidance of self-contradiction. A rational principle, furthermore, must be capable of universalization, i.e., it must apply to all persons in all situations.

His basic principle is that "we should act only according to a maxim which can be universalized." This basic principle resembles the Golden Rule, which, as we know, tells us to "Do unto others as we would have them do unto us." Kant shows how the violation of this principle involves inconsistency.

Consider the person who makes a lying promise, that is, one who makes a promise that he does not intend to keep. The "maxim" of his act is that "one may tell a lie when it is convenient to do so." Can this maxim be universalized? Can the liar say: Let everyone do what I am doing? No, says Kant. The liar "gets away" with his lie because others believe him. But if everyone lied when it was convenient to do so, then mutual trust would disappear and no one would believe anyone, so that a liar could derive no benefit from his lie.

Do not lie or steal, says Kant, not because "Honesty is the best policy" (though it probably is), or because "Crime doesn't pay" (though it usually doesn't) but because such conduct is morally wrong. Morality demands that we universalize our conduct, that we give others the privileges we claim for ourselves (insofar as they are similar to us in relevant characteristics and in similar situations), and the liar and thief cannot do this without self-contradiction. For lying and stealing, if universalized, would frustrate the goals of the liar and thief. The one would not be believed, and the other would find that the rights of property had disappeared, so that he could not enjoy his ill-gotten gains in peace.

Slavery (or any form of coercion except for crimes), is wrong. A slave is treated as if he were a purposeless thing, and his dignity as a fellow human being is disregarded. Can anyone be willing for everyone to be treated in like fashion, including himself? The contradiction is manifest, for no one can wish that his own wishes be frustrated. Slavery is wrong, says Kant, even though a minority of slaves may contribute to "the greatest happiness of the greatest number," for nothing that violates the basic principle of morality or justice can be right. And the rightness of these principles, he argues, is a necessary consequence of rational thinking. If the universalization of one's act leads to the defeat of one's own purposes, Kant holds, the act involves inconsistencies and self-contradiction, and the maxim of such an action cannot be an acceptable principle to a rational man.

In this chapter we have tried to show the relevance of logic in value judgments. The law of rationality is relevant here. We ought to justify our value judgments by reasons. We have shown how value standards may be used in making such judgments, and we have discussed the possibility of justifying the value standards by logic. Whether such justification can finally be achieved or not, the acceptance of such standards is far from being an arbitrary matter. We shall now sum up the different ways in which logic helps us to clarify our standards in the field of ethics.

1. Logic clarifies what we *mean* by right and wrong, in terms of our moral standards.

2. Logic helps us to determine whether a particular judgment makes sense in terms of these standards. We ought to work out the consequences that follow from our choices. We may find that we are defeating our own ends. Many people have supported the mandatory death penalty for kidnapping on the ground that it will effectively discourage the commission of this crime. But one should also consider some of the undesirable consequences that result from a law of this kind. The death penalty–for kidnapping as such–eliminates any inducement to the kidnapper to bring his victim back alive, and juries will also be reluctant to render a verdict of guilty in cases not involving murder, for a guilty verdict will mean the death penalty. If we want victims brought back alive, and if we want juries to do their duty, we may wish to revise our approval of the mandatory death penalty for kidnapping.

3. Logical analysis may also show us that we are striving for the wrong ends, as many Socialists discovered when they saw that the abolition of private property in Russia did not bring about

the elimination of cruelty and oppression. They also discovered that the State can be a harsh exploiter of the working man.

4. Logical analysis may also reveal self-inconsistencies in our own thinking. Few of us, perhaps, are as inconsistent as was the Mexican Society for the Prevention of Cruelty to Animals when it raised a considerable sum of money in a benefit performance at the bull ring. But we are sometimes as inconsistent as was King David–though in other contexts–when he condemned the rich man (in Nathan's parable) for taking away the poor man's little ewe lamb. David himself had sent Uriah to his death in order to possess the beautiful Bathsheba.

We see, then, that logic is relevant in all human problems: in problems of values as well as those of a scientific nature. To dismiss judgments of value as mere matters of opinion, and not subject to discussion, is to invite an irrationalist attitude, an attitude which dismisses the criteria of logical analysis, rational deliberation, and the testing of our opinions by experience.

Reason is opposed to dogmatism, fanaticism, and obscurantism. The rational way of life offers no panaceas: the rational individual recognizes the complexities of human problems, and the difficulties in proving one side or the other in controversial issues. But there is no human problem that is inherently insoluble, and if we try hard enough, using the best methods that the human race has so far devised for thinking about these problems, we are justified in the faith that we shall solve them, one by one. The best methods, as we have seen, require working out the probable consequences of our ideas, and testing them in experience.

Many years ago Socrates taught that "the unexamined life is not worth living": the life that is not scrutinized by intelligence is a life not fit for a human being. Reason–or intelligence–is not all, but it is our greatest asset. The rational path leads to the enlightenment of the human mind and brings us illumination in place of darkness.

INDEX